# GENESIS

THE IGNATIUS CATHOLIC STUDY BIBLE

REVISED STANDARD VERSION
SECOND CATHOLIC EDITION

# GENESIS

With Introduction, Commentary, and Notes

by

Scott Hahn and Curtis Mitch

and

with Study Questions by

Dennis Walters

IGNATIUS PRESS SAN FRANCISCO

Published with ecclesiastical approval

Original Catholic RSV Bible text:
*Nihil Obstat:* Thomas Hanlon, S.T.L., L.S.S., Ph.L.
*Imprimatur:* ✝ Peter W. Bartholome, D.D.
Bishop of Saint Cloud, Minnesota
May 11, 1966

Introduction, commentaries and notes:
*Nihil obstat:* Rev. Msgr. J. Warren Holleran, S.T.D.
*Imprimatur:* ✝ Most Reverend George Niederauer
Archbishop of San Francisco
August 24, 2010

The *nihil obstat* and *imprimatur* are official declarations that a book or pamphlet is free of doctrinal or moral error. No implication is contained therein that those who have granted the *nihil obstat* and *imprimatur* agree with the contents, opinions, or statements expressed.

Second Catholic Edition approved by the
National Council of the Churches of Christ in the USA

Cover art: *Abraham Receives the Promise of Three Angels*
Kunsthistorisches Museum, Vienna
Erich Lessing / Art Resource, N.Y.

Cover design by Riz Boncan Marsella

Maps by David Notley
Camway Creative Limited

Published by Ignatius Press in 2010


ISBN 978-1-58617-433-0 (PB)
ISBN 978-1-68149-122-6 (eBook)

Printed in the United States of America ♾

# CONTENTS

# INTRODUCTION TO
# THE IGNATIUS CATHOLIC STUDY BIBLE

*by Scott Hahn, Ph.D.*

You are approaching the "word of God". This is the title Christians most commonly give to the Bible, and the expression is rich in meaning. It is also the title given to the Second Person of the Blessed Trinity, God the Son. For Jesus Christ became flesh for our salvation, and "the name by which he is called is The Word of God" (Rev 19:13; cf. Jn 1:14).

The word of God is Scripture. The Word of God is Jesus. This close association between God's *written* word and his *eternal* Word is intentional and has been the custom of the Church since the first generation. "All Sacred Scripture is but one book, and this one book is Christ, 'because all divine Scripture speaks of Christ, and all divine Scripture is fulfilled in Christ'[1]" (CCC 134). This does not mean that the Scriptures are divine in the same way that Jesus is divine. They are, rather, divinely inspired and, as such, are unique in world literature, just as the Incarnation of the eternal Word is unique in human history.

Yet we can say that the inspired word resembles the incarnate Word in several important ways. Jesus Christ is the Word of God incarnate. In his humanity, he is like us in all things, except for sin. As a work of man, the Bible is like any other book, except without error. Both Christ and Scripture, says the Second Vatican Council, are given "for the sake of our salvation" (*Dei Verbum* 11), and both give us God's definitive revelation of himself. We cannot, therefore, conceive of one without the other: the Bible without Jesus, or Jesus without the Bible. Each is the interpretive key to the other. And because Christ is the subject of all the Scriptures, St. Jerome insists, "Ignorance of the Scriptures is ignorance of Christ"[2] (CCC 133).

When we approach the Bible, then, we approach Jesus, the Word of God; and in order to encounter Jesus, we must approach him in a prayerful study of the inspired word of God, the Sacred Scriptures.

**Inspiration and Inerrancy** The Catholic Church makes mighty claims for the Bible, and our acceptance of those claims is essential if we are to read the Scriptures and apply them to our lives as the Church intends. So it is not enough merely to nod at words like "inspired", "unique", or "inerrant". We have to understand what the Church means by these terms, and we have to make that understanding our own. After all, what we believe about the Bible will inevitably influence the way we read the Bible. The way we read the Bible, in turn, will determine what we "get out" of its sacred pages.

These principles hold true no matter what we read: a news report, a search warrant, an advertisement, a paycheck, a doctor's prescription, an eviction notice. How (or whether) we read these things depends largely upon our preconceived notions about the reliability and authority of their sources—and the potential they have for affecting our lives. In some cases, to misunderstand a document's authority can lead to dire consequences. In others, it can keep us from enjoying rewards that are rightfully ours. In the case of the Bible, both the rewards and the consequences involved take on an ultimate value.

What does the Church mean, then, when she affirms the words of St. Paul: "All Scripture is inspired by God" (2 Tim 3:16)? Since the term "inspired" in this passage could be translated "God-breathed", it follows that God breathed forth his word in the Scriptures as you and I breathe forth air when we speak. This means that God is the primary author of the Bible. He certainly employed human authors in this task as well, but he did not merely assist them while they wrote or subsequently approve what they had written. God the Holy Spirit is the *principal* author of Scripture, while the human writers are *instrumental* authors. These human authors freely wrote everything, and only those things, that God wanted: the word of God in the very words of God. This miracle of dual authorship extends to the whole of Scripture, and to every one of its parts, so that whatever the human authors affirm, God likewise affirms through their words.

The principle of biblical inerrancy follows logically from this principle of divine authorship. After all, God cannot lie, and he cannot make mistakes. Since the Bible is divinely inspired, it must be without error in everything that its divine and human authors affirm to be true. This means that biblical inerrancy is a mystery even broader in scope than infallibility, which guarantees for us that the Church will always teach the truth concerning faith and morals. Of course the mantle of inerrancy likewise covers faith and morals, but it extends even farther to ensure that all the facts and events of salvation history are accurately presented for us in the Scriptures. Inerrancy is our guarantee that the words and deeds of God found in the Bible are unified and true, declaring with one voice the wonders of his saving love.

[1] Hugh of St. Victor, *De arca Noe* 2, 8: PL 176, 642: cf. ibid. 2, 9: PL 176, 642–43.

[2] *DV* 25; cf. Phil 3:8 and St. Jerome, *Commentariorum in Isaiam libri xviii*, prol.: PL 24, 17b.

The guarantee of inerrancy does not mean, however, that the Bible is an all-purpose encyclopedia of information covering every field of study. The Bible is not, for example, a textbook in the empirical sciences, and it should not be treated as one. When biblical authors relate facts of the natural order, we can be sure they are speaking in a purely descriptive and "phenomenological" way, according to the way things appeared to their senses.

**Biblical Authority** Implicit in these doctrines is God's desire to make himself known to the world and to enter a loving relationship with every man, woman, and child he has created. God gave us the Scriptures not just to inform or motivate us; more than anything he wants to save us. This higher purpose underlies every page of the Bible, indeed every word of it.

In order to reveal himself, God used what theologians call "accommodation". Sometimes the Lord stoops down to communicate by "condescension"—that is, he speaks as humans speak, as if he had the same passions and weakness that we do (for example, God says he was "sorry" that he made man in Genesis 6:6). Other times he communicates by "elevation"—that is, by endowing human words with divine power (for example, through the Prophets). The numerous examples of divine accommodation in the Bible are an expression of God's wise and fatherly ways. For a sensitive father can speak with his children either by condescension, as in baby talk, or by elevation, by bringing a child's understanding up to a more mature level.

God's word is thus saving, fatherly, and personal. Because it speaks directly to us, we must never be indifferent to its content; after all, the word of God is at once the object, cause, and support of our faith. It is, in fact, a test of our faith, since we see in the Scriptures only what faith disposes us to see. If we believe what the Church believes, we will see in Scripture the saving, inerrant, and divinely authored revelation of the Father. If we believe otherwise, we see another book altogether.

This test applies not only to rank-and-file believers but also to the Church's theologians and hierarchy, and even the Magisterium. Vatican II has stressed in recent times that Scripture must be "the very soul of sacred theology" (*Dei Verbum* 24). As Joseph Cardinal Ratzinger, Pope Benedict XVI echoed this powerful teaching with his own, insisting that, "The *normative theologians* are the authors of Holy Scripture" (emphasis added). He reminded us that Scripture and the Church's dogmatic teaching are tied tightly together, to the point of being inseparable: "Dogma is by definition nothing other than an interpretation of Scripture." The defined dogmas of our faith, then, encapsulate the Church's infallible interpretation of Scripture, and theology is a further reflection upon that work.

**The Senses of Scripture** Because the Bible has both divine and human authors, we are required to master a different sort of reading than we are used to. First, we must read Scripture according to its *literal* sense, as we read any other human literature. At this initial stage, we strive to discover the meaning of the words and expressions used by the biblical writers as they were understood in their original setting and by their original recipients. This means, among other things, that we do not interpret everything we read "literalistically", as though Scripture never speaks in a figurative or symbolic way (it often does!). Rather, we read it according to the rules that govern its different literary forms of writing, depending on whether we are reading a narrative, a poem, a letter, a parable, or an apocalyptic vision. The Church calls us to read the divine books in this way to ensure that we understand what the human authors were laboring to explain to God's people.

The literal sense, however, is not the only sense of Scripture, since we interpret its sacred pages according to the *spiritual* senses as well. In this way, we search out what the Holy Spirit is trying to tell us, beyond even what the human authors have consciously asserted. Whereas the literal sense of Scripture describes a historical reality—a fact, precept, or event—the spiritual senses disclose deeper mysteries revealed through the historical realities. What the soul is to the body, the spiritual senses are to the literal. You can distinguish them; but if you try to separate them, death immediately follows. St. Paul was the first to insist upon this and warn of its consequences: "God ... has qualified us to be ministers of a new covenant, not in a written code but in the Spirit; for the written code kills, but the Spirit gives life" (2 Cor 3:5–6).

Catholic tradition recognizes three spiritual senses that stand upon the foundation of the literal sense of Scripture (see CCC 115). (**1**) The first is the *allegorical* sense, which unveils the spiritual and prophetic meaning of biblical history. Allegorical interpretations thus reveal how persons, events, and institutions of Scripture can point beyond themselves toward greater mysteries yet to come (OT) or display the fruits of mysteries already revealed (NT). Christians have often read the Old Testament in this way to discover how the mystery of Christ in the New Covenant was once hidden in the Old and how the full significance of the Old Covenant was finally made manifest in the New. Allegorical significance is likewise latent in the New Testament, especially in the life and deeds of Jesus recorded in the Gospels. Because Christ is the Head of the Church and the source of her spiritual life, what was accomplished in Christ the Head during his earthly life prefigures what he continually produces in his members through grace. The allegorical sense builds up the virtue of faith. (**2**) The second is the *tropological* or *moral* sense, which reveals how the actions of God's people in the Old Testament and the life of Jesus in the New Testament prompt us to form virtuous habits in our own lives. It therefore draws from Scripture warnings against sin and vice as well as inspirations to pursue holiness and purity. The moral sense is intended to build up the virtue of charity. **(3)** The third is the *anagogical* sense, which points upward to heavenly glory. It shows us how countless events in the Bible prefigure our final union with God in eternity and how things that are "seen" on earth are figures of things "unseen" in heaven. Because the anagogical sense leads us to contemplate our destiny, it is meant to build up the virtue of hope. Together with the literal sense, then, these spiritual senses draw out the fullness of what God wants to give us through his Word and as such comprise what ancient tradition has called the "full sense" of Sacred Scripture.

All of this means that the deeds and events of the Bible are charged with meaning beyond what is immediately apparent to the reader. In essence, that meaning is Jesus Christ and the salvation he died to give us. This is especially true of the books of the New Testament, which proclaim Jesus explicitly; but it is also true of the Old Testament, which speaks of Jesus in more hidden and symbolic ways. The human authors of the Old Testament told us as much as they were able, but they could not clearly discern the shape of all future events standing at such a distance. It is the Bible's divine Author, the Holy Spirit, who could and did foretell the saving work of Christ, from the first page of the Book of Genesis onward.

The New Testament did not, therefore, abolish the Old. Rather, the New fulfilled the Old, and in doing so, it lifted the veil that kept hidden the face of the Lord's bride. Once the veil is removed, we suddenly see the world of the Old Covenant charged with grandeur. Water, fire, clouds, gardens, trees, hills, doves, lambs—all of these things are memorable details in the history and poetry of Israel. But now, seen in the light of Jesus Christ, they are much more. For the Christian with eyes to see, water symbolizes the saving power of Baptism; fire, the Holy Spirit; the spotless lamb, Christ crucified; Jerusalem, the city of heavenly glory.

The spiritual reading of Scripture is nothing new. Indeed, the very first Christians read the Bible this way. St. Paul describes Adam as a "type" that prefigured Jesus Christ (Rom 5:14). A "type" is a real person, place, thing, or event in the Old Testament that foreshadows something greater in the New. From this term we get the word "typology", referring to the study of how the Old Testament prefigures Christ (CCC 128–30). Elsewhere St. Paul draws deeper meanings out of the story of Abraham's sons, declaring, "This is an allegory" (Gal 4:24). He is not suggesting that these events of the distant past never really happened; he is saying that the events both happened *and* signified something more glorious yet to come.

The New Testament later describes the Tabernacle of ancient Israel as "a copy and shadow of the heavenly sanctuary" (Heb 8:5) and the Mosaic Law as a "shadow of the good things to come" (Heb 10:1). St. Peter, in turn, notes that Noah and his family were "saved through water" in a way that "corresponds" to sacramental Baptism, which "now saves you" (1 Pet 3:20–21). It is interesting to note that the expression translated as "corresponds" in this verse is a Greek term that denotes the fulfillment or counterpart of an ancient "type".

We need not look to the apostles, however, to justify a spiritual reading of the Bible. After all, Jesus himself read the Old Testament this way. He referred to Jonah (Mt 12:39), Solomon (Mt 12:42), the Temple (Jn 2:19), and the brazen serpent (Jn 3:14) as "signs" that pointed forward to him. We see in Luke's Gospel, as Christ comforted the disciples on the road to Emmaus, that "beginning with Moses and all the prophets, he interpreted to them in all the Scriptures the things concerning himself" (Lk 24:27). It was precisely this extensive spiritual interpretation of the Old Testament that made such an impact on these once-discouraged travelers, causing their hearts to "burn" within them (Lk 24:32).

**Criteria for Biblical Interpretation** We, too, must learn to discern the "full sense" of Scripture as it includes both the literal and spiritual senses together. Still, this does not mean we should "read into" the Bible meanings that are not really there. Spiritual exegesis is not an unrestrained flight of the imagination. Rather, it is a sacred science that proceeds according to certain principles and stands accountable to sacred tradition, the Magisterium, and the wider community of biblical interpreters (both living and deceased).

In searching out the full sense of a text, we should always avoid the extreme tendency to "over-spiritualize" in a way that minimizes or denies the Bible's literal truth. St. Thomas Aquinas was well aware of this danger and asserted that "all other senses of Sacred Scripture are based on the literal" (*STh* I, 1, 10, *ad* 1, quoted in CCC 116). On the other hand, we should never confine the meaning of a text to the literal, intended sense of its human author, as if the divine Author did not intend the passage to be read in the light of Christ's coming.

Fortunately the Church has given us guidelines in our study of Scripture. The unique character and divine authorship of the Bible call us to read it "in the Spirit" (*Dei Verbum* 12). Vatican II outlines this teaching in a practical way by directing us to read the Scriptures according to three specific criteria:

1. We must "[b]e especially attentive 'to the content and unity of the whole Scripture'" (CCC 112).

2. We must "[r]ead the Scripture within 'the living Tradition of the whole Church'" (CCC 113).

3. We must "[b]e attentive to the analogy of faith"

(CCC 114; cf. Rom 12:6).

These criteria protect us from many of the dangers that ensnare readers of the Bible, from the newest inquirer to the most prestigious scholar. Reading Scripture out of context is one such pitfall, and probably the one most difficult to avoid. A memorable cartoon from the 1950s shows a young man poring over the pages of the Bible. He says to his sister: "Don't bother me now; I'm trying to find a Scripture verse to back up one of my preconceived notions." No doubt a biblical text pried from its context can be twisted to say something very different from what its author actually intended.

The Church's criteria guide us here by defining what constitutes the authentic "context" of a given biblical passage. The first criterion directs us to the literary context of every verse, including not only the words and paragraphs that surround it, but also the entire corpus of the biblical author's writings and, indeed, the span of the entire Bible. The *complete* literary context of any Scripture verse includes every text from Genesis to Revelation—because the Bible is a unified book, not just a library of different books. When the Church canonized the Book of Revelation, for example, she recognized it to be incomprehensible apart from the wider context of the entire Bible.

The second criterion places the Bible firmly within the context of a community that treasures a "living tradition". That community is the People of God down through the ages. Christians lived out their faith for well over a millennium before the printing press was invented. For centuries, few believers owned copies of the Gospels, and few people could read anyway. Yet they absorbed the gospel—through the sermons of their bishops and clergy, through prayer and meditation, through Christian art, through liturgical celebrations, and through oral tradition. These were expressions of the one "living tradition", a culture of living faith that stretches from ancient Israel to the contemporary Church. For the early Christians, the gospel could not be understood apart from that tradition. So it is with us. Reverence for the Church's tradition is what protects us from any sort of chronological or cultural provincialism, such as scholarly fads that arise and carry away a generation of interpreters before being dismissed by the next generation.

The third criterion places scriptural texts within the framework of faith. If we believe that the Scriptures are divinely inspired, we must also believe them to be internally coherent and consistent with all the doctrines that Christians believe. Remember, the Church's dogmas (such as the Real Presence, the papacy, the Immaculate Conception) are not something *added* to Scripture; rather, they are the Church's infallible interpretation *of* Scripture.

**Using This Study Guide** This volume is designed to lead the reader through Scripture according to the Church's guidelines—faithful to the canon, to the tradition, and to the creeds. The Church's interpretive principles have thus shaped the component parts of this book, and they are designed to make the reader's study as effective and rewarding as possible.

*Introductions*: We have introduced the biblical book with an essay covering issues such as authorship, date of composition, purpose, and leading themes. This background information will assist readers to approach and understand the text on its own terms.

*Annotations*: The basic notes at the bottom of every page help the user to read the Scriptures with understanding. They by no means exhaust the meaning of the sacred text but provide background material to help the reader make sense of what he reads. Often these notes make explicit what the sacred writers assumed or held to be implicit. They also provide a great deal of historical, cultural, geographical, and theological information pertinent to the inspired narratives—information that can help the reader bridge the distance between the biblical world and his own.

*Cross-References*: Between the biblical text at the top of each page and the annotations at the bottom, numerous references are listed to point readers to other scriptural passages related to the one being studied. This follow-up is an essential part of any serious study. It is also an excellent way to discover how the content of Scripture "hangs together" in a providential unity. Along with biblical cross-references, the annotations refer to select paragraphs from the *Catechism of the Catholic Church*. These are not doctrinal "proof texts" but are designed to help the reader interpret the Bible in accordance with the mind of the Church. The *Catechism* references listed either handle the biblical text directly or treat a broader doctrinal theme that sheds significant light on that text.

*Topical Essays, Word Studies, Charts*: These features bring readers to a deeper understanding of select details. The *topical essays* take up major themes and explain them more thoroughly and theologically than the annotations, often relating them to the doctrines of the Church. Occasionally the annotations are supplemented by *word studies* that put readers in touch with the ancient languages of Scripture. These should help readers to understand better and appreciate the inspired terminology that runs throughout the sacred books. Also included are various *charts* that summarize biblical information "at a glance".

*Icon Annotations*: Three distinctive icons are interspersed throughout the annotations, each one corresponding to one of the Church's three criteria for biblical interpretation. Bullets indicate the passage or passages to which these icons apply.

Notes marked by the book icon relate to the

"content and unity" of Scripture, showing how particular passages of the Old Testament illuminate the mysteries of the New. Much of the information in these notes explains the original context of the citations and indicates how and why this has a direct bearing on Christ or the Church. Through these notes, the reader can develop a sensitivity to the beauty and unity of God's saving plan as it stretches across both Testaments.

Notes marked by the dove icon examine particular passages in light of the Church's "living tradition". Because the Holy Spirit both guides the Magisterium and inspires the spiritual senses of Scripture, these annotations supply information along both of these lines. On the one hand, they refer to the Church's doctrinal teaching as presented by various popes, creeds, and ecumenical councils; on the other, they draw from (and paraphrase) the spiritual interpretations of various Fathers, Doctors, and saints.

Notes marked by the keys icon pertain to the "analogy of faith". Here we spell out how the mysteries of our faith "unlock" and explain one another. This type of comparison between Christian beliefs displays the coherence and unity of defined dogmas, which are the Church's infallible interpretations of Scripture.

**Putting It All in Perspective** Perhaps the most important context of all we have saved for last: the interior life of the individual reader. What we get out of the Bible will largely depend on how we approach the Bible. Unless we are living a sustained and disciplined life of prayer, we will never have the reverence, the profound humility, or the grace we need to see the Scriptures for what they really are.

You are approaching the "word of God". But for thousands of years, since before he knit you in your mother's womb, the Word of God has been approaching you.

*One Final Note.* The volume you hold in your hands is only a small part of a much larger work still in production. Study helps similar to those printed in this booklet are being prepared for *all* the books of the Bible and will appear gradually as they are finished. Our ultimate goal is to publish a single, one-volume Study Bible that will include the entire text of Scripture, along with all the annotations, charts, cross-references, maps, and other features found in the following pages. Individual booklets will be published in the meantime, with the hope that God's people can begin to benefit from this labor before its full completion.

We have included a long list of Study Questions in the back to make this format as useful as possible, not only for individual study, but for group settings and discussions as well. The questions are designed to help readers both "understand" the Bible and "apply" it to their lives. We pray that God will make use of our efforts and yours to help renew the face of the earth! «

# INTRODUCTION TO GENESIS

**Author and Date** Nowhere does the Book of Genesis identify its author. The vast stretch of Jewish and Christian tradition credits the work, along with the rest of the Pentateuch (the Books of Exodus, Leviticus, Numbers, and Deuteronomy), to Moses. This would mean that Genesis was first put into writing during the lifetime of the Lawgiver, which has been dated in either the 1400s or the 1200s B.C.

Modern scholarship has largely abandoned the tradition of Mosaic authorship in favor of a theory of multiple authorship. This newer paradigm, called the Documentary Hypothesis, holds that Genesis (and the Pentateuch as a whole) is the work of several writers whose contributions were pieced together into a single literary work long after the time of Moses. Documentary scholars generally contend that Genesis is a composite of two sources of epic narrative (labeled "J" and "E" for the Yahwist and Elohist sources) that were joined together and later expanded by the additions of a priestly writer (labeled "P" for the Priestly source). On this hypothesis, the composition of Genesis began around 900 B.C. and came to an end around 400 B.C., sometime after the return of the Jews from the Babylonian Exile. Most who adopt this view acknowledge that the stories in Genesis are often much older than their written form, and some would allow that certain parts of its contents may indeed be Mosaic in origin.

Studies of the Book of Genesis within its Near Eastern context tend to confirm both the antiquity and the authenticity of its traditions. Comparative evidence can be read to suggest an origin for the Genesis stories in the second millennium B.C. at a time roughly contemporary with the historical Moses. For example, the storyline of Gen 1–11 shows striking affinities with creation and flood stories from Mesopotamia that date back to the early second millennium. Parallels extend both to the broad outline of primeval history (*Sumerian King List, Sumerian Flood Tale, Atrahasis Epic*) as well as to specific details about creation (*Enuma Elish*), the flood (*Gilgamesh Epic*), and the origin of diverse human languages (*Enmerkar Epic*). In similar fashion, the patriarchal narratives of Gen 12–50 are consistent with our knowledge of the cultural conditions of the ancient Near East in the early second millennium. The names of the Patriarchs are characteristic of the archaic name types prevalent at this time (e.g., Isaac, Jacob, Ishmael, Joseph); the journeys of the Patriarchs back and forth across Near Eastern lands mirror the freedom of mobility that then prevailed (e.g., Gen 11:31; 12:4–5, 9–10; 13:1; 24:10; 28:6–7; 37:28); and the situation described in Gen 14:1–4 fits with the geopolitical conditions of greater Mesopotamia before the Old Babylonian kingdom gained control over the region around 1750 B.C. and made alliances between local monarchs a thing of the past. Furthermore, several of the legal and domestic customs played out in the lives of the Patriarchs find parallels in second-millennium texts from Babylon, Mari, and Nuzi (see notes on Gen 15:3, 16:1–6, and 31:39).

None of this evidence strictly demands that Genesis be dated before the first millennium B.C. However, it may be said to favor a greater antiquity for the work than is often accepted. For example, it is true that some of the Near Eastern literature that parallels the primeval stories of Genesis continued to be read (and updated) well into the first millennium, but virtually all of the works in question were first composed in the second or third millennium. Dating the stories of Gen 1–11 around the time of Moses and the founding of the nation of Israel puts them close to the period of composition, when works of this particular type were being produced in the Near East. So too, it seems more probable than not that the stories compiled in Gen 12–50, whose historical reliability is firmly supported (see note on 12:1—50:26), took written form before the second millennium came to a close. At least it is difficult to believe that authentic memories of the patriarchal period survived intact long after the period of Moses. This would require an extraordinarily tenacious oral tradition that scholars are generally unwilling to accept. By the same token, given the evolution of social, cultural, and political conditions in the Near East, it is unlikely that authors working during the period of the Israelite monarchy and even later could accurately recreate the circumstances of life that obtained in patriarchal times. Had they been the first to put the Book of Genesis into written form, most likely they would have described Israel's ancestors in situations and surroundings reflective of their own times and experiences. The comparative data can thus be read as broadly consistent with the tradition of Mosaic authorship, even if it fails to demonstrate it in a conclusive way.

It is also of relevance that the Pontifical Biblical Commission twice in the twentieth century addressed the origin of the Pentateuch. Although its pronouncements are not per se considered binding teachings of the Church today, they illustrate the wisdom of the Church in cautioning scholars against a premature and uncritical rejection of longstanding traditions associated with the Bible. At its first intervention, the Commission judged that the modern arguments used to support the Documentary Hypothesis were insufficiently strong to overturn the tradition of Mosaic authorship. The Commission did not thereby insist that Moses penned the entire text of the Pentateuch with his own hand, but it considered several scenarios to be compatible with the traditional thesis: (1) Moses may have utilized secretaries to assist with the writing; (2) he may have incorporated oral and written sources into the work; and (3) scribes in later centuries may be said to have made additions and modifications to the text in an effort to modernize the Pentateuch for later generations of readers (*On the Mosaic Authenticity of the Pentateuch*, June 27, 1906). The second intervention of the Commission invited scholars to study further the sources and composition of the Pentateuch with the tools of modern literary criticism and with the help of allied sciences. Optimism was expressed that this effort would reveal the profound role of Moses as an author and lawgiver, even if it found that a certain development of Mosaic Law took place after the time of Moses (*Letter to Cardinal Suhard*, January 16, 1948).

In the final analysis, Catholic scholarship is not bound to espouse any particular view of the authorship and date of Genesis (or the Pentateuch). Scholars are free to investigate the historical background of the book within the doctrinal framework of Scripture's divine inspiration and without disparagement of the Church's tradition. A range of views, from the substantial Mosaic authorship of Genesis to the Mosaic origin of its sources and traditions to the notion that Genesis is indebted to Moses in a more indirect way, is allowable. Still, for reasons given above and elsewhere, it remains a defensible position that the Book of Genesis is substantially Mosaic, at least in the antiquity of its traditions and quite possibly in its authorship as well.

**Structure** Genesis can be divided neatly into two major movements. Chapters 1–11 cover the distant aeons of *primeval* history, while chapters 12–50 cover the shorter span of *patriarchal* history. These two movements, differing in scope and perspective, create a funnel effect: the primeval narrative is cosmic in scope; it stretches across undateable ages; and it presents a world that is steadily beaten down by sin. In contrast, the patriarchal narrative narrows the focus to a single family instead of the human family as a whole; it slows the pace of the story to four generations; and it outlines God's plan to restore the world to a state of blessing. Within these two halves, the internal structure of Genesis is marked off by the recurring formula "these are the generations" or "these are the descendants" or "this is the history" (Heb. *'elleh toledot*). Eleven times the underlying Hebrew expression occurs in Genesis, each time pointing the way forward to a new phase or development in the story, usually with reference to a significant ancestor (2:4; 5:1; 6:9; 10:1; 11:10, 27; 25:12, 19; 36:1, 9; 37:2).

**Title** The Hebrew title for Genesis consists of its opening phrase, *bere'shit*, meaning "in the beginning". The Greek Septuagint entitles the book *genesis*, meaning "origin" or "birth", as does the Latin Vulgate. These headings correctly indicate that Genesis is a book of beginnings. It narrates the origin of the world (chap. 1), the origin of the human race (chap. 2), the origin of sin and suffering (chap. 3), the origin of nations (chap. 10), the origin of languages (chap. 11), and the origin of Israel as a tribal family descended from Abraham, Isaac, and Jacob (chaps. 12–50).

**Literary Background** A sound interpretation of Genesis depends in part on a sound evaluation of its literary form. This has proven to be a formidable challenge in the case of Gen 1–11, which resists easy classification among the surviving genres of ancient literature. The Catholic Church has never taken an official position on its form, though several statements made in the twentieth century offer important guidance for its interpretation. The first is a response of the Pontifical Biblical Commission, which maintained that the first three chapters of Genesis recount "things that actually happened", with the twofold proviso that Genesis does not offer a strictly scientific description of creation, nor must everything stated in these chapters be understood in a strictly literal way (*On the Historical Character of Genesis 1–3*, June 30, 1909). Several decades later the Biblical Commission sent a letter to the Archbishop of Paris contending that Gen 1–11 is a "popular description" of the world's beginning that expresses fundamental truths in "figurative language" (*Letter to Cardinal Suhard*, January 16, 1948). Pope Pius XII referred back to this letter in a 1950 encyclical in which he clarified that the first eleven chapters of Genesis "pertain to history in a true sense" and so must not be reduced to the level of "myths" (*Humani Generis* 38–39). Most recently, the *Catechism of the Catholic Church* affirms the creation of the world, along with the original holiness and fall of the first couple, as real historical events that Scripture describes in symbolic and figurative ways (CCC 337, 362, 375, 390, 396).

Guided by these pronouncements and informed by contemporary biblical scholarship, it seems best to say that Gen 1–11 occupies a unique position between history and myth. On the one hand, these chapters offer a *historical* account of primeval times that explains the existence and conditions of the world as we know it. The historicity of such things as the creation of the cosmos by God, the creation of man and woman, the unity of the human race, the testing and fall of man from a state of grace and original innocence, etc., cannot be compromised, for these constitute the essential pillars of the biblical world view and remain basic presuppositions of the Christian faith. On the other hand, the first eleven chapters of Genesis exhibit notable parallels with the *mythological* traditions of the ancient Near East. These ancient myths of origin abound with poetic imagery and symbolic representations of the mysteries that pertain to divine and human realities. Of course, Genesis differs from the myths of Israel's neighbors in having an objective grounding in history, and at several points Genesis is anti-mythological in intention (see note on 1:1—2:4). Nevertheless, this did not prevent the sacred writer from utilizing common cultural forms of expression, also used by the mythmakers of the ancient world, in order to make his description of primeval history understandable to his contemporaries.

All things considered, then, Gen 1–11 may be regarded as historical in substance but mythopoeic in expression. Its narrative is anchored in realities and events of the past, and yet its description of those events makes use of the poetic symbolism and figurative modes of speech that once had a broad currency in biblical times. For the literary form of the patriarchal narratives in Gen 12–50, see note on 12:1—50:26.

**Themes** The Book of Genesis is a historical and theological introduction to the Bible. It lays the indispensable groundwork for the rest of biblical revelation. For this reason, the book adopts a universal and religious perspective: the world is the stage of the Genesis drama, and God is the main Actor behind the scenes of history and human affairs that it records. This broad perspective is most evident in the early chapters, which encompass the divine creation of the cosmos, the formation and fall of the human race, the epidemic spread of moral and spiritual corruption, the universal flood, and the scattering of peoples over the earth (chaps. 1–11). But concern for the world at large, though less obvious on the surface, remains at the center of the patriarchal narratives as well, where God's promises for the future continue to propel the story forward (chaps. 12–50).

In many ways, the theology of Genesis comes to expression in its preoccupation with "covenants". This is not strange in itself, since covenants were very much a part of social and political life in the ancient Near East. But unlike their ancient counterparts, several covenants in Genesis involve God, not simply as the witness or enforcer of a human arrangement, but as a full partner in forging covenant bonds with the world and pledging his love and loyalty to the human race. God thus makes covenants with creation (see note on 1:1—2:4), with Adam (2:15–17), with Noah and the world (9:8–17), and with Abraham and his descendants (15:18–21; 17:1–21; 22:16–18, etc.). Two of these covenants, the Adamic and the Abrahamic, occasion events that mark the low point and the high point of the Genesis narrative. (**1**) The *Adamic* covenant is the primeval bond that unites the human family with God the Creator in a state of blessing. However, when this relationship is tested, the covenant is broken by the rebellion of the first couple (3:6) and the original blessings are exchanged for the discipline of divine curses (3:16–19). From that point on, everything goes downhill, as the plot bottoms out under the avalanche of human iniquity that follows, with envy, murder, bigamy, violence, impurity, and pride wreaking havoc throughout the world (4:6–11, 19, 23; 6:11; 9:22; 11:1–9). (**2**) The *Abrahamic* covenant is God's solution to the broken Adamic covenant. At first, his covenant with Abraham is simply the pledge of a new homeland (15:18; 17:8) and a future dynasty of kings (17:6, 16). But at the summit of the Genesis story, when Abraham is tested as Adam was, God responds to the faith and obedience of the patriarch by swearing a covenant oath to restore his blessings to the world through Abraham's offspring (22:16–18). It is this pledge, according to the NT, that envisions God's worldwide plan of redemption in Jesus Christ (Acts 3:25–26; Gal 3:10–29).

The Book of Genesis, then, is protological as well as prophetic. It looks back on the earliest phase of human existence as the beginning phase of salvation history, focusing on the generations that paved the way for the founding of Israel as a covenant people. But it also looks forward to the future realization of the divine plan, when the curses of the Adamic covenant are slowly but eventually reversed by the blessings of the Abrahamic. Insofar as man's rebellion and estrangement from the Lord are dilemmas that go unresolved within the storyline of Genesis, the book presents itself as the first chapter in this larger story of redemptive history.

**Christian Perspective** Christianity sees the mystery of salvation prophesied and prefigured in multiple ways in Genesis. (**1**) The first man, Adam, is a type of the divine man, Jesus Christ, who assumes headship over the human race to repair the damage done by Adam's rebellion (chaps. 2–3; Rom 5:12–21). (**2**) The blessings of Eden, with its flowing rivers and tree of life, point to the blessings of eternal life that await us in heaven (2:8–14; Rev 22:1–5). (**3**) The vanquishing of the serpent is realized when Christ reigns victorious in the lives of his disciples (3:15; Rom 16:20). (**4**) The raging waters of the flood prefigure the saving waters of Baptism (chaps. 6–8; 1 Pet 3:20–21). (**5**) Melchizedek, the priest-king who offers bread and wine, is a type of Christ the King and his priestly offering of the Eucharist under the same visible signs (14:17–20; Mt 26:26–29; Heb 7:1–19). (**6**) Abraham is the archetype of the believer, and his faith in the power and goodness of God is the same faith that animates the lives of the Christian faithful (15:1–6; Rom 4:1–12; Gal 3:6–9). (**7**) The offering and return of Isaac, not spared by his anguished father, foreshadow the dying and rising of Jesus, the beloved Son who was not spared by his Father but was handed over for the world's salvation (22:1–14; Rom 8:32; Heb 11:17–19). (8) The expectation of an international ruler from the royal line of Judah is realized in Christ, who reigns over all nations as the Lion of the tribe of Judah (49:9–11; Rev 5:5). «

## OUTLINE OF GENESIS

1. **Primeval History (chaps. 1–11)**
   A. The Story of Creation (1:1—2:25)
   B. The Fall of Adam and Eve (3:1–24)
   C. The Descendants of Adam (4:1—5:32)
   D. The Story of the Flood (6:1—9:19)
   E. The Descendants of Noah (9:20—10:32)
   F. The Tower of Babel (11:1–9)
   G. The Descendants of Shem (11:10–32)

2. **Patriarchal History (chaps. 12–50)**
   A. The Story of Abraham (12:1—25:11)
   B. The Descendants of Ishmael (25:12–18)
   C. The Story of Isaac (25:19—26:35)
   D. The Story of Jacob (27:1—35:29)
   E. The Descendants of Esau (36:1–43)
   F. The Story of Joseph (37:1—48:22)
   G. The Blessing of the Twelve Tribes (49:1–27)
   H. The Death of Jacob and Joseph (49:28—50:26)

THE FIRST BOOK OF MOSES COMMONLY CALLED

# GENESIS

## Six Days of Creation and the Sabbath

1 In the beginning God created[a] the heavens
and the earth. 2 The earth was without form and
void, and darkness was upon the face of the deep;
and the Spirit[b] of God was moving over the face of
the waters.
3 And God said, "Let there be light"; and there

**1:1:** Jn 1:1.

**1:1—2:25** Genesis begins with two accounts of creation. The first is grand in scope and majestic in tone; it stresses the Lordship of God over all things and describes his actions as an almighty voice that brings the world into being (1:1—2:4). The second is narrower in focus and more intimate in description; it emphasizes the closeness of the Lord to his creation and describes his actions in more humanlike terms (2:5–25). It is possible these were once independent accounts having different dates of origin. Regardless, their juxtaposition in Genesis makes for a balanced depiction of God's transcendence and immanence in relation to the world (CCC 289).

**1:1—2:4** The first creation account affirms a cosmic event at the beginning of history. It offers neither a literal nor a scientific description of how the world was made; rather, it asserts theological truths about God and creation in a symbolic way (CCC 337). The account should not be interpreted as a revealed timetable about the actual historical sequence of creation, nor should the author's prescientific view of the cosmos be mistaken for divinely inspired teaching about the physical constitution of the natural world. Its main teachings include the following. (**1**) The entire universe owes its existence to God as Creator and Lord. (**2**) Each and every part of creation is good in the eyes of God. (**3**) God established a hierarchy among created things, as seen in the ascending movement of the account, from inanimate things to animate creatures to the human race as the crown of the material world. (**4**) Creation shows forth the power of God, who speaks the universe into existence, the wisdom of God, who arranges all things into a symphony of natural beauty and harmony, and the goodness of God, who bestows life and blessing gratuitously. (**5**) The creation story exhibits an apologetic interest in countering the mythological world views of the ancient Near East. According to the pagan myths, a pantheon of deities existed in the beginning; the gods were embodied in nature and had humanlike needs and imperfections; the world was born out of a struggle between the gods; and man was created only to be exploited by the gods. In contrast, Genesis teaches that only one God exists, that he stands outside of time, that he is altogether distinct from the natural world, and that he blessed mankind, making man the bearer of his image. In addition to these considerations, the seven-day structure of the account is best viewed as a literary device for communicating the following points. (**6**) Six days of work followed by one day of rest underscores the obligation of man to lay aside his labor and honor the Creator every seventh day (Ex 20:8–11). (**7**) The founding of the world in seven days parallels the building of the Tabernacle according to seven commands (Ex 40:16–33) and the dedication of the Temple in seven days (1 Kings 8:65) after seven years of construction (1 Kings 6:38). Also, the description of God resting on the seventh day (2:2–3) has links with ancient concepts of a temple, which is considered a place of divine rest (2 Chron 6:41; Ps 132:14; Sir 24:11; Is 66:1). The creation week in Genesis thus reflects the belief that the world is a cosmic sanctuary (see topical essay: *Theology of the Temple* at 2 Chron 5). (**8**) Seven days of divine speech hint that God established a covenant with creation. Not only does the Hebrew for "seven" share a common root with the verb for "swearing a covenant oath" (see 21:27–32), but in later Jewish tradition, God is said to have founded the world through his oath (*1 Enoch* 69, 15–27; *Sifre Deuteronomy* 330) (on creation, see CCC 282–87, 337–44).

**1:1 the beginning:** The moment when time and space burst into existence by a creative act of God. The date of the event cannot be ascertained from the biblical data. **created:** The Hebrew expression hints at God's unique ability to create *ex nihilo*, i.e., out of nothing, without reliance on preexisting materials. This is how creation came to be understood in Jewish (2 Mac 7:28) and Christian theology (Rom 4:17) (CCC 290, 296–97). **the heavens and the earth:** The totality of creation, which includes all things seen and unseen, material as well as spiritual (Neh 9:6; Col 1:16).

**1:2 earth was without form:** The first thing created, as portrayed in the description, is an amorphous mass of land submerged in water. This is conceived as the raw material from which God then shapes the world into its recognizable parts. **the deep:** The cosmic ocean that forms the seas (Ps 33:7) and was thought to lie beneath the earth in Semitic cosmology (Ex 20:4). Here it is said to engulf the earth (Ps 104:6) before dry land emerges from its depths (1:9). **the Spirit of God:** Some render this phrase "a wind from God" or even "a mighty wind". Both translations are possible from a grammatical standpoint. However, the RSV translation is preferable because (**1**) the same expression is used elsewhere in the Pentateuch as a reference to God's Spirit (Gen 41:38; Ex 31:3; 35:31; Num 24:2), (**2**) elsewhere in the Bible the divine Spirit is associated with God's creative work (Job 33:4; Ps 104:30), and (**3**) the preferred interpretation throughout Christian history takes it as a reference to the Holy Spirit (CCC 703). **moving:** I.e., hovering or fluttering like an eagle over its young (Deut 32:11). • *Allegorically*, the Holy Spirit was carried upon the waters as upon a chariot and brought forth the newborn world as a type of Baptism (St. Jerome, *Letters* 69).

**1:3 God said:** The universe is created by divine utterance (Ps 33:6–9). In several creation myths of the Near East, the world emerged out of a conflict between rival gods; in Genesis, the word of God goes forth unchallenged, meeting no resistance or rival. • According to the NT, the creative word is not simply a power but a Person—God the Son, through whom all things were made (Jn 1:1–3; Heb 1:2; CCC 291). • One who pays close attention will recognize the Father, the Son, and the Spirit in the beginning. The Father creates heaven and earth, the Spirit moves over the waters, and the Son, who acts while the Father is speaking, separates the light from the darkness (St. Ambrose, *The Holy Spirit* 2, 1).

[a] Or *When God began to create.*
[b] Or *wind.*

was light. 4 And God saw that the light was good;
and God separated the light from the darkness.
5 God called the light Day, and the darkness he called
Night. And there was evening and there was morning, one day.
6 And God said, "Let there be a firmament in the
midst of the waters, and let it separate the waters
from the waters." 7 And God made the firmament
and separated the waters which were under the
firmament from the waters which were above the firmament. And it was so. 8 And God called the
firmament Heaven. And there was evening and
there was morning, a second day.
9 And God said, "Let the waters under the heavens be gathered together into one place, and let the
dry land appear." And it was so. 10 God called the
dry land Earth, and the waters that were gathered
together he called Seas. And God saw that it was
good. 11 And God said, "Let the earth put forth vegetation, plants yielding seed, and fruit trees bearing
fruit in which is their seed, each according to its kind,
upon the earth." And it was so. 12 The earth brought
forth vegetation, plants yielding seed according to
their own kinds, and trees bearing fruit in which is
their seed, each according to its kind. And God saw
that it was good. 13 And there was evening and there
was morning, a third day.
14 And God said, "Let there be lights in the
firmament of the heavens to separate the day from
the night; and let them be for signs and for seasons

---

**1:4 good:** Indicates that creation corresponds perfectly to the divine purpose for which it was made. Emphasis on the goodness of the natural world punctuates the account (1:10, 12, 18, 21, 25, 31).

**1:5 Day ... Night:** The organization of time, with its recurring cycles of daylight and darkness, is the work of the first day. **day:** The Hebrew word *yom* is capable of designating various durations of time but normally denotes a 24-hour day. Nevertheless, the seven "days" of creation are not intended to be read as literal history. Keeping in mind the symbolic nature of the account (CCC 337), the enumeration of "days" serves the purpose of promoting Sabbath observance, among other things (see note on 1:1—2:4). Perhaps the clearest indication that Genesis employs temporal language in a figurative way is the fact that light is created on day 1, together with the evening and morning, and yet the sun and the moon are not created until day 4.

**1:6 firmament:** The Hebrew term is related to a verb that means "hammer out" (see Ex 39:3). This suggests the ancient Israelites imagined the firmament as a hammered bowl that is placed over the world like a roof or dome, holding up waters above the earth and separating them from the seas below. This ancient cosmology has a phenomenological basis: to the unaided senses, the sky looks like an enormous vault, and its blueness may have suggested the idea of an ocean suspended overhead. Modern readers must recognize that the author's world view is one of his cultural assumptions, not one of his inspired assertions; thus, the cosmological presuppositions of the author should not be taken as revealed propositions to be accepted by faith. The Church, following the wisdom of St. Augustine (*On the Literal Interpretation of Genesis* 2, 9), maintains that the Bible does not contain any properly scientific teaching about the nature of the physical universe (Leo XIII, *Providentissimus Deus* 39).

**1:8 Heaven:** Can also be translated "sky" or "heavens" (the Hebrew term is an archaic plural). It is uncertain what concept the Israelites had of multiple heavens. In later Jewish tradition, the lowest level of heaven was thought to be the atmosphere, and the highest level was the dwelling place of God. Different forms of the tradition counted three heavens (2 Cor 12:2; *Testament of Levi* 2, 7–10) or seven heavens (Talmud, *b. Ḥagigah* 12b). Scripture elsewhere conceptualizes the heavens as a cosmic tent (Ps 104:2; Is 40:22) that is stretched over the earth (Is 42:5; Zech 12:1).

**1:14 days and years:** The solar and lunar cycles determined the agricultural and liturgical seasons of the Israelite calendar (Ps 104:19; Hos 2:11; Gal 4:10; CCC 347).

## The Framework of Seven Days

Genesis pictures the newly created world in a state of primeval chaos. Submerged in water and shrouded in darkness, it is a place that is unfit for habitation and life. The author conveys this idea by describing it as something "without form and void" (Gen 1:2). This twofold problem of formlessness and emptiness is important because it sets the stage for the days of creation that follow, where God imposes order on the chaos in two phases: on days 1–3 he *forms* the world into its temporal and spatial dimensions, and on days 4–6 he *fills* the world with its designated rulers. Genesis thus arranges the creation account in symmetrical fashion, with the first three days corresponding to the second three days (cf. St. Thomas Aquinas, *Summa Theologiae* 1, 70, 1). The seventh day stands apart as the day when God rested from his work. Inherent in this literary format is the message that the cosmos, in its artistic design and orderliness, bears witness to the consummate wisdom of the Creator (cf. Ps 19:1; Wis 13:5; Rom 1:20).

| Formlessness ▼ | | Emptiness ▼ |
|---|---|---|
| **Day 1.** Day and Night | ▸ | **Day 4.** Sun, Moon, and Stars |
| **Day 2.** Sea and Sky | ▸ | **Day 5.** Fish and Birds |
| **Day 3.** Land and Vegetation | ▸ | **Day 6.** Man and Animals |
| **Day 7.** The Sabbath Rest | | |

and for days and years, [15]and let them be lights in the firmament of the heavens to give light upon the earth." And it was so. [16]And God made the two great lights, the greater light to rule the day, and the lesser light to rule the night; he made the stars also. [17]And God set them in the firmament of the heavens to give light upon the earth, [18]to rule over the day and over the night, and to separate the light from the darkness. And God saw that it was good. [19]And there was evening and there was morning, a fourth day.

20 And God said, "Let the waters bring forth swarms of living creatures, and let birds fly above the earth across the firmament of the heavens." [21]So God created the great sea monsters and every living creature that moves, with which the waters swarm, according to their kinds, and every winged bird according to its kind. And God saw that it was good. [22]And God blessed them, saying, "Be fruitful and multiply and fill the waters in the seas, and let birds multiply on the earth." [23]And there was evening and there was morning, a fifth day.

24 And God said, "Let the earth bring forth living creatures according to their kinds: cattle and creeping things and beasts of the earth according to their kinds." And it was so. [25]And God made the beasts of the earth according to their kinds and the cattle according to their kinds, and everything that creeps upon the ground according to its kind. And God saw that it was good.

26 Then God said, "Let us make man in our image, after our likeness; and let them have dominion over the fish of the sea, and over the birds of the air, and over the cattle, and over all the earth, and over every creeping thing that creeps upon the earth." [27]So God created man in his own image, in the image of God he created him; male and female he created them. [28]And God blessed them, and God said to them, "Be fruitful and multiply, and fill the earth and subdue it; and have dominion over the fish of the sea and over the birds of the air and over every living thing that moves upon the earth." [29]And God said, "Behold, I have given you every plant yielding seed which is upon the face of all

**1:26, 27:** Gen 5:1; Mt 19:4; Mk 10:6; Col 3:10; Jas 3:9.

**1:16 greater light ... lesser light ... stars:** Israel was forbidden to worship these luminaries, which were deified as gods in the Near Eastern world (Deut 4:19). This may explain why the sun and moon are not mentioned by name in the creation account, for the Hebrew terms resemble the names of the Semitic sun and moon gods. Later passages in Genesis compare the sun, moon, and stars to a family representing father, mother, and children (15:5; 22:17; 37:9–10).

**1:21 sea monsters:** Large aquatic animals as distinct from small ones, which are called "swarms of living creatures" (1:20). The sea monsters are symbols of evil in biblical poetry, just as they represented primal forces of chaos in Canaanite mythology (Ps 74:13–14; Is 27:1; Ezek 29:3). In contrast to these myths, Genesis insists that God created the mighty sea creatures; they are not preexistent powers that God faced as rivals in the beginning.

**1:22 blessed them:** God endowed them with the creative power to reproduce their species. The divine gift of fertility is always viewed as a blessing in the Bible, especially in connection with human procreation (1:28; Deut 28:4; 30:19; Ps 128:3–4; CCC 1652).

**1:26 Let us:** The plural expression does not imply a belief in multiple gods. It may be read as (**1**) a plural of majesty, in which God speaks as a king representing his court or the fullness of his authority (cf. Ezra 4:18); (**2**) a plural of deliberation, in which God decides to create man after considering his options (Is 6:8); (**3**) a plural of self-exhortation, in which God urges himself into action (11:7); or (**4**) a plural of assembly, in which God addresses his intention to the heavenly host of angels (cf. Job 38:4–7). • Christian tradition detects in this idiom a hint that God himself is a communion of Divine Persons, later revealed as the Trinity (Mt 28:19; 2 Cor 13:14). Scripture elsewhere indicates that creation is the work, not only of the Father, but also of the Son (Jn 1:1–3; Heb 1:2) and the Spirit (Job 33:4; Ps 104:30).

**1:27 male and female:** The sexual distinction between man and woman is willed by God, as is its purpose to reproduce the human race (1:28). • The image of God is not only borne by individuals but is also expressed through man and woman as a couple. From the image of the natural family, then, we can infer that God, in the mystery of his inner life, is a community of persons united by a bond of love and shared life (cf. John Paul II, *Mulieris dignitatem* 7).

**1:28 subdue:** The Hebrew means "bring into subjection" (2 Chron 28:10; Jer 34:11). Man is not given license to abuse creation but is called to harness its potential for good. He is to use his creative abilities to manage the earth's resources for the building of human civilization. In the theology of Genesis, man is the steward of God's world, not its owner or master in any absolute sense (CCC 373, 2415–17).

**1:29 every plant:** Man and animals are supplied with a diet of natural produce (1:30). Neither is a carnivore in the

### Word Study

#### *Image and Likeness* (Gen 1:26)

*Tselem* and *demut* (Heb.): the first term often denotes a physical "representation" of something in two (Ezek 23:14) or three dimensions (Num 33:52; 1 Sam 6:5; Ezek 16:17), and the second term refers to a "pattern" (2 Kings 16:10) or visible "resemblance" of something (Is 40:18; Ezek 1:5). Genesis associates this word pair with *royal authority*, as when the first man and woman are given dominion to rule over creation (Gen 1:26); with the relational concept of *sonship*, as when a father produces an image of himself in a son (Gen 5:3); and with the *sanctity* of human life, as when the Lord pledges to avenge the dignity of human life against murderous violence (9:5–6). A similar complex of ideas had currency in the political ideology of the ancient Near East, where the kings of Mesopotamia and Egypt were said to be "sons" fashioned in the "image" of their patron deity. Thus, what was typically the prerogative of a ruling monarch in distinction from his subjects, Genesis applies to every human person in distinction from the plants and animals. Other aspects of the divine image include man's rational intelligence, his dignity as a person, his moral awareness, and his unique capacity for a personal relationship with God (CCC 343, 355–58).

the earth, and every tree with seed in its fruit; you
shall have them for food. [30]And to every beast of
the earth, and to every bird of the air, and to everything that creeps on the earth, everything that has
the breath of life, I have given every green plant for
food." And it was so. [31]And God saw everything
that he had made, and behold, it was very good.
And there was evening and there was morning, a
sixth day.

2 Thus the heavens and the earth were
finished, and all the host of them. [2]And on the
seventh day God finished his work which he had
done, and he rested on the seventh day from all his
work which he had done. [3]So God blessed the seventh day and hallowed it, because on it God rested
from all his work which he had done in creation.

### Another Account of Creation

4 These are the generations of the heavens and the
earth when they were created.

In the day that the LORD God made the earth and
the heavens, [5]when no plant of the field was yet in the
earth and no herb of the field had yet sprung up—
for the LORD God had not caused it to rain upon the
earth, and there was no man to till the ground; [6]but a
mist[c] went up from the earth and watered the whole
face of the ground—[7]then the LORD God formed man
of dust from the ground, and breathed into his nostrils the breath of life; and man became a living soul.
[8]And the LORD God planted a garden in Eden, in the
east; and there he put the man whom he had formed.
[9]And out of the ground the LORD God made to grow
every tree that is pleasant to the sight and good for

**2:1–3:** Ex 20:11. **2:2:** Heb 4:4, 10. **2:7:** 1 Cor 15:45, 47. **2:9:** Rev 2:7; 22:2, 14, 19.

beginning, since the shedding of lifeblood, which is necessary for the consumption of meat, is inconsistent with the harmony between creatures that reigns in the primeval state. Not until the disharmony of sin invades the world are animals given as food, and then only as a divine concession (9:3–4).

**1:31 very good:** God is pleased and delighted with the whole ensemble of creation. This final assessment comes after he approves its individual parts (1:4, 10, 12, 18, 21, 25).

**2:2 rested:** God institutes the Sabbath by setting the example for its observance. For man, to bear the image of God means to bear the responsibility of imitating God in the weekly rhythm of labor and rest (Ex 20:8–11). Hence, the point is not that God had grown tired after creating the world, but that we have need of rest when we labor in imitation of him. Strictly speaking, God's work of sustaining the universe continues throughout history (Jn 5:16–17; Heb 1:3), as does his work of creation, e.g., each time he creates a human soul at conception (Pius XII, *Humani Generis* 36) (CCC 366, 2172–73). The Sabbath, which is set apart for the worship of God and the contemplation of his works, is the sign of his covenant with creation (Ex 31:12–17; CCC 346). • The NT interprets the weekly Sabbath rest as a sign of the eternal rest that awaits us in heaven (Heb 4:1–10).

**2:3 hallowed it:** God sanctifies the seventh day and makes it a holy day (Is 58:13). The lesson is that work is ordered to worship, lest man become a slave to his labor and fail to acknowledge his total dependence on the Lord (CCC 347, 2175–76).

**2:4–25** The second creation account describes the formation of the first human couple. The story is historical in content but symbolic in description (CCC 362, 375), its message being conveyed through images once familiar in the epic and mythopoeic literature of the ancient Near East. The setting is the garden of Eden, which represents the state of grace. Man, who is created outside the garden, is placed there by God (2:8) to show that he is raised to a level of divine blessedness that is above his natural state (CCC 374–78). The sacredness of this original situation is underscored by indications that Genesis imagines paradise as a primeval sanctuary. Like the Tabernacle and Temple of later times, the garden is (**1**) entered from the east (3:24; Ex 27:13; Ezek 47:1), (**2**) home to angelic guardians called cherubim (3:24; 1 Kings 6:23–28), (**3**) adorned with trees (2:9; Josh 24:26; 1 Kings 6:29–32), (**4**) the source of sacred waters (2:10; Ezek 47:1–12; Joel 3:18), and (**5**) the place where God dwells with his people on the earth (3:8; Lev 26:12; 2 Sam 7:6). According to one Jewish tradition, Eden is the Holy of Holies, i.e., the most sacred estate within the cosmic Temple of the world (*Jubilees* 8, 19). See note 1:1—2:4.

**2:4 These are the generations:** A formula that introduces new phases of history and narrative in Genesis. See introduction: *Structure*. **LORD God:** The first term in Hebrew is "Yahweh", the personal name of God revered by Israel. The second term is the common noun for a deity and is used throughout the first creation account (1:1—2:4). Used together, Genesis teaches that the God of Israel ("Yahweh") is none other than the Creator of the universe ("God").

**2:5 no plant:** In the second creation account, man is formed before the vegetation and animals; in the first account, man is created after the vegetation and animals (1:11, 20–26). The discrepancy does not amount to a contradiction insofar as the first account is not meant to be a chronological description of the actual stages of creation. See note on 1:1—2:4.

**2:7 God formed man:** Evokes the image of a potter shaping a vessel out of clay (Job 10:9; Is 45:9). There is a wordplay in Hebrew between "man" (*'adam*) and the "ground" (*'adamah*) from which he is made (Sir 33:10). The creation of man out of dirt or clay is an ancient motif paralleled in Egyptian (*Great Hymn to Khnum*) and Mesopotamian literature (*Atrahasis Epic*; *Gilgamesh Epic*). **dust:** Symbolic of human mortality (3:19). **breath of life:** The animating principle that makes man a living creature like the animals (see 2:19; 7:21–22). However, man is unique in that God has made him a composite of matter and spirit, a being who possesses a body and a rational soul (Wis 15:11; CCC 362–66). The animation of human bodies by divine breath is paralleled in Egyptian texts (*Instruction for King Merikare*; *Great Hymn to Aton*). • According to Catholic theology, Adam was not only created with natural or biological life, but was infused with the supernatural life of grace and holiness. Thus, from his first breath, Adam was an "upright" (Eccles 7:29) "son of God" (Lk 3:38) (CCC 374–76).

**2:8 garden:** The Greek Septuagint translates this as "paradise". See word study: *Paradise* at 2 Cor 12:3. **in the east:** I.e., east of Palestine. The geographical data in 2:10–14 suggest a location in Mesopotamia (modern Iraq).

**2:9 tree of life:** An ancient symbol of immortality and divine wisdom (Prov 3:18). Its fruit was thought to confer everlasting life (3:22). **knowledge of good and evil:** Not a moral awareness of right and wrong, which man possessed from the beginning as a rational creature, but the legal authority to determine what is good and evil (see 2 Sam 14:17; 1 Kings 3:9). Adam will presume to wield this authority over the moral order, though it belongs exclusively to God. Overstepping his bounds, he will attempt to break free from the limits of being a creature who is made to love and serve God with the free submission of his will (Sir 15:15; CCC 396). See notes on 3:6 and 3:22.

[c]Or *flood*.

food, the tree of life also in the midst of the garden,
and the tree of the knowledge of good and evil.
10 A river flowed out of Eden to water the garden,
and there it divided and became four rivers. 11The
name of the first is Pi′shon; it is the one which flows
around the whole land of Hav′ilah, where there is
gold; 12and the gold of that land is good; bdellium
and onyx stone are there. 13The name of the second
river is Gi′hon; it is the one which flows around the
whole land of Cush. 14And the name of the third
river is Tigris, which flows east of Assyria. And the
fourth river is the Euphra′tes.
15 The LORD God took the man and put him in
the garden of Eden to till it and keep it. 16And the
LORD God commanded the man, saying, "You may
freely eat of every tree of the garden; 17but of the tree
of the knowledge of good and evil you shall not eat,
for in the day that you eat of it you shall die."
18 Then the LORD God said, "It is not good that
the man should be alone; I will make him a helper
fit for him." 19So out of the ground the LORD God
formed every beast of the field and every bird of
the air, and brought them to the man to see what
he would call them; and whatever the man called
every living creature, that was its name. 20The man
gave names to all cattle, and to the birds of the air,
and to every beast of the field; but for the man there
was not found a helper fit for him. 21So the LORD
God caused a deep sleep to fall upon the man, and
while he slept took one of his ribs and closed up its
place with flesh; 22and the rib which the LORD God
had taken from the man he made into a woman and
brought her to the man. 23Then the man said,

"This at last is bone of my bones
 and flesh of my flesh;
she shall be called Woman,[d]
 because she was taken out of Man."[e]

24Therefore a man leaves his father and his mother
and clings to his wife, and they become one flesh.
25And the man and his wife were both naked, and
were not ashamed.

### The Fall of Man

3 Now the serpent was more subtle than
any other wild creature that the LORD God had

**2:24:** Mt 19:5; Mk 10:7; 1 Cor 6:16; Eph 5:31. **3:1:** Rev 12:9; 20:2.

**2:15–17** The terms and conditions of the Adamic covenant (Sir 14:17). The tree of life and the tree threatening death represent the twin sanctions of the covenant—the blessing and the curse (see Deut 30:19). Adam was to learn from these boundaries that God is not his equal but his Father and Lord. The arrangement is an ordeal designed to test Adam's faith and filial obedience.

**2:15 till ... keep:** The command to "keep" the garden may be translated as a command to "guard" it, as in 3:24. In this case, a threat to the order of paradise is implied, and the appearance of the serpent in 3:1 is anticipated. Moreover, the two Hebrew verbs in question are used elsewhere in the Pentateuch for the liturgical duties of priests and Levites serving as ministers and guardians over the Tabernacle (Num 3:7–8; 8:26; 18:5–6). Their use here implies that man's work of cultivating and keeping watch over the garden is likewise a form of divine service. Rabbinic tradition thus considered Adam a priest (*Genesis Rabbah* 16, 7). For Eden as a sacred sanctuary, see note on 2:4–25.

**2:17 you shall die:** Mortality as well as the spiritual death of estrangement from God are the curse for transgressing the Adamic covenant (Sir 14:17; CCC 1008).

**2:18 a helper fit for him:** Anticipates the creation of woman, though other living creatures are fashioned first (2:19). The fact that woman comes last is not the result of trial and error, but is God's way of teaching man that he is fundamentally different from the animals, despite certain natural features and functions they share in common. Lower life forms cannot supply the love, help, and companionship man needs to be whole.

**2:20 gave names:** Adam's first act of sovereignty over the animal kingdom (1:26). In the ancient world, to name something was to exercise authority over it.

**2:21–24** The institution of the marriage covenant, which is designed by God to be intimate (one flesh, 2:24), heterosexual (man and woman, 2:23), mutually supportive (helper, 2:18), and procreative (multiply, 1:28). For indications that the Bible considers marriage a covenant, see Ezek 16:8 and Mal 2:14. • Jesus teaches from this text that God designed marriage to be a permanent union of the spouses (Mt 19:3–9). As such, it symbolizes the unbreakable bond between Christ and his spiritual bride, the Church (Eph 5:21–33).

**2:22 the rib:** The first woman is created from the substance of the first man (1 Cor 11:8). Her sexual distinction from the man shows that the two are literally "made for each other". That she is taken from his side rather than from his head or feet is also significant—it shows that she is equal in dignity to the man, not above him or below him (CCC 369, 371). • *Allegorically*, the sleep of Adam foreshadows the death of Christ; and Eve, coming from Adam's side, is a type of the Church, the true mother of all the living (Tertullian, *On the Soul* 43).

**2:23 my bones ... my flesh:** An idiom for natural kinship (29:14; Judg 9:2). The bride becomes the kinswoman of the groom and his family through the covenant of marriage. **Woman ... Man**: The poem makes a wordplay on "man" (*'ish*) and "woman" (*'ishshah*), which are also the terms for "husband" and "wife" in biblical Hebrew.

**2:24 clings:** The term indicates fidelity to one's partner in a covenant relationship (Deut 10:20; 30:20; Josh 23:8).

**2:25 naked ... not ashamed:** Points to the innocence and original integrity of Adam and Eve. At this point, their lives are untouched by sin, and their sexual drive is under complete control. The expression also hints at their vulnerability, since the term "naked" (*'arummim*) resembles the term "subtle" (*'arum*), which characterizes the serpent in the next verse (3:1).

**3:1–24** The account of the Fall affirms a primeval event using figurative language (CCC 390). It indicates that man, at the beginning of his history, rebelled against his Creator and brought sin and misery into the world. As Genesis presents it, the immediate effects of man and woman transgressing the original covenant (2:16–17) include shame (3:7), strife (3:12), suffering (3:16–19), and separation from the Lord (3:23–24). Its lasting effects, including death (3:19) and a disordered propensity toward evil (6:5), are passed down to the entire human family (CCC 390, 400). For the propagation of Original Sin (human nature deprived of sanctifying grace) and the fallen inclinations (concupiscence) that come with it, see notes on Rom 5:12 and 7:23.

**3:1 the serpent:** A personal agent of evil that Scripture later identifies as Satan (Rev 12:9). The serpent has been

[d]Heb *ishshah.*
[e]Heb *ish.*

made. He said to the woman, "Did God say, 'You shall not eat of any tree of the garden'?" [2]And the woman said to the serpent, "We may eat of the fruit of the trees of the garden; [3]but God said, 'You shall not eat of the fruit of the tree which is in the midst of the garden, neither shall you touch it, lest you die.'" [4]But the serpent said to the woman, "You will not die. [5]For God knows that when you eat of it your eyes will be opened, and you will be like God, knowing good and evil." [6]So when the woman saw that the tree was good for food, and that it was a delight to the eyes, and that the tree was to be desired to make one wise, she took of its fruit and ate; and she also gave some to her husband, and he ate. [7]Then the eyes of both were opened, and they knew that they were naked; and they sewed fig leaves together and made themselves aprons.

8 And they heard the sound of the LORD God walking in the garden in the cool of the day, and the man and his wife hid themselves from the presence of the LORD God among the trees of the garden. [9]But the LORD God called to the man, and said to him, "Where are you?" [10]And he said, "I heard the sound of you in the garden, and I was afraid, because I was naked; and I hid myself." [11]He said, "Who told you that you were naked? Have you eaten of the tree of which I commanded you not to eat?" [12]The man said, "The woman whom you gave to be with me, she gave me fruit of the tree, and I ate." [13]Then the LORD God said to the woman, "What is this that you have done?" The woman said, "The serpent beguiled me, and I ate." [14]The LORD God said to the serpent,

"Because you have done this,
  cursed are you above all cattle,
  and above all wild animals;
upon your belly you shall go,
  and dust you shall eat
  all the days of your life.

---

**3:4:** 2 Cor 11:3. **3:13:** 2 Cor 11:3. **3:14, 15:** Rev 12:9; 20:2.

---

commonly considered (**1**) a mythopoeic image that represents the devil (or at least the diabolical) in a literary way, (**2**) the visible form assumed by the devil in the garden, or (**3**) a real serpent whose body is possessed and manipulated by the devil, much as demons are capable of speaking through bodily creatures and controlling their actions (cf. Mk 5:1–13). Whatever the case, Satan was driven by envy to rob man of his blessings and bring death into the world (Wis 2:24; CCC 391, 2539). Jesus thus refers to him as "a murderer from the beginning" (Jn 8:44). Note, too, that the Hebrew term *naḥash* often refers to a snake (49:17), but in poetic and apocalyptic texts it can refer to a draconic sea serpent that represents opposition to the Lord (Job 26:13; Is 27:1; Amos 9:3). In the ancient Near East, serpents were symbolic of divinity and fertility as well as the threat of cosmic chaos. **subtle:** In the sense of "cunning". Notice that Satan uses half-truths to seduce and mislead: he claims that the couple will not die (3:4), that their eyes will be opened (3:5), and that they will become like God (3:5). These assurances all seem to come true at one level, since after eating the forbidden fruit, Adam and Eve continue to live for many years (5:5), their eyes are opened (3:7), and they in some sense become like God (3:22). However, in the light of God's intentions, these promised gains turn out to be painful losses (CCC 392, 2847). **not eat of any tree . . . ?:** The question insinuates that God is an obstacle to human fulfillment. In particular, it raises doubts about the Lord's generosity and goodwill, as though Adam and Eve were deprived of much more than God provided them. This is a complete distortion of the divine allowance in 2:16 (CCC 215).

**3:3 neither shall you touch:** A curious addition to the divine commandment in 2:17. It may imply that Eve is beginning to slip on the serpent's suggestion that God is unreasonably restrictive (3:1; CCC 399).

**3:4 You will not die:** A bold contradiction of 2:17 that denies the truthfulness of God and his word.

**3:5 God knows:** The accusation makes God look jealous and self-interested, as though he is withholding life's finest blessings from the couple in order to safeguard his prerogatives. Satan, meanwhile, is posing as a friend who has the woman's best interests in mind. **like God, knowing:** The expression could also be translated: "like gods, knowing . . ." (as in the Greek LXX and Latin Vulgate). Either translation implies the belief that deities possess powers and perfections not shared by humans.

**3:6 her husband:** These words are followed in the Hebrew text by the phrase "with her", indicating that Adam was present when Eve committed the sin. **and he ate:** Unlike Eve, who was deceived by the serpent after engaging him in dialogue (3:13; 1 Tim 2:14), Adam bows without resistance to the wishes of his wife (3:17) and asserts himself against the commandment given to him by the Lord (2:17). Tradition holds that Adam, having surrendered his trust in God, committed a sin of pride in wanting to be "like God, knowing good and evil" (3:5). His desire was not to discern the difference between good and evil, but to determine what was good and evil for himself, independently of God (cf. John Paul II, *Dominum et Vivificantem* 36) (CCC 397–98). See note on 2:9. • In the theology of Paul, Christ is the counterimage of Adam. Just as Adam, by his transgression, made us sinners subject to death, so Christ, by his obedience, secured the grace that makes us heirs of eternal life (Rom 5:12–21; 1 Cor 15:20–22). • Christ conquered the devil with the same weapons the devil used against us: a virgin, a tree, and death. These tokens of our demise have now become the tokens of our victory. Instead of Eve, there is Mary; instead of the tree of knowledge, there is the wood of the Cross; and instead of Adam's death, there is the death of Christ (St. John Chrysostom, *On the Cemetery and the Cross*).

**3:7 sewed fig leaves:** The couple, awakened to the disorder of sin, attempt to cover their shame and guilt. The effort proves unsatisfactory, for God reclothes them with animal skins in 3:21—perhaps a faint intimation that sin must be dealt with by blood sacrifice (Lev 17:11; Heb 9:22).

**3:8–13** Interrogated by the Lord, Adam shifts the blame to Eve (3:12), and Eve shifts the blame to the serpent (3:13). Sin has sown division and discord between the spouses in addition to shattering their relationship with God (CCC 1606–7).

**3:8 walking:** A humanlike description of God that stresses his closeness to man and woman in Eden. The expression in Hebrew elsewhere describes the Lord dwelling in his sanctuary in the midst of Israel (Lev 26:12; 2 Sam 7:6). See note on 6:6.

**3:9 Where are you?:** Not a literal inquiry of Adam's whereabouts, but an invitation for Adam to confess his wrongdoing and seek forgiveness.

**3:14 upon your belly:** Animals that go on the belly are declared an abomination by the Mosaic Law (Lev 11:42). **dust you shall eat:** An idiom for suffering a humiliating defeat (Ps 72:9; Is 65:25; Mic 7:17).

[15]I will put enmity between you and the woman,
and between your seed and her seed;
he shall bruise your head,
and you shall bruise his heel."
[16]To the woman he said,
"I will greatly multiply your pain in childbearing;
in pain you shall bring forth children,
yet your desire shall be for your husband,
and he shall rule over you."
[17]And to Adam he said,
"Because you have listened to the voice of your wife, and have eaten of the tree
of which I commanded you,
'You shall not eat of it,'
cursed is the ground because of you;
in toil you shall eat of it all the days of your life;
[18]thorns and thistles it shall bring forth to you;
and you shall eat the plants of the field.
[19]In the sweat of your face
you shall eat bread
till you return to the ground,
for out of it you were taken;
you are dust,
and to dust you shall return."

20 The man called his wife's name Eve,[f] because
she was the mother of all living. [21]And the LORD God
made for Adam and for his wife garments of skins,
and clothed them.

22 Then the LORD God said, "Behold, the man has
become like one of us, knowing good and evil; and
now, lest he put forth his hand and take also of the
tree of life, and eat, and live for ever"—[23]therefore the
LORD God sent him forth from the garden of Eden, to
till the ground from which he was taken. [24]He drove
out the man; and at the east of the garden of Eden
he placed the cherubim, and a flaming sword which
turned every way, to guard the way to the tree of life.

### Cain and Abel

4 Now Adam knew Eve his wife, and she conceived and bore Cain, saying, "I have gotten[g]

**3:17, 18:** Heb 6:8. **3:22, 24:** Rev 2:7; 22:2, 14, 19.

**3:15 I will put enmity:** A crucial verse in Genesis, which some think is an etiology that explains the origin of man's instinctive fear of snakes. More likely, the proverbial antagonism between men and snakes was evoked for the purpose of symbolizing man's ongoing struggle against sin and evil, which is personified by the serpent (cf. 4:7; Sir 21:2). In any case, neither interpretation captures the full meaning of the text, which foretells the eventual triumph of the woman and her offspring over Satan after a protracted period of hostility. **your seed:** The devil's accomplices in doing evil, including wicked men, who constitute his spiritual offspring (Jn 8:44). In Genesis, Cain and his line of godless descendants are the first to fulfill this role (4:8, 17–24; 1 Jn 3:12). **her seed:** The righteous descendants of the woman, initially linked with Abel (4:4) and the godly line of Seth (4:26; 5:6–32). **he shall:** The Hebrew could be read individually ("he shall") or collectively ("they shall"). The earliest known Jewish interpretation of this text takes the offspring of the woman to be an individual man (Gk. *autos*, "he" in the Greek LXX). **bruise:** Or, "crush" (as in Job 9:17). Victory over the satanic deceiver is assured: the serpent will sustain a fatal *head* injury, while the woman's offspring will suffer only a biting on the *heel*. At least one Jewish tradition connects this triumph with the coming of a messianic king (*Palestinian Targum*). • Christian tradition gives this text a messianic interpretation (Christ is the individual who tramples the devil underfoot: Heb 2:14; 1 Jn 3:8; St. Irenaeus *Against Heresies* 3, 23, 7), an ecclesiological interpretation (the Church is the offspring that shares in his victory: Rom 16:20; Rev 12:17), and a mariological interpretation (Mary is the promised woman who bears the Redeemer: Vatican II, *Lumen Gentium* 55). This passage has long been called the "first gospel" (Lat. *protoevangelium*) and stands out as the first revelation of God's mercy in Scripture (CCC 410–11).

**3:16–19** Suffering is imposed as the temporal consequence of sin. Eve and her descendants will suffer as wives (spousal domination) and mothers (painful childbirth). Adam and his descendants will suffer as family providers (toilsome labor for food) (CCC 1609).

**3:17 cursed:** A curse of futility and decay grips the earth, making the production of food an extremely tedious process. This is in contrast to the superabundance of food that was easily accessible in the garden (2:9, 16). See note on Rom 8:22. **toil:** Labor itself is not a curse of the Fall, since man was charged with tilling the soil from the beginning (2:15). The point is that his work will now become wearisome. • Jesus accepted thorns in order to cancel the curse that brought thorns from the ground, and he was buried in the earth so that the ground, cursed by sin, might receive a blessing. From the tree of the garden came sin, but sin expired with the tree of the Savior (St. Cyril of Jerusalem, *Catechesis* 13, 18–19).

**3:19 to dust you shall return:** Physical death, which is the separation of body and soul, is part of the curse inherited by Adam's descendants (Rom 5:14; 1 Cor 15:22). Once the womb of man (2:7), the ground now becomes the tomb of man (Eccles 12:7) (CCC 400).

**3:20 his wife's name:** The Hebrew name for "Eve" (*ḥawwah*) resembles the term "living" (*ḥay*).

**3:22 become like one of us:** Man has acted the part of a god by presuming to exercise lordship over the moral order and redefine what is good and evil in opposition to his Creator (cf. Is 5:20). Only in this disordered way has his transgression made him like God. Adam would have attained true godliness had he humbly obeyed the Father as Jesus did (Phil 2:5–8). For possible meanings of the plural "us", see note on 1:26.

**3:23 God sent him forth:** By expulsion and exile, Adam learns that the most devastating effect of sin is separation from God and his blessings.

**3:24 cherubim:** Represent angels who guard the holiness of God's presence here in the garden as they will later do in the Tabernacle of Moses (Ex 25:18) and the Temple of Solomon (1 Kings 6:23–28) (CCC 332). For other links between Eden and these Israelite sanctuaries, see note on 2:4–25. **guard:** Angelic sentries are posted to keep the defiled couple from reentering paradise. This may be seen as an act of divine mercy, lest fallen man eat of the tree of life and "live for ever" in a state of spiritual separation from God (3:22).

**4:1–26** The prophecy of 3:15 begins to materialize in history, with the offspring of the serpent (Cain, 1 Jn 3:12) attacking the righteous offspring of the woman (Abel, Heb 11:4). The human family continues to grow apart as the line of Cain becomes ever more evil (4:19, 23–24) and the line of Seth develops a close relationship with the Lord (4:26; 5:22; 6:9). See note on 3:15.

**4:1 knew:** A biblical euphemism for sexual relations. **a man:** The Hebrew name "Cain" (*qayin*) resembles the expression "I have gotten" (*qaniti*). **help of the LORD:** Man and

[f] The name in Hebrew resembles the word for *living*.
[g] Heb *qanah*, get.

a man with the help of the LORD." 2And again, she
bore his brother Abel. Now Abel was a keeper of
sheep, and Cain a tiller of the ground. 3In the course
of time Cain brought to the LORD an offering of the
fruit of the ground, 4and Abel brought some of the
firstlings of his flock and of their fat portions. And
the LORD had regard for Abel and his offering, 5but
for Cain and his offering he had no regard. So Cain
was very angry, and his countenance fell. 6The
LORD said to Cain, "Why are you angry, and why
has your countenance fallen? 7If you do well, will
you not be accepted? And if you do not do well, sin
is lurking at the door; its desire is for you, but you
must master it."
8 Cain said to Abel his brother, "Let us go out to
the field."[h] And when they were in the field, Cain
rose up against his brother Abel, and killed him.
9Then the LORD said to Cain, "Where is Abel your
brother?" He said, "I do not know; am I my brother's keeper?" 10And the LORD said, "What have you
done? The voice of your brother's blood is crying to
me from the ground. 11And now you are cursed from
the ground, which has opened its mouth to receive
your brother's blood from your hand. 12When you
till the ground, it shall no longer yield to you its
strength; you shall be a fugitive and a wanderer on
the earth." 13Cain said to the LORD, "My punishment
is greater than I can bear. 14Behold, you have driven
me this day away from the ground; and from your
face I shall be hidden; and I shall be a fugitive and
a wanderer on the earth, and whoever finds me will
slay me." 15Then the LORD said to him, "Not so![i] If
any one slays Cain, vengeance shall be taken on him
sevenfold." And the LORD put a mark on Cain, lest
any who came upon him should kill him. 16Then
Cain went away from the presence of the LORD, and
dwelt in the land of Nod,[j] east of Eden.

**Beginnings of Civilization**

17 Cain knew his wife, and she conceived and
bore E'noch; and he built a city, and called the name
of the city after the name of his son, Enoch. 18To
E'noch was born I'rad; and Irad was the father of
Mehu'ja-el, and Mehuja-el the father of Methu'sha-el,
and Methusha-el the father of La'mech. 19And
La'mech took two wives; the name of the one was
A'dah, and the name of the other Zillah. 20A'dah
bore Ja'bal; he was the father of those who dwell
in tents and have cattle. 21His brother's name was
Ju'bal; he was the father of all those who play the
lyre and pipe. 22Zillah bore Tu'bal-cain; he was the
forger of all instruments of bronze and iron. The sister of Tubal-cain was Na'amah.
23 La'mech said to his wives:
"A'dah and Zillah, hear my voice;
you wives of Lamech, hearken to what I say:
I have slain a man for wounding me,
a young man for striking me.
24If Cain is avenged sevenfold,
truly La'mech seventy-sevenfold."
25 And Adam knew his wife again, and she bore
a son and called his name Seth, for she said, "God
has appointed for me another child instead of Abel,

---

**4:4:** Heb 11:4. **4:8:** 1 Jn 3:12.

---

woman can only bring forth children in cooperation with God (Ps 139:13). This is one reason why children are always considered a divine blessing in the Bible (1:28; 22:17; Ps 127; 128).

**4:4 firstlings:** First-born animals represent the choice picks of the flock, i.e., those that are suitable as divine offerings (Ex 13:2). Abel thus offers his best to God as a sacrificial act of faith (Heb 11:4). Cain, however, appears to offer something less—at least no indication is given that his sacrifice was made from the "firstfruits" of his harvest. Insofar as the external act of worship is a reflection of the interior disposition of the worshiper, it is no surprise that God looked with favor on Abel's offering but not on Cain's (4:5). See note on Lev 1:9.

**4:6 angry:** Cain is enraged by the favor shown to Abel and thinks himself the victim of injustice. Instead of trying to emulate his brother, he allows envy to take hold and finally decides to eliminate him. Cain thus follows the way of the devil, which is the way of envy that leads to murder (Wis 2:24; Jn 8:44; 1 Jn 3:12) (CCC 2538–39).

**4:7 lurking:** Sin is like a predator ready to pounce on the unaware. Though cautioned to resist this deadly force, Cain is entirely mastered by it: in addition to his negligent worship (4:5), he resents Abel in his heart (4:5), murders him with hands (4:8), and then lies to God with his tongue (4:9). The reality of sin in primeval times presupposes that the natural moral law is in effect and that it prohibits crimes like fratricide (CCC 401, 2259).

[h] Sam Gk Syr Compare Vg: Heb lacks *Let us go out to the field.*
[i] Gk Syr Vg: Heb *Therefore.*
[j] That is *Wandering.*

**4:8 let us go out:** Suggests that the murder of Abel is a premeditated act rather than a crime of passion.

**4:9 Where is Abel . . . ?:** God questions the sinner in order to draw forth contrition and give him an opportunity for confession. Cain refuses this mercy as Adam had done before him (3:9–12).

**4:10 blood is crying to me:** I.e., for vengeance (Is 26:21; Rev 6:10; CCC 1867, 2268).

**4:11 you are cursed:** Cain is banished from the soil he once cultivated as a farmer (4:2). He is now forced to roam aimlessly and restlessly in a state of exile (4:16).

**4:13 greater than I can bear:** A childish cry of self-pity.

**4:15 a mark:** A visible sign of protection and divine mercy. It seems that Cain fears retribution from his family for the murder of innocent Abel (5:4).

**4:17–24** The descendants of Cain were technologically advanced and yet morally debased. To their credit, they were pioneers of urbanization (4:17), pastoral culture (4:20), instrumental music (4:21), and metalworking (4:22). To their shame, however, they were the first to engage in murder (4:23), polygamy (4:19), and vindictive violence (4:23–24). The point of presenting the genealogy in this way is not to say that scientific progress is evil or incompatible with religious obligations. Rather, it shows that advances in material civilization come with the danger of moral and spiritual decline. The more a culture is enamored with human achievements, the more it risks forgetting about God and its responsibilities toward him.

**4:24 seventy-sevenfold:** The number 77 (or possibly 490) signifies unlimited vengeance.

**4:25 another child:** The Hebrew name "Seth" (*shet*) resembles the word "appointed" (*shat*).

for Cain slew him." [26]To Seth also a son was born,
and he called his name E'nosh. At that time men
began to call upon the name of the LORD.

### Adam's Descendants to Noah

5 This is the book of the generations of Adam.
When God created man, he made him in the likeness of God. [2]Male and female he created them, and
he blessed them and named them Man when they
were created. [3]When Adam had lived a hundred and
thirty years, he became the father of a son in his own
likeness, after his image, and named him Seth. [4]The
days of Adam after he became the father of Seth
were eight hundred years; and he had other sons and
daughters. [5]Thus all the days that Adam lived were
nine hundred and thirty years; and he died.

6 When Seth had lived a hundred and five years,
he became the father of E'nosh. [7]Seth lived after the
birth of E'nosh eight hundred and seven years, and
had other sons and daughters. [8]Thus all the days of
Seth were nine hundred and twelve years; and he
died.

9 When E'nosh had lived ninety years, he
became the father of Ke'nan. [10]E'nosh lived after the
birth of Ke'nan eight hundred and fifteen years, and
had other sons and daughters. [11]Thus all the days
of E'nosh were nine hundred and five years; and he
died.

12 When Ke'nan had lived seventy years, he
became the father of Ma-hal'alel. [13]Ke'nan lived
after the birth of Ma-hal'alel eight hundred and forty
years, and had other sons and daughters. [14]Thus all
the days of Ke'nan were nine hundred and ten years;
and he died.

15 When Ma-hal'alel had lived sixty-five years,
he became the father of Jar'ed. [16]Ma-hal'alel lived
after the birth of Jar'ed eight hundred and thirty
years, and had other sons and daughters. [17]Thus
all the days of Ma-hal'alel were eight hundred and
ninety-five years; and he died.

18 When Jar'ed had lived a hundred and sixty-
two years he became the father of E'noch. [19]Jared
lived after the birth of E'noch eight hundred years,
and had other sons and daughters. [20]Thus all the
days of Jar'ed were nine hundred and sixty-two
years; and he died.

21 When E'noch had lived sixty-five years, he
became the father of Methu'selah. [22]E'noch walked
with God after the birth of Methu'selah three hundred years, and had other sons and daughters.
[23]Thus all the days of E'noch were three hundred
and sixty-five years. [24]E'noch walked with God; and
he was not, for God took him.

25 When Methu'selah had lived a hundred
and eighty-seven years, he became the father of

---

**5:1:** Gen 1:27. **5:24:** Heb 11:5.

---

**4:26 call upon the name:** A reference to prayer and worship (Mal 1:11) in which God's name is praised (Ps 66:2, 4) and petitioned for help (Joel 2:32). The religious actions of the Patriarchs are often described in these terms (12:8; 13:4; 21:33; 26:25). The meaning of the statement in this context is difficult to determine. Perhaps it denotes the resumption of public worship since Cain and Abel first offered sacrifices to God—an event that sparked jealousy and ended in bloodshed (4:3–8). The verb **began** would thus carry the meaning "began again" (CCC 2569). **the LORD:** Indicates that the one true God, known to Israel as Yahweh or LORD, was worshiped from earliest times. For the revelation of the divine name, see note on Ex 6:3.

**5:1–32** The genealogy of Adam through the line of Seth. Certain contrasts between Seth's line and Cain's line in 4:17–24 are highlighted, most notably in the *second* (Cain, Seth) and *seventh* generation (Lamech, Enoch). In the second generation, Cain founds a city and "names" it after his son, Enoch (Gen 4:17); Seth and his son, Enosh, instead of seeking their own glory, call upon the "name" of the Lord (4:25–26). In the seventh generation, Lamech flaunts his reputation as a murderer and bigamist (4:18–24); Enoch, however, walks with God and is caught up to heaven (5:21–24). Cain thus fathers a wicked family line, and Seth, a righteous family line. This is confirmed by the flood that follows: it destroys the line of Cain, but the line of Seth is preserved through righteous Noah (5:32; 6:9).

**5:1 the generations:** A formula that introduces new phases of history and narrative in Genesis. See introduction: *Structure*.

**5:3 likeness ... image:** Terms here associated with sonship in relation to a father. See word study: *Image and Likeness* at 1:26.

**5:4 other sons and daughters:** Unnamed children of Adam and Eve. The fact that several male and female offspring were born to the first couple explains how marriages could take place in primeval times and how the world could become populated from a single human pair. Marriage between brothers and sisters was a matter of necessity at first, even though sexual union between close relatives was later prohibited (Lev 18:6–18; cf. St. Augustine, *City of God* 15, 16).

**5:5 nine hundred and thirty years:** Adam's age falls within the range of 777 (Lamech, 5:31) to 969 years (Methuselah, 5:27) that characterizes the era before the flood. There is as yet no positive solution to the mystery of these enormous lifespans. Modern anthropology holds that the human species (called *homo sapiens*) is around 40,000 years old, that prehistoric man lived a fairly short life, and that human longevity slowly increased rather than decreased over the millennia. The Bible, however, as well as ancient Near Eastern writings (e.g., *Sumerian King List*) concur in giving the ancients an immensely long life, especially before the flood. Various approaches have been taken to explain this phenomenon in Genesis. (**1**) Some take the ages at face value and maintain the literal truth of the genealogies; however, this results in putting Adam less than 2000 years before Abraham and makes the human race only about 6000 years old. (**2**) Others have proposed converting the "years" into "months", but this creates a situation in which some of the figures are children at the time they are said to bear children of their own. (**3**) Still others take the names of the Patriarchs to refer to "clans" rather than individuals, yet this fails to explain why some of the names clearly concern individuals, such as Adam, Cain, Enoch, and Noah. (**4**) Perhaps the best hypothesis, and one that would help to explain both the biblical and Near Eastern data, is that giving primeval figures extremely long lives was a way of conceptualizing the great antiquity of mankind. In other words, this may be simply a literary technique used to assert the remarkable age of the human race itself.

**5:21–24** Seven generations from Adam, **Enoch** walked with God in righteousness and was taken into heaven without experiencing death (Heb 11:5). According to later

La'mech. 26 Methu'selah lived after the birth of La'-
mech seven hundred and eighty-two years, and
had other sons and daughters. 27 Thus all the days
of Methu'selah were nine hundred and sixty-nine
years; and he died.
28 When La'mech had lived a hundred and
eighty-two years, he became the father of a son,
29 and called his name Noah, saying, "Out of
the ground which the LORD has cursed this one
shall bring us relief from our work and from the
toil of our hands." 30 La'mech lived after the birth
of Noah five hundred and ninety-five years, and
had other sons and daughters. 31 Thus all the days
of La'mech were seven hundred and seventy-seven
years; and he died.
32 After Noah was five hundred years old,
Noah became the father of Shem, Ham, and Ja'pheth.

### The Wickedness of Mankind

6 When men began to multiply on the face of
the ground, and daughters were born to them,
2 the sons of God saw that the daughters of men were
fair; and they took to wife such of them as they chose.
3 Then the LORD said, "My spirit shall not abide in
man for ever, for he is flesh, but his days shall be a
hundred and twenty years." 4 The Neph'ilim were on
the earth in those days, and also afterward, when

**6:4:** Num 13:33.

traditions, Enoch was a model of repentance (Sir 44:16), a visionary prophet (Jude 14–15), and the author of nonbiblical apocalyptic books (e.g., *1 Enoch, 2 Enoch*) (CCC 2569).

**5:29 called his name:** The Hebrew name "Noah" (*noaḥ*) resembles the verb for "bring relief" (*naḥam*).

**6:1–4** A critical event in the Genesis narrative, where the righteous line of Seth (**sons of God**) intermarries with the godless line of Cain (**daughters of men**) and becomes corrupted (except for Noah, 6:8–9). On top of the violence and moral decadence spreading over the earth, this is the final outrage that moves God to pour out his wrath in the waters of the flood. This interpretation appears in rabbinic tradition (*Genesis Rabbah* 26, 5–7; *b. Sanhedrin* 108a) and in the Church Fathers (St. John Chrysostom, *Homilies on Genesis* 22, 8; St. Augustine, *City of God* 15, 23; St. Ephraem, *Commentary on Genesis* 6, 3). Another interpretation, also represented in Jewish and Christian antiquity, holds that the **sons of God** are not men but rebel angels called the Watchers who took the form of men and had sexual relations with women (*1 Enoch* 6–7; *Jubilees* 5, 1; 7, 21; St. Justin Martyr, *First Apology* 5, 2; St. Clement of Alexandria *Christ the Teacher* 3, 2). See note on Jude 6.

**6:2 saw ... fair ... took:** The same Hebrew expressions are used in the same sequence in 3:6 ("saw ... good ... took"), hinting that the sons of God replicate the original sin of Eve.

**6:3 My spirit:** The breath of life that God infuses into man to make him alive (2:7; Job 27:3; Eccles 12:7). **hundred and twenty years:** Seems to impose a limit so that man's lifetime will not run beyond 120 years. Although the life-span of subsequent generations begins to plummet after this point, the limit never takes full effect until the end of the Pentateuch, when Moses dies at 120 years of age (Deut 34:7). Another possibility is that the 120 years refers, not to a reduced life-span, but to a time of forbearance in which God grants an opportunity for sinners to repent before the onset of the flood (cf. St. Jerome, *Hebrew Questions on Genesis* 6, 3; St. John Chrysostom, *Homilies on Genesis* 25, 4).

**6:4 Nephilim:** Remembered as a people of magnificent strength and stature from ancient times (Num 13:31–33).

### The Family Line of Adam

Genesis sets forth a genealogical chain of 23 links from the person of Adam to the people of Israel (set in bold and numbered below). It focuses on a chosen line, blessed and preserved by God, that runs from Adam to Israel through the righteous figures of Seth, Noah, and Shem in Gen 1–11 and through Abraham, Isaac, and Jacob in Gen 12–50.

***The Chosen Line***

| | | | |
|---|---|---|---|
| 1. | **Adam** (Gen 2:7) | 13. | **Shelah** (Gen 11:12) |
| | Cain (Gen 4:1) | 14. | **Eber** (Gen 11:14) |
| | Abel (Gen 4:2) | 15. | **Peleg** (Gen 11:16) |
| 2. | **Seth** (Gen 5:3) | 16. | **Reu** (Gen 11:18) |
| 3. | **Enosh** (Gen 4:26; 5:6) | 17. | **Serug** (Gen 11:20) |
| 4. | **Kenan** (Gen 5:9) | 18. | **Nahor** (Gen 11:22) |
| 5. | **Mahalalel** (Gen 5:12) | 19. | **Terah** (Gen 11:24) |
| 6. | **Jared** (Gen 5:15) | 20. | **Abram** (Gen 11:26) |
| 7. | **Enoch** (Gen 5:18) | | Nahor (Gen 11:26) |
| 8. | **Methuselah** (Gen 5:21) | | Haran (Gen 11:26) |
| 9. | **Lamech** (Gen 5:25) | | Ishmael (Gen 16:15) |
| 10. | **Noah** (Gen 5:28–29) | 21. | **Isaac** (Gen 21:3) |
| 11. | **Shem** (Gen 5:32) | | Others (Gen 25:1–2) |
| | Ham (Gen 5:32) | | Esau (Gen 25:25) |
| | Japheth (Gen 5:32) | 22. | **Jacob** (Gen 25:26) |
| 12. | **Arpachshad** (Gen 11:10) | 23. | **The Twelve Tribes of Israel** (Gen 35:22–26) |

the sons of God came in to the daughters of men, and
they bore children to them. These were the mighty
men that were of old, the men of renown.

5 The LORD saw that the wickedness of man was
great in the earth, and that every imagination of the
thoughts of his heart was only evil continually. [6]And
the LORD was sorry that he had made man on the
earth, and it grieved him to his heart. [7]So the LORD
said, "I will blot out man whom I have created from
the face of the ground, man and beast and creeping
things and birds of the air, for I am sorry that I have
made them." [8]But Noah found favor in the eyes of
the LORD.

9 These are the generations of Noah. Noah was
a righteous man, blameless in his generation; Noah
walked with God. [10]And Noah had three sons, Shem,
Ham, and Ja'pheth.

### Noah Makes the Ark as God Commands

11 Now the earth was corrupt in God's sight, and
the earth was filled with violence. [12]And God saw
the earth, and behold, it was corrupt; for all flesh
had corrupted their way upon the earth. [13]And
God said to Noah, "I have determined to make an
end of all flesh; for the earth is filled with violence
through them; behold, I will destroy them with the
earth. [14]Make yourself an ark of gopher wood; make
rooms in the ark, and cover it inside and out with
pitch. [15]This is how you are to make it: the length of
the ark three hundred cubits, its breadth fifty cubits,
and its height thirty cubits. [16]Make a roof[k] for the
ark, and finish it to a cubit above; and set the door
of the ark in its side; make it with lower, second,
and third decks. [17]For behold, I will bring a flood of
waters upon the earth, to destroy all flesh in which
is the breath of life from under heaven; everything
that is on the earth shall die. [18]But I will establish
my covenant with you; and you shall come into the
ark, you, your sons, your wife, and your sons' wives
with you. [19]And of every living thing of all flesh, you
shall bring two of every sort into the ark, to keep
them alive with you; they shall be male and female.
[20]Of the birds according to their kinds, and of the
animals according to their kinds, of every creeping
thing of the ground according to its kind, two of
every sort shall come in to you, to keep them alive.
[21]Also take with you every sort of food that is eaten,
and store it up; and it shall serve as food for you and
for them." [22]Noah did this; he did all that God commanded him.

### The Great Flood

7 Then the LORD said to Noah, "Go into the
ark, you and all your household, for I have seen
that you are righteous before me in this generation.
[2]Take with you seven pairs of all clean animals, the

---

**6:6 the LORD was sorry:** The expression should not be taken literally, as though God could be moved or swayed by an emotional wave of regret. Scripture teaches that God does not change as man does (Mal 3:6), nor does he repent as man does (Num 23:19). The Bible often describes the thoughts and actions of God in human terms in order to make the mystery of God more understandable to human minds. Another class of figurative or anthropomorphic expressions includes those that describe God as having physical features such as hands (Ex 7:5), arms (Hos 11:3), feet (Ex 24:10), white hair (Dan 7:9), and a face (Ps 27:8). These and similar word pictures help to communicate the personal nature of God.

**6:9—9:19** Noah and the flood. (**1**) *Compositionally*, the account may have been compiled from two independent flood stories that were skillfully woven together. Scholars who hold this view base their hypothesis on alleged tensions within the account and typically speak of the flood narrative as a composite of Yahwist (J) and Priestly (P) traditions. (**2**) *Comparatively*, the episode in Genesis has close affinities with other flood stories from ancient Mesopotamia, especially the *Gilgamesh Epic*. (**3**) *Chronologically*, the deluge lasts for ten and a half months: the floodwaters rise for 40 days (7:4), remain for a total of five months (7:24), and then recede for five and a half months (8:3-13). (**4**) *Theologically*, the flood brings about a new creation, cleansing the old world of the bloodstains of violence (4:10, 23; 6:11). Several parallels with the creation story bring this out: the land is once again engulfed by the deep (1:2; 7:11); the land reemerges dry from the water (1:9; 8:13); Noah and his family are blessed and made fruitful to multiply (1:28; 9:1); man's dominion over the animals is reaffirmed (1:26; 9:2); a food supply is given (1:29; 9:3); and God renews his commitment to continue the daily and seasonal cycles (1:14; 8:22). • The NT interprets the flood as a foreshadowing of Baptism, which cleanses the believer of sin and confers the grace of salvation in Christ (1 Pet 3:20-21; CCC 701, 1219). • *Allegorically*, the ark of Noah is a figure of the one Church, and the baptism of the world, which purified and redeemed it, corresponds to the saving Baptism of the Church (St. Cyprian, *Letters* 68). The family of Noah is saved by water and wood, just as the family of Christ is saved by Baptism, which represents the suffering of the Cross. And as every kind of animal was aboard the ark, so believers from all nations are enclosed in the Church (St. Augustine, *Against Faustus* 12, 14-15).

**6:9 the generations:** A formula that introduces new phases of history and narrative in Genesis. See introduction: *Structure*. **righteous ... blameless:** Means that Noah lived by the law of God (cf. Lk 1:6). At this early point in history, he observed the natural moral law inscribed on the heart (Rom 2:14-15). His obedience to the Lord continues throughout the narrative (6:22; 7:5, 16).

**6:14-22** Noah is instructed to build an ark (6:14-16), load it with animals (6:19-20), stock it with food (6:21), and then board it with his family (6:18; 7:1).

**6:14 gopher wood:** An unidentified species of wood.

**6:15 length ... breadth ... height:** With an 18-inch cubit, the ark measured about 440 feet long, 73 feet wide, and 44 feet high, roughly the size of a naval battleship. Inside it was divided into three floors or decks (6:16).

**6:18 establish my covenant:** Or, "confirm my covenant". The Hebrew expression indicates the *renewal* of an already existing covenant rather than the *ratification* of an entirely new covenant. Understood in this way, it presupposes God's original covenant with creation. See note on 1:1—2:4.

**7:1 all your household:** A family of eight persons in all: Noah, his wife, his three sons, and his three daughters-in-law (7:13; 1 Pet 3:20).

**7:2 seven pairs:** Added to the general command of taking "two" of every animal aboard the ark (6:19). The rationale for this additional requirement emerges from the larger context of the story: the *single* pairs of unclean animals will go forth to repopulate the earth after the flood, whereas *seven* pairs of clean animals are needed so that sacrifices can

---

[k]Or *window*.

male and his mate; and a pair of the animals that are not clean, the male and his mate; [3]and seven pairs of the birds of the air also, male and female, to keep their kind alive upon the face of all the earth. [4]For in seven days I will send rain upon the earth forty days and forty nights; and every living thing that I have made I will blot out from the face of the ground." [5]And Noah did all that the LORD had commanded him.

6 Noah was six hundred years old when the flood of waters came upon the earth. [7]And Noah and his sons and his wife and his sons' wives with him went into the ark, to escape the waters of the flood. [8]Of clean animals, and of animals that are not clean, and of birds, and of everything that creeps on the ground, [9]two and two, male and female, went into the ark with Noah, as God had commanded Noah. [10]And after seven days the waters of the flood came upon the earth.

11 In the six hundredth year of Noah's life, in the second month, on the seventeenth day of the month, on that day all the fountains of the great deep burst forth, and the windows of the heavens were opened. [12]And rain fell upon the earth forty days and forty nights. [13]On the very same day Noah and his sons, Shem and Ham and Ja'pheth, and Noah's wife and the three wives of his sons with them entered the ark, [14]they and every beast according to its kind, and all the cattle according to their kinds, and every creeping thing that creeps on the earth according to its kind, and every bird according to its kind, every bird of every sort. [15]They went into the ark with Noah, two and two of all flesh in which there was the breath of life. [16]And they that entered, male and female of all flesh, went in as God had commanded him; and the LORD shut him in.

17 The flood continued forty days upon the earth; and the waters increased, and bore up the ark, and it rose high above the earth. [18]The waters prevailed and increased greatly upon the earth; and the ark floated on the face of the waters. [19]And the waters prevailed so mightily upon the earth that all the high mountains under the whole heaven were covered; [20]the waters prevailed above the mountains, covering them fifteen cubits deep. [21]And all flesh died that moved upon the earth, birds, cattle, beasts, all swarming creatures that swarm upon the earth, and every man; [22]everything on the dry land in whose nostrils was the breath of life died. [23]He blotted out every living thing that was upon the face of the ground, man and animals and creeping things and birds of the air; they were blotted out from the earth. Only Noah was left, and those that were with him in the ark. [24]And the waters prevailed upon the earth a hundred and fifty days.

### The Flood Subsides

8 But God remembered Noah and all the beasts and all the cattle that were with him in the ark. And God made a wind blow over the earth, and the waters subsided; [2]the fountains of the deep and the windows of the heavens were closed, the rain from the heavens was restrained, [3]and the waters receded from the earth continually. At the end of a hundred and fifty days the waters had abated; [4]and in the seventh month, on the seventeenth day of the month, the ark came to rest upon the mountains of Ar'arat. [5]And the waters continued to abate until the tenth month; in the tenth month, on the first day of the month, the tops of the mountains were seen.

6 At the end of forty days Noah opened the window of the ark which he had made, [7]and sent forth a raven; and it went to and fro until the waters were dried up from the earth. [8]Then he sent forth a dove from him, to see if the waters had subsided from the face of the ground; [9]but the dove found no place to set her foot, and she returned to him to the ark, for the waters were still on the face of the whole earth. So he put forth his hand and took her and brought her into the ark with him. [10]He waited another seven days, and again he sent forth the dove out of the ark; [11]and the dove came back to him in the evening, and behold, in her mouth a freshly plucked olive leaf; so

**7:7:** Mt 24:38; Lk 17:27.

be offered after the flood without making the clean animals extinct (8:20). The number seven may also symbolize the covenant that follows (see note on 1:1—2:4). **clean:** Permissible to sacrifice (8:20) and eat (Lev 11:47).

**7:4 forty days:** Symbolic of a period of testing. See note on Lk 4:2.

**7:11 great deep ... windows:** The floodwaters are pictured surging up from the subterranean ocean below and pouring down through openings in the solid firmament above (cf. Ps 78:23; Jon 2:3; Mal 3:10). See notes on 1:2 and 1:6.

**7:19 mountains ... covered:** Recalls the status of the earth in the beginning, before God called back the waters on the third day of creation (1:9; Ps 104:6-9).

**7:20 fifteen cubits:** The waters rise nearly 23 feet above the mountaintops. Besides stressing the extent of divine judgment, the author also sees this as God's provision to keep the ark from running aground on the submerged peaks.

**7:21 all flesh died:** The flood is a universal disaster, drowning the entire population of man, along with every beast and bird of the earth. The only land-dwelling creatures to escape the waters of judgment are aboard the ark.

**8:1 God remembered Noah:** Both the midpoint and turning point of the flood narrative, when God begins to drain the prevailing waters off the earth. **wind:** The Hebrew term can also be rendered "Spirit". Along with other parallels to the creation story, this detail recalls how the Spirit of God hovered over the primordial waters (1:2) before the dry land appeared (1:9). See note on 6:9—9:19.

**8:4 Ararat:** A mountainous region in historical Armenia (Is 37:38; Jer 51:27). It is known in ancient Assyrian texts as the kingdom of Urartu, which was located near the headwaters of the Tigris and Euphrates rivers (in eastern Turkey).

**8:6-12** Noah sends out a **raven** and a **dove** in search of habitable land. The raven, which is forced to return, is an unclean species (Lev 11:15), whereas the dove, which never returns from its final mission, is taken from the extra pairs of clean birds taken aboard the ark (7:3). See note on 7:2.

**8:11 olive leaf:** A traditional symbol of peace.

Noah knew that the waters had subsided from the
earth. 12 Then he waited another seven days, and
sent forth the dove; and she did not return to him
any more.

13 In the six hundred and first year, in the
first month, the first day of the month, the waters
were dried from off the earth; and Noah removed
the covering of the ark, and looked, and behold,
the face of the ground was dry. 14 In the second
month, on the twenty-seventh day of the month,
the earth was dry. 15 Then God said to Noah, 16 "Go
forth from the ark, you and your wife, and your
sons and your sons' wives with you. 17 Bring forth
with you every living thing that is with you of
all flesh—birds and animals and every creeping
thing that creeps on the earth—that they may breed
abundantly on the earth, and be fruitful and multiply upon the earth." 18 So Noah went forth, and his
sons and his wife and his sons' wives with him.
19 And every beast, every creeping thing, and every
bird, everything that moves upon the earth, went
forth by families out of the ark.

### God's Promise to Noah

20 Then Noah built an altar to the LORD, and
took of every clean animal and of every clean bird,
and offered burnt offerings on the altar. 21 And
when the LORD smelled the pleasing odor, the
LORD said in his heart, "I will never again curse
the ground because of man, for the imagination of
man's heart is evil from his youth; neither will I
ever again destroy every living creature as I have
done. 22 While the earth remains, seedtime and harvest, cold and heat, summer and winter, day and
night, shall not cease."

### The Covenant with Noah

9 And God blessed Noah and his sons, and said to
them, "Be fruitful and multiply, and fill the
earth. 2 The fear of you and the dread of you shall be
upon every beast of the earth, and upon every bird
of the air, upon everything that creeps on the ground
and all the fish of the sea; into your hand they are
delivered. 3 Every moving thing that lives shall be
food for you; and as I gave you the green plants, I
give you everything. 4 Only you shall not eat flesh
with its life, that is, its blood. 5 For your lifeblood I
will surely require a reckoning; of every beast I will
require it and of man; of every man's brother I will
require the life of man. 6 Whoever sheds the blood of
man, by man shall his blood be shed; for God made
man in his own image. 7 And you, be fruitful and
multiply, bring forth abundantly on the earth and
multiply in it."

8 Then God said to Noah and to his sons with
him, 9 "Behold, I establish my covenant with you
and your descendants after you, 10 and with every
living creature that is with you, the birds, the cattle,
and every beast of the earth with you, as many as
came out of the ark.[1] 11 I establish my covenant with
you, that never again shall all flesh be cut off by the
waters of a flood, and never again shall there be a
flood to destroy the earth." 12 And God said, "This
is the sign of the covenant which I make between
me and you and every living creature that is with
you, for all future generations: 13 I set my bow in the
cloud, and it shall be a sign of the covenant between
me and the earth. 14 When I bring clouds over the
earth and the bow is seen in the clouds, 15 I will
remember my covenant which is between me and

---

**9:4:** Lev 7:26, 27; 17:10–14; Deut 12:16, 23.

---

**8:13 the first month, the first day:** The waters are gone by the beginning of the new year, signifying a new beginning for the world. This marks ten and a half months since the flood began (7:11). Noah and his family stay aboard the ark for another two months, meaning they will have lived in the vessel for over a year (8:14–16).

**8:17 be fruitful and multiply:** A renewal of the blessing and mandate given to the fish and birds at creation (1:22).

**8:20—9:17** The Noahic covenant. Ratified in response to Noah's obedience (6:22) and expressed in the sign of the rainbow (9:13), it features God taking upon himself the unconditional obligation—despite the persistence of sin (8:21)—to maintain the stability of the natural order (8:22) without the threat of another flood (9:11). The Noahic covenant is a renewal of the covenant that God established with creation in the beginning. See note on 6:18.

**8:21 man's heart is evil:** The floodwaters cleanse the home of man but leave his heart unchanged. See word study: *Heart* at Deut 30:6. • The problem of sin awaits its final solution in the waters of Baptism, which cleanse the heart from sin and renew it with the life and love of the Spirit (Acts 2:38; 15:8–9; Rom 5:5; CCC 1219).

**9:1 Be fruitful and multiply:** A renewal of the blessing and mandate given to the first couple at creation (1:28). Noah thus becomes a new Adam, who fathers the human family after the flood through his three sons (9:7, 18–19).

**9:2 into your hand:** Reaffirms man's dominion over the animal kingdom (1:26; CCC 2417).

**9:3 food for you:** The human diet of plants and fruits can now be supplemented with meat, so long as it is drained of blood (9:4). In the Bible, blood is considered a sacred substance because it bears within it the life of the creature, which must be respected (Lev 17:10–14). See note on 1:29.

**9:6 his blood be shed:** Murder is a crime against the sanctity of human life, and man is held fully responsible for the destruction of that life (CCC 2258). Homicide thus merits the stiffest penalty: capital punishment (Lev 24:17). The Lord can delegate to men, whether individuals (Num 35:19) or states (Rom 13:4), the judicial authority to avenge wrongful deaths. However, according to OT standards, a policy of strict proportion (one life is taken for one life lost) must be observed; otherwise, a single homicide might spark an ongoing blood feud that leaves many persons dead as a result.

**9:13 my bow:** The Hebrew term for a rainbow is the same term used for a hunting (27:3) or military bow (Lam 2:4). This has given rise to different explanations of the sign. (**1**) Some see the rainbow as a sign of *peace*. They picture God hanging up his bow in the sky, retiring it from service and signifying that he has ended his battle with the sinful world. (**2**) Others interpret the rainbow as a sign of God's *covenant oath*. They envision the bow pulled back and pointed up at heaven, signifying that God will be forever faithful to his pledge, for he threatens himself with a curse should he fail to uphold the terms of the Noahic covenant.

---

[1] Gk: Heb repeats *every beast of the earth*.

you and every living creature of all flesh; and the waters shall never again become a flood to destroy all flesh. [16]When the bow is in the clouds, I will look upon it and remember the everlasting covenant between God and every living creature of all flesh that is upon the earth." [17]God said to Noah, "This is the sign of the covenant which I have established between me and all flesh that is upon the earth."

### Noah and His Sons

18 The sons of Noah who went forth from the ark were Shem, Ham, and Ja'pheth. Ham was the father of Canaan. [19]These three were the sons of Noah; and from these the whole earth was peopled.

20 Noah was the first tiller of the soil. He planted a vineyard; [21]and he drank of the wine, and became drunk, and lay uncovered in his tent. [22]And Ham, the father of Canaan, saw the nakedness of his father, and told his two brothers outside. [23]Then Shem and Ja'pheth took a garment, laid it upon both their shoulders, and walked backward and covered the nakedness of their father; their faces were turned away, and they did not see their father's nakedness. [24]When Noah awoke from his wine and knew what his youngest son had done to him, [25]he said,

"Cursed be Canaan;
a slave of slaves shall he be to his brothers."

[26]He also said,

"Blessed by the LORD my God be Shem;[m]
and let Canaan be his slave.
[27]God enlarge Ja'pheth,
and let him dwell in the tents of Shem;
and let Canaan be his slave."

28 After the flood Noah lived three hundred and fifty years. [29]All the days of Noah were nine hundred and fifty years; and he died.

### Nations Descended from Noah

**10** These are the generations of the sons of Noah, Shem, Ham, and Ja'pheth; sons were born to them after the flood.

2 The sons of Ja'pheth: Gomer, Ma'gog, Ma'dai, Ja'van, Tu'bal, Me'shech, and Ti'ras. [3]The sons of Gomer: Ash'kenaz, Ri'phath, and Togar'mah. [4]The sons of Ja'van: Eli'shah, Tar'shish, Kittim, and Do'danim. [5]From these the coastland peoples spread. These are the sons of Ja'pheth[n] in their

---

**9:16 everlasting covenant:** The Noahic covenant remains in force as long as "the earth remains" (8:22), that is, "for all future generations" (9:12) (CCC 71).

**9:20–27** Introduces the next phase of the Genesis story, showing that just as Adam's family line split between the righteous (Seth) and the wicked (Cain), so Noah's family line divides into the blessed (Shem) and the cursed (Ham). The Shemite line is a continuation of the righteous Sethite line through Noah (5:1–32).

**9:20 the first tiller:** I.e., after the flood. The first agriculturalists to appear in Genesis are Adam (2:15) and Cain (4:2). Another possible translation is: "Noah, a man of the soil, was the first to plant a vineyard."

**9:22 saw the nakedness of his father:** Variously interpreted to mean that Ham looked perversely upon his naked father (voyeurism), that he emasculated his father (castration), or that he sexually abused his father (homosexual incest). More likely, the expression is an idiom for maternal incest, where (**1**) a father's nakedness is an indirect way of referring to the nakedness of his wife (as in Lev 18:7), and (**2**) "seeing" nakedness is synonymous with "uncovering" the nakedness of a close relative to engage in sexual relations (as in Lev 20:17). So understood, Ham is guilty of having sexual relations with his mother, and this explains why a curse falls, not on himself, but on his son, Canaan, who would seem to be the child conceived of this sinful union (9:25). It is otherwise difficult to understand why Canaan, who plays no role in the story at all, is mentioned five times in the immediate context (9:18, 22, 25, 26, 27). The account of Ham's perversity thus supplies the backstory of *how* he became the father of Canaan and the Canaanites. For a parallel episode in Genesis where drunkenness leads to incest with a parent and the birth of nations that become traditional enemies of Israel, see 19:30–38.

**9:23 covered the nakedness of their father:** Supposing the use of the idiom in Lev 18:7, this means that Shem and Japheth discretely covered their naked and violated mother.

**9:24 youngest son:** This detail hints that Ham resorts to maternal incest as a bid for power, hoping to seize the more exalted blessings intended for Noah's first-born, Shem. As other examples illustrate, unlawful relations with another man's wives or concubines is often linked with perverse ambitions to usurp his authority (e.g., Reuben, 35:22; 49:3–4; Absalom, 2 Sam 16:20–23). Near Eastern literature gives further examples of sexual aggression in the context of family power struggles.

**9:26 Blessed by the LORD my God be Shem:** Or, better, "Blessed be the LORD, the God of Shem" (see textual note *m*). The blessing is unique, for this is the first time in Scripture that God is identified as the patron and protector of an individual. The Patriarchs will later share this same privilege ("the God of Abraham, the God of Isaac, and the God of Jacob", Ex 3:6). **Canaan be his slave:** The curse upon Canaan goes into effect when Israel, who descends from Shem through Abraham (11:10–26), seizes the Promised Land and makes the Canaanite survivors of the Conquest into forced laborers (Josh 16:10; 17:13; Judg 1:28, 33; 1 Kings 9:20–21).

**9:27 God enlarge Japheth:** The Hebrew name "Japheth" (*yepet*) resembles the verb "enlarge" (*yapt*). **dwell in the tents of Shem:** Envisions a lasting fraternal friendship between Japheth and Shem.

**9:28–29** Rounds off the genealogical record of Noah (5:28–32) after the intermission of the flood story and its aftermath (6:1—9:27).

**10:1–32** The table of nations, an inventory of the national, geographic, and linguistic diversity of the ancient Near East. (**1**) *Numerically*, it lists a total of 70 nations: 14 from Japheth (10:2–5), 30 from Ham (10:6–20), and 26 from Shem (10:21–31). (**2**) *Genealogically*, it asserts the unity of the human family stemming from Noah's three sons (10:32). (**3**) *Chronologically*, it stands before the Tower of Babel narrative (11:1–9), yet it presents a map of the world and its languages as it existed after the Babel incident. (**4**) *Geographically*, it outlines a general pattern of migration and settlement with the Japhethites concentrated in Asia Minor and the islands of the Mediterranean, the Hamites spread across northern Africa and up into Syria-Palestine, and the Shemites settled in Mesopotamia and across the Arabian peninsula. Palestine is situated in the very center of this world map, reinforcing the central importance of the Holy Land in the theological world view of Israel (Ezek 5:5; 38:12).

**10:1 These are the generations:** A formula that introduces new phases of history and narrative in Genesis. See introduction: *Structure*.

---

[m]Or *Blessed be the* LORD, *the God of Shem.*

[n]Compare verses 20, 31. Heb lacks *These are the sons of Japheth.*

lands, each with his own language, by their families,
in their nations.
6 The sons of Ham: Cush, Egypt, Put, and
Canaan. [7]The sons of Cush: Seba, Hav'ilah, Sab-
tah, Ra'amah, and Sab'teca. The sons of Raamah:
Sheba and De'dan. [8]Cush became the father of
Nimrod; he was the first on earth to be a mighty
man. [9]He was a mighty hunter before the LORD;
therefore it is said, "Like Nimrod a mighty hunter
before the LORD." [10]The beginning of his kingdom was Ba'bel, E'rech, and Accad, all of them in
the land of Shi'nar. [11]From that land he went into
Assyria, and built Nin'eveh, Reho'both-Ir, Ca'lah,
and [12]Re'sen between Nin'eveh and Ca'lah; that
is the great city. [13]Egypt became the father of
Lu'dim, An'amim, Leha'bim, Naph'tuhim, [14]Path-
ru'sim, Caslu'him (whence came the Philis'tines), and
Caph'torim.
15 Canaan became the father of Si'don his first-
born, and Heth, [16]and the Jeb'usites, the Am'orites, the Gir'gashites, [17]the Hi'vites, the Arkites,
the Si'nites, [18]the Ar'vadites, the Zem'arites, and
the Ha'mathites. Afterward the families of the
Canaanites spread abroad. [19]And the territory of the
Canaanites extended from Si'don, in the direction of
Ge'rar, as far as Gaza, and in the direction of Sodom,
Gomor'rah, Admah, and Zeboi'im, as far as La'sha.
[20]These are the sons of Ham, by their families, their
languages, their lands, and their nations.
21 To Shem also, the father of all the children of
E'ber, the elder brother of Ja'pheth, children were
born. [22]The sons of Shem: E'lam, Asshur, Arpach'-
shad, Lud, and Ar'am. [23]The sons of Ar'am: Uz, Hul,
Ge'ther, and Mash. [24]Arpach'shad became the father
of She'lah; and Shelah became the father of E'ber.
[25]To E'ber were born two sons: the name of the one
was Pe'leg,° for in his days the earth was divided,
and his brother's name was Joktan. [26]Joktan became
the father of Almo'dad, She'leph, Haz"arma'veth,
Je'rah, [27]Hador'am, U'zal, Diklah, [28]O'bal, Abim'a-el,

**10:6–20** Ham is depicted as a progenitor of Israel's traditional enemies: the Egyptians (10:6), the Canaanites (10:6), the Babylonians (10:10), the Assyrians (10:11), the Philistines (10:14), and the Jebusites (10:16).

**10:10 Babel, Erech, Accad:** Cities in lower Mesopotamia.

**10:19 Sidon ... as far as Gaza:** The land of the Canaanites, which is destined to become the Promised Land of Israel through the Abrahamic covenant (17:8).

**10:21 Shem:** The eponymous ancestor of all Semitic peoples. The Israelites, descended from Shem through the Patriarchs, are among this group, but the two are not equivalent. The Semites constitute a much larger family of peoples spread across the Near East. **Eber:** The eponymous ancestor of all Hebrew peoples. Abraham descended from Shem through Eber and was thus an Eberite or Hebrew (14:13).

**10:24 Arpachshad ... Shelah:** The name "Cainan" appears between these two names in the Greek Septuagint and in Lk 3:36.

° That is *Division*.

**The Nations of Genesis 10**

Sheba, [29]O'phir, Hav'ilah, and Jo'bab; all these were
the sons of Joktan. [30]The territory in which they lived
extended from Me'sha in the direction of Se'phar to
the hill country of the east. [31]These are the sons of
Shem, by their families, their languages, their lands,
and their nations.

32 These are the families of the sons of Noah,
according to their genealogies, in their nations; and
from these the nations spread abroad on the earth
after the flood.

### The Tower of Babel

11 Now the whole earth had one language and
few words. [2]And as men migrated from the
east, they found a plain in the land of Shinar and
settled there. [3]And they said to one another, "Come,
let us make bricks, and burn them thoroughly."
And they had brick for stone, and bitumen for mortar. [4]Then they said, "Come, let us build ourselves
a city, and a tower with its top in the heavens,
and let us make a name for ourselves, lest we be
scattered abroad upon the face of the whole earth."
[5]And the LORD came down to see the city and the
tower, which the sons of men had built. [6]And the
LORD said, "Behold, they are one people, and they
have all one language; and this is only the beginning of what they will do; and nothing that they
propose to do will now be impossible for them. [7]Come,
let us go down, and there confuse their language,
that they may not understand one another's speech."
[8]So the LORD scattered them abroad from there
over the face of all the earth, and they left off building the city. [9]Therefore its name was called Ba'bel,
because there the LORD confused[p] the language
of all the earth; and from there the LORD scattered
them abroad over the face of all the earth.

### Descendants of Shem

10 These are the descendants of Shem. When
Shem was a hundred years old, he became the
father of Arpach'shad two years after the flood;
[11]and Shem lived after the birth of Arpach'shad five
hundred years, and had other sons and daughters.

12 When Arpach'shad had lived thirty-five years,
he became the father of She'lah; [13]and Arpach'shad
lived after the birth of She'lah four hundred and
three years, and had other sons and daughters.

14 When She'lah had lived thirty years, he
became the father of E'ber; [15]and She'lah lived after
the birth of E'ber four hundred and three years, and
had other sons and daughters.

16 When E'ber had lived thirty-four years, he
became the father of Pe'leg; [17]and E'ber lived after
the birth of Pe'leg four hundred and thirty years,
and had other sons and daughters.

18 When Pe'leg had lived thirty years, he became
the father of Re'u; [19]and Pe'leg lived after the birth
of Re'u two hundred and nine years, and had other
sons and daughters.

20 When Re'u had lived thirty-two years, he
became the father of Se'rug; [21]and Re'u lived after
the birth of Se'rug two hundred and seven years,
and had other sons and daughters.

22 When Se'rug had lived thirty years, he
became the father of Na'hor; [23]and Se'rug lived after
the birth of Na'hor two hundred years, and had
other sons and daughters.

24 When Na'hor had lived twenty-nine years, he
became the father of Te'rah; [25]and Na'hor lived after
the birth of Te'rah a hundred and nineteen years,
and had other sons and daughters.

26 When Te'rah had lived seventy years, he
became the father of Abram, Na'hor, and Haran.

### Descendants of Terah

27 Now these are the descendants of Te'rah.
Terah was the father of Abram, Na'hor, and Haran;

---

**11:1–9** The Tower of Babel incident explains the dispersion of groups of people (11:8) and the diversity of their languages (11:9). Both are manifestations of divine judgment on man, whose pride has reached a new and towering height in the form of a mudbrick skyscraper. The tower may have resembled one of the colossal mountain temples, or ziggurats, of ancient Babylon. These sacred elevations were thought to be points of contact between heaven and earth (CCC 57).

**11:2 the land of Shinar:** The broad plain watered by the Tigris and Euphrates rivers (10:10).

**11:3 make bricks:** Monumental architecture in ancient Mesopotamia was typically constructed of kiln-fired bricks. **bitumen:** A natural tar used for mortar joints and weather sealing.

**11:4 make a name for ourselves:** The family of man bands together to build a secular civilization that glorifies human achievement and the strength of social and political unity. The arrogance of this attempt illustrates how sin has come to corrupt, not only individuals, but whole societies and their collective pursuits. Moreover, as the broader context of Genesis shows, the "name" coveted by the sinners at Babel is never acquired; rather, it is Abraham and his descendants whom God promises to bless with a great "name" (12:2). Preparations for this had already been made when God blessed Abraham's ancestor Shem, whose name in Hebrew means "name" (9:26) and whose two genealogies stand immediately before and after the Babel episode (10:21–31; 11:10–26). **lest we be scattered:** The dispersion that is feared by the builders will become the tragic result of their efforts (11:8).

**11:5 the LORD came down:** Implies that man's attempt at reaching the heavens (11:4) has failed, for God still has to descend from on high to inspect the tower.

**11:7 Come, let us:** Echoes the words of the builders in 11:3 and 11:4.

**11:9 Babel:** The name "Babylon" (*babel*), meaning "gate of God", resembles the Hebrew word for "he confused" (*balal*).

**11:10–26** Ten generations stretch from Shem, the first-born of Noah, down to Abram, the first-born of Terah. The author is showing that the Patriarchs stand in the blessed line of Seth (5:3), Noah (5:32), and Shem (11:10). See chart: *The Family Line of Adam* at Gen 5.

**11:16 Eber:** The father of the Hebrews (10:21).

**11:27 these are the descendants:** A formula that introduces new phases of history and narrative in Genesis. See introduction: *Structure*. **Abram:** Abraham, whose name is changed in 17:5.

**11:28 Ur of the Chaldeans:** An ancient city and cultural center built along the Euphrates River in southern Mesopotamia

---

[p] Compare Heb *balal*, confuse.

and Haran was the father of Lot. [28]Haran died before
his father Te'rah in the land of his birth, in Ur of the
Chalde'ans. [29]And Abram and Na'hor took wives;
the name of Abram's wife was Sar'ai, and the name
of Nahor's wife, Milcah, the daughter of Haran the
father of Milcah and Is'cah. [30]Now Sar'ai was barren; she had no child.

31 Te'rah took Abram his son and Lot the son of
Haran, his grandson, and Sar'ai his daughter-in-law,
his son Abram's wife, and they went forth together
from Ur of the Chalde'ans to go into the land of
Canaan; but when they came to Haran, they settled
there. [32]The days of Te'rah were two hundred and
five years; and Terah died in Haran.

## The Call of Abram

12 Now the LORD said to Abram, "Go from
your country and your kindred and your
father's house to the land that I will show you. [2]And
I will make of you a great nation, and I will bless
you, and make your name great, so that you will be
a blessing. [3]I will bless those who bless you, and him
who curses you I will curse; and by you all the families of the earth shall bless themselves."[q]

4 So Abram went, as the LORD had told him; and
Lot went with him. Abram was seventy-five years
old when he departed from Haran. [5]And Abram
took Sar'ai his wife, and Lot his brother's son, and
all their possessions which they had gathered, and
the persons that they had gotten in Haran; and they
set forth to go to the land of Canaan. When they had
come to the land of Canaan, [6]Abram passed through
the land to the place at She'chem, to the Oak[r] of
Mo'reh. At that time the Canaanites were in the
land. [7]Then the LORD appeared to Abram, and said,

**12:1:** Acts 7:3; Heb 11:8. **12:2:** Gen 15:5; 17:4, 5; 18:18; 22:17; 28:14; 32:12; 35:11; 46:3. **12:3:** Gen 18:18; 22:17, 18; 26:4; 28:14; Gal 3:8. **12:7:** Gen 13:15; 15:18; 17:8; 24:7; 26:3; 28:4, 13; 35:12; 48:4; Acts 7:5; Gal 3:16.

(modern Iraq). Reference to the tribal people known as the Chaldeans seems to be a gloss added to the text after the ninth century B.C. to distinguish this city from others in the Near East bearing the same (or a similar) name.

**11:30 Sarai:** Sarah, whose name is changed in 17:15. **was barren:** The wives of the Patriarchs each endured the burden of childlessness (Rebekah, 25:21; Rachel, 29:31). This set the stage for several miracles of divine intervention and blessing (18:13–14; 25:21; 30:22–24).

**11:31 Haran:** A city 600 miles northwest of Ur (in modern Syria). It is mentioned several times in the Mari tablets, which date back to the 18th century B.C.

**11:32 Terah died:** Taken together with the information in 11:26 and 12:4, this verse implies that Terah remained in Haran a full 60 years after Abram left the city for Canaan. The Samaritan Pentateuch differs on this point, saying that Terah lived to be 145 instead of 205, meaning he died the same year that Abram set out from Haran. Stephen follows this Samaritan chronology in Acts 7:4.

**12:1—50:26** The patriarchal narratives. These are often classified as folk tales, legends, or epic sagas; some even consider them the free creations of a later age. However, the stories of the Patriarchs are best regarded as genuine family history. Not only do the main characters and events have a solid claim to historicity, but a number of supporting details have been verified by modern research as well. Several considerations favor the authenticity of Genesis 12–50 and make it unlikely that these chapters were either fabricated by later storytellers or substantially altered with nonhistorical elements in the course of a lengthy oral transmission. (**1**) The patriarchal stories are sober and restrained in dealing with the miraculous. Attention is given to God and his actions, but not in ways that suppress the authentically human dimensions of the narrative. (**2**) The accounts give every impression of being objective. No obvious effort is made to idealize the Patriarchs by hiding their weaknesses or excusing their failures. Despite being the founding fathers of God's holy people, they are sometimes portrayed in an unflattering light: e.g., Abraham and Isaac are less than truthful (20:2, 13; 26:7); Jacob and Rebekah are deceptive (27:5–29); Judah fathers two sons by a prostitute (38:12–30); and most of Jacob's sons—ancestors of the tribes of Israel—struggled with jealousy and hatred (37:4, 11). (**3**) The Patriarchs live at variance with the standards of the Torah later erected for Israel: e.g., Abraham married his paternal half-sister (20:10, contrary to Lev 18:11); Jacob married two sisters at the same time (29:21–30, contrary to Lev 18:18); Jacob consecrated sacred pillars (28:18; 35:14, contrary to Deut 16:22); and both Judah and Simeon married Canaanite women (38:2; 46:10; Ex 6:15, contrary to Deut 7:1–3). Stories of religious heroes would not likely be told in this way unless they were believed to rest on historical facts. (**4**) The Patriarchs always appear as outsiders and sojourners in the land of Canaan. This would probably not be the case if their stories were later inventions; more likely, national propagandists would have made them natives of Canaan, thus giving Israel an ancestral claim to the Promised Land and not simply a theological claim based on an ancient covenant with Yahweh (17:7–8). (**5**) The Patriarchs fit comfortably within the cultural, social, and religious environment of the Middle Bronze Age (2000–1500 B.C.). Archeological finds, though not yet attesting the existence of the Patriarchs as individuals, confirm the general manner of life depicted in Genesis as well as specific features related to adoption, surrogate motherhood, restitution, and even the price of slaves. See notes on 15:3; 16:1–6; 31:39; 37:28.

**12:1—25:11** The story of Abraham, the great grandfather of Israel. He stands tall in biblical history as a pillar of faith, righteousness, and obedience (Heb 11:8–19). But more than just a model of heroic trust in God, Abraham is presented in Genesis as a divinely chosen mediator of worldwide blessings (12:3; 18:17–18; 22:17–18). This promise is reaffirmed with Isaac in 26:3–5 and Jacob in 28:13–14 (CCC 144–47). See topical essay: *The Abrahamic Covenant*.

**12:1 Go . . . I will show you:** An invitation to walk by faith and not by sight (Heb 11:8; CCC 2570).

**12:3 families of the earth:** Refers back to 10:32 and the entire family of man that issues from Noah's sons after the flood (CCC 56). **shall bless themselves:** A recurring promise in the patriarchal narratives (18:18; 22:18; 26:4; 28:14). Though translated in the RSV as reflexive, the verb can also be rendered in the passive voice: "shall be blessed" (see textual note *q*). This is how the text was understood in early Jewish tradition (Greek LXX of Gen 12:3 and Sir 44:21) and in the NT (Acts 3:25; Gal 3:8).

**12:6–9** Abram's initial sweep through Canaan moves from **Shechem** in the central highlands to **Bethel** 20 miles south and then down to the **Negeb** in the deep south of Palestine. On a literal reading of biblical chronology, Abram arrived in Canaan around 2090 B.C.

**12:7 I will give this land:** The first time in Scripture that Canaan (12:5) is designated as the Promised Land intended for the family of Abraham (13:15; 15:7; 17:8). **built there an**

[q] Or *in you all the families of the earth shall be blessed.*

[r] Or *Terebinth.*

"To your descendants I will give this land." So he
built there an altar to the LORD, who had appeared
to him. 8Thence he removed to the mountain on the
east of Bethel, and pitched his tent, with Bethel on
the west and Ai on the east; and there he built an
altar to the LORD and called on the name of the LORD.
9And Abram journeyed on, still going toward the
Neg′eb.

### Abram and Sarai in Egypt

10 Now there was a famine in the land. So
Abram went down to Egypt to sojourn there, for
the famine was severe in the land. 11When he was
about to enter Egypt, he said to Sar′ai his wife, "I
know that you are a woman beautiful to behold;
12and when the Egyptians see you, they will say,
'This is his wife'; then they will kill me, but they
will let you live. 13Say you are my sister, that it
may go well with me because of you, and that
my life may be spared on your account." 14When
Abram entered Egypt the Egyptians saw that
the woman was very beautiful. 15And when the
princes of Pharaoh saw her, they praised her to
Pharaoh. And the woman was taken into Pharaoh's
house. 16And for her sake he dealt well with Abram;
and he had sheep, oxen, he-donkeys, menservants,
maidservants, she-donkeys, and camels.

17 But the LORD afflicted Pharaoh and his
house with great plagues because of Sar′ai,
Abram's wife. 18So Pharaoh called Abram, and
said, "What is this you have done to me? Why

**12:10–20:** Gen 20:1–18; 26:7–11.

**altar:** Abram not only surveys the land of Canaan (13:14–17), he sanctifies it as a place of worship by erecting altars in Shechem (12:7), Bethel (12:8), Hebron (13:18), and Moriah (22:2, 9), and by planting a sacred tree in Beer-sheba (21:33). In addition to building altars, which implies the practice of ritual sacrifice (8:20; 46:1), patriarchal religion also includes tithing (14:20; 28:22), libations (35:14), and calling upon the name of the Lord in prayer (12:8; 21:33; 26:25). The Patriarchs themselves performed acts of public worship and served as priests over their families. See topical essay: *Priesthood in the Old Testament* at Num 18.

**12:10–13:1** No sooner does Abram arrive in Canaan than his family is forced into Egypt. • Parallels with the Exodus story show that Abram is preenacting the Exodus event: like Israel, the patriarch journeys to Egypt because of a famine in Canaan (12:10; 42:1–5), but he eventually comes out (13:1; Ex 12:41) with great wealth (12:16; Ex 12:35–36) because God sends plagues upon the house of Pharaoh (12:17; Ex 7–12).

**12:13 you are my sister:** Technically a half-truth, since Sarai and Abram have different mothers but share the same biological father (20:12). As a result of this tactic, Sarai is taken from Abram into the Pharaoh's royal harem (12:15). Similar episodes appear in 20:1–18 and 26:6–11.

**12:16 maidservants:** Perhaps this is how Sarai acquires Hagar, her Egyptian maid (16:1).

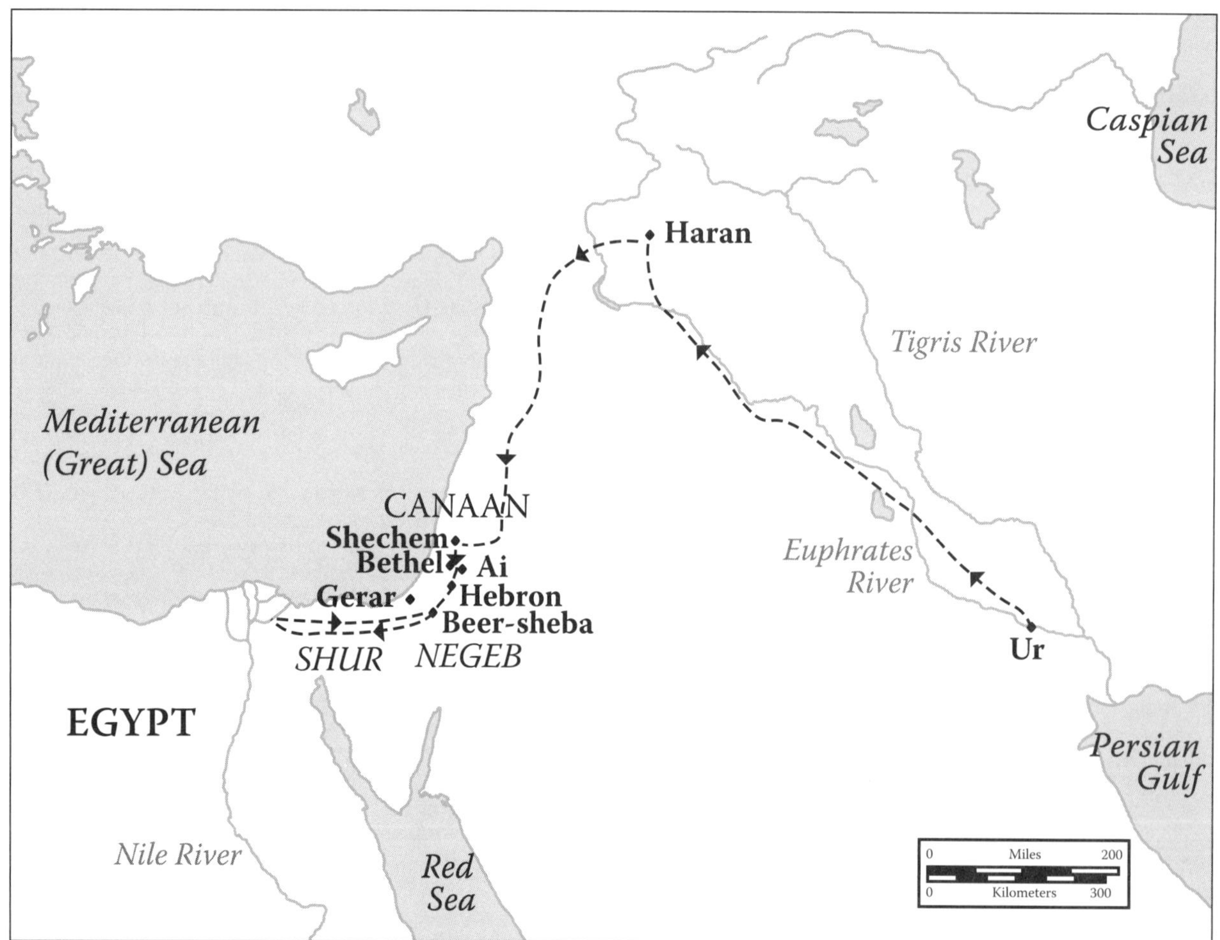


The Journeys of Abraham

did you not tell me that she was your wife? [19]Why
did you say, 'She is my sister,' so that I took her for
my wife? Now then, here is your wife, take her, and
be gone." [20]And Pharaoh gave men orders concerning him; and they set him on the way, with his wife
and all that he had.

### Abram and Lot Separate

13 So Abram went up from Egypt, he and his
wife, and all that he had, and Lot with him,
into the Neg'eb.
2 Now Abram was very rich in cattle, in silver,
and in gold. [3]And he journeyed on from the Neg'eb
as far as Bethel, to the place where his tent had been
at the beginning, between Bethel and Ai, [4]to the
place where he had made an altar at the first; and
there Abram called on the name of the LORD. [5]And
Lot, who went with Abram, also had flocks and
herds and tents, [6]so that the land could not support
both of them dwelling together; for their possessions
were so great that they could not dwell together, [7]and
there was strife between the herdsmen of Abram's
cattle and the herdsmen of Lot's cattle. At that time
the Canaanites and the Per'izzites dwelt in the land.
8 Then Abram said to Lot, "Let there be no strife
between you and me, and between your herdsmen
and my herdsmen; for we are kinsmen. [9]Is not the
whole land before you? Separate yourself from me. If
you take the left hand, then I will go to the right; or
if you take the right hand, then I will go to the left."
[10]And Lot lifted up his eyes, and saw that the Jordan
valley was well watered everywhere like the garden
of the LORD, like the land of Egypt, in the direction
of Zoar; this was before the LORD destroyed Sodom
and Gomor'rah. [11]So Lot chose for himself all the
Jordan valley, and Lot journeyed east; thus they separated from each other. [12]Abram dwelt in the land of
Canaan, while Lot dwelt among the cities of the valley
and moved his tent as far as Sodom. [13]Now the men
of Sodom were wicked, great sinners against the LORD.
14 The LORD said to Abram, after Lot had separated from him, "Lift up your eyes, and look from
the place where you are, northward and southward

**13:15:** Acts 7:5; Gal 3:16.

**13:2-18** Abram and Lot divide their company and go their separate ways. The point is that Lot, of his own free will, chooses to put himself outside the land of promise and into a land of moral corruption (near Sodom, 13:12).

**13:8 kinsmen:** Literally, "brothers", a term used for various family relations beyond that of biological male siblings. The relation between Abram and Lot is that of uncle and nephew (11:27).

**13:10 direction of Zoar:** Lot prefers the Dead Sea valley at the termination of the Jordan River. Genesis tells us this was a lush and fertile region before God scorched it with fire and brimstone (19:24-29; Deut 29:23).

**13:14-17** Reiterates the promise made to Abraham in 12:7. Jacob will receive this same promise (land, 13:15; 28:13) while standing in the same place (Bethel, 13:3; 28:19) and peering out in the same four directions (points of the compass, 13:14; 28:14).

### The Abrahamic Covenant

The story of Abraham begins with the voice of God calling him to a new land (Gen 12:1) and promising him extraordinary blessings for the future (Gen 12:2-3). The divine promise was threefold: (**1**) to make Abraham a *great nation*, (**2**) to make his *name great*, and (**3**) to make him an instrument of *blessing* for the entire world. The first promise is closely connected with the gift of land, which is a necessary foundation for building a nation. The second is closely connected with dynastic kingship, which involves the exaltation and propagation of a royal name. The third is a promise of worldwide blessing mediated through his offspring.

Within Genesis, these three promises are eventually upgraded to the status of divine covenants. The first promise becomes a covenant in Gen 15:7-21, where God swears to rescue the family of Abraham from the oppression of a wicked nation and to give them a new homeland. The second promise becomes a covenant in Gen 17:1-21, where God institutes the rite of circumcision and swears to raise up a dynasty of kings out of Abraham's line. The third promise becomes a covenant oath in Gen 22:16-18, where the Lord swears to multiply the offspring of Abraham and to use them in blessing all nations.

Beyond Genesis, the promises and corresponding covenants reach their fulfillment in three historical stages. The first promise takes shape during the Exodus with the ratification of the Mosaic covenant, which forges the family of Israel into a nation (Ex 19-24) as they prepare to take possession of the Promised Land (in Deuteronomy). The second promise materializes at the founding of the Davidic covenant, where the Lord installs David as king, swearing to give him a great name (2 Sam 7:9) and an everlasting throne (Ps 89:3-4; 132:11-12). The third promise comes to realization in the New Covenant as universal blessings are poured out on the world by Jesus Christ, the messianic descendant of Abraham (Mt 1:1; Acts 3:25-26; Gal 3:14).

| Promises | Covenants | Fulfillments |
|---|---|---|
| 1. Great Nation | Genesis 15 | Mosaic Covenant |
| 2. Great Name | Genesis 17 | Davidic Covenant |
| 3. Worldwide Blessing | Genesis 22 | New Covenant |

«

and eastward and westward; 15 for all the land which you see I will give to you and to your descendants for ever. 16 I will make your descendants as the dust of the earth; so that if one can count the dust of the earth, your descendants also can be counted. 17 Arise, walk through the length and the breadth of the land, for I will give it to you." 18 So Abram moved his tent, and came and dwelt by the Oaks[s] of Mamre, which are at He'bron; and there he built an altar to the LORD.

### Lot's Captivity and Rescue

**14** In the days of Am'raphel king of Shi'nar, Ar'ioch king of Ella'sar, Ched"-or-lao'mer king of E'lam, and Ti'dal king of Goi'im, 2 these kings made war with Be'ra king of Sodom, Bir-sha king of Gomor'rah, Shi'nab king of Admah, Sheme'ber king of Zeboi'im, and the king of Be'la (that is, Zoar). 3 And all these joined forces in the Valley of Siddim (that is, the Salt Sea). 4 Twelve years they had served Ched"-or-lao'mer, but in the thirteenth year they rebelled. 5 In the fourteenth year Ched"-or-lao'mer and the kings who were with him came and subdued the Reph'aim in Ash'teroth-karna'im, the Zu'zim in Ham, the E'mim in Sha'veh-kir"iatha'im, 6 and the Horites in their Mount Se'ir as far as El-par'an on the border of the wilderness; 7 then they turned back and came to Enmish'pat (that is, Ka'desh), and subdued all the country of the Amal'ekites, and also the Am'orites who dwelt in Haz'azon-ta'mar. 8 Then the king of Sodom, the king of Gomor'rah, the king of Admah, the king of Zeboi'im, and the king of Be'la (that is, Zoar) went out, and they joined battle in the Valley of Siddim 9 with Ched"-or-lao'mer king of E'lam, Ti'dal king of Goi'im, Am'raphel king of Shi'nar, and Ar'ioch king of Ella'sar, four kings against five. 10 Now the Valley of Siddim was full of bitumen pits; and as the kings of Sodom and Gomor'rah fled, some fell into them, and the rest fled to the mountain. 11 So the enemy took all the goods of Sodom and Gomor'rah, and all their provisions, and went their way; 12 they also took Lot, the son of Abram's brother, who dwelt in Sodom, and his goods, and departed.

13 Then one who had escaped came, and told Abram the Hebrew, who was living by the Oaks[s] of Mamre the Am'orite, brother of Eshcol and of A'ner; these were allies of Abram. 14 When Abram heard that his kinsman had been taken captive, he led forth his trained men, born in his house, three hundred and eighteen of them, and went in pursuit as far as Dan. 15 And he divided his forces against them by night, he and his servants, and routed them and pursued them to Ho'bah, north of Damascus. 16 Then he brought back all the goods, and also brought back his kinsman Lot with his goods, and the women and the people.

### Melchizedek Blesses Abram

17 After his return from the defeat of Ched"-or-lao'mer and the kings who were with him, the king of

---

**14:17–20:** Heb 7:1–10.

---

**13:18 Hebron:** In the hill country of lower Palestine, about 20 miles south of Jerusalem.

**14:1–12** An alliance of four kings from Mesopotamia (14:1) makes war on five vassal kings from the Dead Sea valley (14:2). Under the leadership of Chedorlaomer, the eastern coalition subdues the entire region and plunders the cities of Sodom and Gomorrah (14:11). Abram's nephew Lot is among the prisoners of war being hauled back to Mesopotamia (14:12).

**14:5–6** The subjugation of people and settlements east of the Jordan River (Deut 2:10–20).

**14:13 the Hebrew:** Abram is a descendant of Eber. See note on 10:21. **allies of Abram:** Or, "Abram's overlords". The expression implies that Abram made a treaty covenant with Mamre, Eschol, and Aner that obligated these men to help him as their vassal in time of need.

**14:14 Dan:** A city at the northern extremity of Palestine named after Dan, the fifth son of Jacob (30:4–6). In Abram's day it was known as "Laish" (Judg 18:27–29).

**14:16 all the goods:** The spoils of people and property that Abram recovered from the Mesopotamian army during his nighttime raid (14:15).

**14:17 the King's Valley:** In the near vicinity of Jerusalem (cf. 2 Sam 18:18).

**14:18 Melchizedek:** A royal title or throne name meaning "king of righteousness" (Heb 7:2). He is the first person in the Bible to be called a **priest** and is mentioned elsewhere in the OT only in Ps 110:4. The identity of Melchizedek is a mystery. Modern scholars tend to view him as a pagan priest of the Canaanite high god, El, although this deity was deemed the father of the gods in Canaanite mythology, not the "maker of heaven and earth" (14:19). In Jewish tradition, Melchizedek is named in the Dead Sea Scrolls as a heavenly judge and eschatological deliverer (11QMelch) or is identified as Shem, the first-born of Noah (*Targum Neofiti* at Gen 14:18), an ancient figure who outlives Abraham, according to a literal reading of the Genesis genealogies (11:10–26; 25:7). Christian tradition sees him as a type of the royal-priestly Messiah (Heb 5–7) and has identified him as an angel, as a manifestation of the pre-incarnate Christ, or as the patriarch Shem. See topical essay: *The Order of Melchizedek* at Heb 7. **Salem:** A shorter name for ancient Jerusalem, as indicated by Scripture (Ps 76:2) and the testimony of Jewish tradition (e.g., Dead Sea Scrolls, 1QapGen 22, 13). Canonically, it is significant that Jerusalem is a center of kingship and priesthood under Melchizedek even before it is made the political and spiritual capital of Israel under David (2 Sam 5–6). **bread and wine:** The elements of a celebratory meal. These may have been communion portions of a thanksgiving sacrifice offered to God after a successful campaign (14:17), or they may suggest that a covenant is forged between Abraham and Melchizedek and is sealed with a sacred meal (cf. 31:44–46; Josh 9:14–15). • *Allegorically*, in the actions of the priest Melchizedek the sacrament of the Lord is prefigured; for Melchizedek is a type of Jesus Christ, who offered the bread and wine of Melchizedek, that is, his body and blood (St. Cyprian, *Letters* 63, 4). This interpretation, shared by many Church Fathers, is implicit in the Roman Canon of the Mass ("the bread and wine offered by your priest Melchisedech", *Eucharistic Prayer I*) (CCC 1333). **God Most High:** The Hebrew is *'el 'elyon*, a title given to Yahweh in 14:22.

---

[s] Or *Terebinths.*

Sodom went out to meet him at the Valley of Sha′veh
(that is, the King's Valley). [18]And Mel-chiz′edek king
of Salem brought out bread and wine; he was priest
of God Most High. [19]And he blessed him and said,

"Blessed be Abram by God Most High,
maker of heaven and earth;
[20]and blessed be God Most High,
who has delivered your enemies into your hand!"

And Abram gave him a tenth of everything.
[21]And the king of Sodom said to Abram, "Give me
the persons, but take the goods for yourself." [22]But
Abram said to the king of Sodom, "I have sworn
to the LORD God Most High, maker of heaven and
earth, [23]that I would not take a thread or a sandal-
thong or anything that is yours, lest you should say,
'I have made Abram rich.' [24]I will take nothing but
what the young men have eaten, and the share of
the men who went with me; let A′ner, Eshcol, and
Mamre take their share."

### God's Covenant with Abram

15 After these things the word of the LORD
came to Abram in a vision, "Fear not,
Abram, I am your shield; your reward shall be
very great." [2]But Abram said, "O Lord GOD, what
will you give me, for I continue childless, and the
heir of my house is Elie′zer of Damascus?" [3]And
Abram said, "Behold, you have given me no offspring; and a slave born in my house will be my
heir." [4]And behold, the word of the LORD came to
him, "This man shall not be your heir; your own
son shall be your heir." [5]And he brought him outside and said, "Look toward heaven, and number
the stars, if you are able to number them." Then
he said to him, "So shall your descendants be."
[6]And he believed the LORD; and he reckoned it to
him as righteousness.

7 And he said to him, "I am the LORD who brought
you from Ur of the Chalde′ans, to give you this land
to possess." [8]But he said, "O Lord GOD, how am I to
know that I shall possess it?" [9]He said to him, "Bring
me a heifer three years old, a she-goat three years
old, a ram three years old, a turtledove, and a young
pigeon." [10]And he brought him all these, cut them in
two, and laid each half over against the other; but
he did not cut the birds in two. [11]And when birds of
prey came down upon the carcasses, Abram drove
them away.

12 As the sun was going down, a deep sleep
fell on Abram; and behold, a dread and great darkness fell upon him. [13]Then the LORD said to Abram,

---

**15:4:** Gen 17:16, 21; 18:10; 21:2. **15:5:** Rom 4:18; Heb 11:12. **15:6:** Rom 4:3, 9, 22, 23; Gal 3:6. **15:13, 14:** Acts 7:6, 7.

---

**14:19 Blessed be Abram:** Blessings are invoked upon others by Patriarchs (9:26–27; 27:27–29) and priests in the Pentateuch (Lev 9:22; Num 6:22–27).

**14:20 gave him a tenth:** Anticipates later Mosaic Law, which required the lay tribes of Israel to pay tithes to the clerical tribe of Levi for spiritual services (Num 18:21–24). See note on Heb 7:4–10.

**14:22 I have sworn:** Literally, "I have raised my hand", a gesture that accompanied the swearing of oaths in biblical antiquity (Deut 32:40; Rev 10:5–6).

**15:1–6** A critical juncture in the spiritual journey of Abram. He clings to the Lord's *promise* of many descendants (13:16) and a land inheritance (12:7; 13:14–15), but he is forced to wrestle with the unsolved *problem* of childlessness (15:2). As later in 22:1–14, God is giving him an opportunity to be tested and found faithful (1 Mac 2:52) (CCC 2374, 2570).

**15:3 a slave:** A childless couple adopting a legal heir is a Near Eastern practice known from the Nuzi tablets of the 15th century B.C. and from an Old Babylonian text from Larsa.

**15:4 your own son:** Literally, "one coming from your body". The child in view is Isaac, whose conception will be a divine miracle (21:1–3) and who will grow up to inherit Abram's estate (25:5).

**15:6 believed the LORD:** Abram trusts in the promise of offspring despite old age (12:4) and the inability of his wife to bear children (11:30). This is not the first time he has put his faith in God in the Genesis narrative. Long before this point, we see Abram building a relationship of trust with the Lord: he obeys the voice of Lord (12:1), builds altars in honor of the Lord (12:7; 13:18), calls on the Lord in prayer (12:8), and swears an oath in the name of the Lord (14:22–23). From the day that God called him, Abram's whole life has been an adventure in faith (as noted in Heb 11:8–19). • The NT looks to Abram as the model believer of ancient times. From him we learn that faith is the indispensable foundation of a living relationship with God in every age (Rom 4:1–25; Gal 3:6–9). **righteousness:** Indicates a right relationship with God. One is established in righteousness by putting faith in God's word and by faithful adherence to his covenant (Deut 6:25; Ps 106:31). Abram is counted a loyal friend of God precisely on this basis (Jas 2:23).

**15:7 I am the LORD:** God will address Israel in these terms at Sinai (Ex 20:2). • The link is typological as well as verbal: both here and during the Exodus he leads his elect (Abraham, Israel) from a land of idolatry (Ur, Egypt) to the land of promise (Josh 24:2–3, 14).

**15:8 how am I to know ...?:** Up to this point, Abram has received only promises of land (12:7; 13:15; 15:7). Now God lays his uncertainties to rest by strengthening his promise with a covenant oath (15:18). For the absolute certainty attained when God adds an oath to a promise, see Heb 6:13–18.

**15:9 heifer ... she-goat ... ram ... turtledove ... pigeon:** Anticipates the sacrifices deemed suitable by later Levitical law (Lev 1:2, 10, 14).

**15:10 cut them in two:** A covenant ratification ceremony. Dividing animal carcasses and walking between the pieces is a ritual enactment of the threat of a curse that a covenant partner invokes upon himself when he swears an oath to ratify the agreement (Jer 34:18). Here it is God, appearing as smoke and fire, who puts himself under the threat of a curse as he moves through the slaughtered beasts and swears to grant land to the family of Abram (15:17–21). See topical essay: *The Abrahamic Covenant* at Gen 12. **did not cut the birds:** Anticipates a requirement of later Levitical law (Lev 1:17).

**15:12–14** The first announcement of the Exodus in the Pentateuch. The effect is to show Abram that the promise of land and nationhood (12:1–2) will not materialize in his own lifetime but are the hope of a future generation.

**15:12 a deep sleep:** Recalls the deep sleep of Adam in 2:21.

**15:13 four hundred years:** A round number approximating the 430 years that Israel dwelt in Egypt (Ex 12:40). Initially, the Israelites were honored guests in the land (47:1–6), but eventually they were oppressed and made slaves (Ex 1:8–14).

"Know of a surety that your descendants will be sojourners in a land that is not theirs, and will be slaves there, and they will be oppressed for four hundred years; 14but I will bring judgment on the nation which they serve, and afterward they shall come out with great possessions. 15As for yourself, you shall go to your fathers in peace; you shall be buried in a good old age. 16And they shall come back here in the fourth generation; for the iniquity of the Am′orites is not yet complete."

17 When the sun had gone down and it was dark, behold, a smoking fire pot and a flaming torch passed between these pieces. 18On that day the LORD made a covenant with Abram, saying, "To your descendants I give this land, from the river of Egypt to the great river, the river Euphra′tes, 19the land of the Kenites, the Ken′izzites, the Kad′monites, 20the Hittites, the Per′izzites, the Reph′aim, 21the Am′orites, the Canaanites, the Gir′gashites and the Jeb′usites."

### The Birth of Ishmael

16 Now Sar′ai, Abram's wife, bore him no children. She had an Egyptian maid whose name was Hagar; 2and Sar′ai said to Abram, "Behold now, the LORD has prevented me from bearing children; go in to my maid; it may be that I shall obtain children by her." And Abram listened to the voice of Sar′ai. 3So, after Abram had dwelt ten years in the land of Canaan, Sar′ai, Abram's wife, took Hagar the Egyptian, her maid, and gave her to Abram her husband as a wife. 4And he went in to Hagar, and she conceived; and when she saw that she had conceived, she looked with contempt on her mistress. 5And Sar′ai said to Abram, "May the wrong done to me be on you! I gave my maid to your embrace, and when she saw that she had conceived, she looked on me with contempt. May the LORD judge between you and me!" 6But Abram said to Sar′ai, "Behold, your maid is in your power; do to her as you please." Then Sarai dealt harshly with her, and she fled from her.

7 The angel of the LORD found her by a spring of water in the wilderness, the spring on the way to Shur. 8And he said, "Hagar, maid of Sar′ai, where have you come from and where are you going?" She said, "I am fleeing from my mistress Sarai." 9The angel of the LORD said to her, "Return to your mistress, and submit to her." 10The angel of the LORD also said to her, "I will so greatly multiply your descendants that they cannot be numbered for multitude."

**15:18:** Gen 17:2, 7, 9–14, 21.

**15:16 the fourth generation:** Equivalent to the 400 years in 15:13. Other possible translations of the expression include "the fourth age" and "the fourth lifetime".

**15:18 I give this land:** The land promised to Abram will have to be wrested from the ten nations who occupy it (15:19–21). **river of Egypt:** Either an eastern branch of the Nile or the smaller Brook of Egypt (modern Wadi el-Arish) that juts across the desert stretch of north Sinai between Canaan and Egypt (Num 34:5). **river Euphrates:** Flows southeast through the Mesopotamian plain and empties into the Persian Gulf. Solomon's kingdom will finally extend to the banks of the upper Euphrates in the tenth century B.C. (1 Kings 4:21).

**16:1–6** Distressed by infertility, Sarai makes a fateful decision to give Hagar to the embrace of her husband. The fallout is tension in the home (16:4), retaliation (16:6), and the birth of a wild and contentious son (16:12). Archeological finds have shown that surrogate motherhood by a servant girl or concubine was indeed practiced in the ancient Near East. Childless couples could resort to such measures to produce a family heir (attested in the Nuzi tablets and the Babylonian *Code of Hammurabi* 144–45). Sarai's actions are understandable against the background of this domestic custom. For other examples of this practice in Genesis, see 30:1–6 and 30:9–13.

**16:2 children by her:** Evidence suggests that a man's lawful wife had maternal rights over a child born to a surrogate mother. **Abram listened:** An ominous note recalling how Adam listened to the voice of his wife in the garden (3:17). Perhaps it also foreshadows what follows: the Hebrew for "listened" (*yishma'*) is the verbal root of the name "Ishmael" (*yishma'e'l*), who is the child born as a result of Sarai's counsel.

**16:3 the Egyptian:** Hagar is a descendant of Ham (10:6). This makes her son, Ishmael, half-Hamitic (through Hagar) and half-Semitic (through Abram).

**16:6 dealt harshly:** The same verb is rendered "oppressed" in 15:13. This sets up a reversal in the Pentateuch: the oppression of Hagar will backfire when Sarai's great grandson, Joseph, is taken as a slave to Egypt by the "Ishmaelites" (39:1) and the family of Israel who follows him there is "oppressed" by the Egyptians (Ex 1:12).

**16:7 the way to Shur:** A desert route leading from Canaan to Egypt. It is implied that Hagar is fleeing back to her homeland (16:1).

**16:10 multiply your descendants:** Numerous descendants will spring from Hagar (through Ishmael, 17:20), just as they will from Abram (through Isaac, 15:4–5). For Ishmael's genealogy, see 25:12–18.

### Word Study

#### *Angel of the LORD* (16:7)

*Mal'ak YHWH* (Heb.): The "angel" or "messenger" of Yahweh. Sometimes this figure appears to be a messenger of God sent from heaven to speak in God's name (Gen 22:11–18; Judg 6:12). At other times, however, he appears to be an actual manifestation of God and a sounding forth of his own divine voice (Ex 3:2–6). For theological and other reasons, this messenger is most likely an angel who mediates the words of God to the world and manifests his divine presence in visible and audible ways. The angel of the Lord is said to be endowed with divine wisdom (2 Sam 14:17), and among his many tasks, he is called upon to lead the people of Israel (Ex 23:20), to thwart the enemies of Israel (Num 22:31–34), to send divine judgments on Israel (2 Sam 24:16), and to announce the birth of significant children in Israel (Gen 16:11; Judg 13:3), including the Messiah (Mt 1:20–21). The Bible also refers to this heavenly figure as "the angel of God" (Gen 21:17; 31:11; Ex 14:19).

11 And the angel of the LORD said to her, "Behold, you are with child, and shall bear a son; you shall call his name Ish'mael;[t] because the LORD has given heed to your affliction. 12 He shall be a wild donkey of a man, his hand against every man and every man's hand against him; and he shall dwell over against all his kinsmen." 13 So she called the name of the LORD who spoke to her, "You are a God of seeing"; for she said, "Have I really seen God and remained alive after seeing him?"[u] 14 Therefore the well was called Be'er-la'hai-roi;[v] it lies between Ka'desh and Be'red.

15 And Hagar bore Abram a son; and Abram called the name of his son, whom Hagar bore, Ish'mael. 16 Abram was eighty-six years old when Hagar bore Ish'mael to Abram.

### The Sign of the Covenant

17 When Abram was ninety-nine years old the LORD appeared to Abram, and said to him, "I am God Almighty;[w] walk before me, and be blameless. 2 And I will make my covenant between me and you, and will multiply you exceedingly." 3 Then Abram fell on his face; and God said to him, 4 "Behold, my covenant is with you, and you shall be the father of a multitude of nations. 5 No longer shall your name be Abram,[x] but your name shall be Abraham;[y] for I have made you the father of a multitude of nations. 6 I will make you exceedingly fruitful; and I will make nations of you, and kings shall come forth from you. 7 And I will establish my covenant between me and you and your descendants after you throughout their generations for an everlasting covenant, to be God to you and to your descendants after you. 8 And I will give to you, and to your descendants after you, the land of your sojournings, all the land of Canaan, for an everlasting possession; and I will be their God."

9 And God said to Abraham, "As for you, you shall keep my covenant, you and your descendants after you throughout their generations. 10 This is my covenant, which you shall keep, between me and you and your descendants after you: Every male among you shall be circumcised. 11 You shall be circumcised in the flesh of your foreskins, and it shall be a sign of the covenant between me and you. 12 He that is eight days old among you shall be circumcised; every male throughout your generations, whether born in your house, or bought with your money from any foreigner who is not of your offspring, 13 both he that is born in your house and he that is bought with your money, shall be circumcised. So shall my covenant be in your flesh an everlasting covenant. 14 Any uncircumcised male who is not circumcised in the flesh of his foreskin shall be cut off from his people; he has broken my covenant."

**17:5:** Rom 4:17. **17:7:** Lk 1:55; Gal 3:16. **17:8:** Acts 7:5. **17:10:** Acts 7:8. **17:11–14:** Gen 17:24; 21:4.

**16:12 a wild donkey:** Aggressive and untamed, Ishmael will be a desert dweller and skilled archer, always wrangling with his kinsmen (21:20–21).

**16:13 alive after seeing him?:** The ancients believed that seeing God directly would bring instant death (32:30; Ex 33:20; Judg 13:22).

**16:16 eighty-six years old:** Ishmael is born 11 years after Abram first set foot in Canaan (12:4–5).

**17:1–21** The Abrahamic covenant of circumcision. It follows the pattern of a Near Eastern treaty covenant, meaning that a superior party or suzerain (God, 17:1–8) lays obligations on an inferior party or vassal (Abraham, 17:9–13) under the threat of a curse (cut off, 17:14). This is the second of three covenants that God makes with the patriarch. See topical essay: *The Abrahamic Covenant* at Gen 12.

**17:1 ninety-nine years old:** Marks 13 years since the birth of Ishmael (16:16). **God Almighty:** The Hebrew is *'el shadday*, the name of God known in the patriarchal period (28:3; 35:11; Ex 6:3; Job 5:17). The meaning of the name is uncertain, possibly "God of the mountain".

**17:4 father of ... nations:** Several ancient peoples descend from Abraham: the Israelites (from Isaac and Jacob, 21:1–3; 35:22–26), the Ishmaelites (from Ishmael, 17:20; 25:12–18), the Edomites (from Esau, 36:1–43), and the Midianites and others (from the sons of his second wife, Keturah, 25:1–4). • The NT reveals that God destined Abraham to be the spiritual father of all who imitate his faith, regardless of their nationality (Rom 4:11–12; Gal 3:6–9) (CCC 59, 1819).

**17:5 Abram ... Abraham:** The original name, meaning "exalted father", is expanded to mean "father of a multitude". In biblical times, a change in one's name signaled a change in one's mission and destiny (17:15; 35:10; Jn 1:42).

**17:6 kings shall come:** A royal dynasty will stem from Abraham and Sarah (17:16) through the genealogical line of their great grandson, Judah (49:8–10). This promise is first realized with the founding of the Israelite monarchy under King David (from Judah's son, Perez, Ruth 4:18–22) and comes to its ultimate fulfillment in Jesus the Messiah (from David's royal son, Solomon, Mt 1:1–18).

**17:11 sign of the covenant:** Circumcision is the sign of the Abrahamic covenant and will later serve as a rite of initiation into the liturgical life of Israel (Ex 12:48; Lev 12:3). Theologically, circumcision of the flesh points inward to the circumcision of the heart, i.e., it summons the descendants of Abraham to cut away the stubbornness of fallen human nature in order to follow the Lord's ways blamelessly (17:1; Deut 10:16). Historically, circumcision was practiced among many peoples of the Near East (Jer 9:25–26) and is still observed today as a religious rite among Jews (at eight days, like Isaac, 17:12) and Muslims (at age 13, like Ishmael, 17:25). • Baptism is the counterpart to circumcision as the initiation rite of the New Covenant. With Baptism, however, which is administered to males and females alike, the grace of the sacrament effects the interior circumcision of the heart that the cutting of the flesh merely signified (Rom 2:28–29; Col 2:11–12). See note on Deut 30:6.

**17:14 shall be cut off:** The curse for transgressing the circumcision covenant is signified by the rite itself: unless the foreskin is excised, the offender will be excised from the covenant people.

**17:15–21** God's promise to give Abraham a son in 15:4 is now defined more precisely: the boy will be **Isaac** (not Ishmael); his mother will be **Sarah** (not Hagar); and he will be born **next year** (not in the unspecified future).

**17:15 Sarai ... Sarah:** Variations of the same name, both meaning "princess". Its royal overtones become more

[t] That is *God hears.*
[u] Cn: Heb *have I even here seen after him who sees me?*
[v] That is *the well of one who sees and lives.*
[w] Heb *El Shaddai.*
[x] That is *exalted father.*
[y] Here taken to mean *father of a multitude.*

15 And God said to Abraham, "As for Sar'ai your
wife, you shall not call her name Sarai, but Sarah
shall be her name. 16I will bless her, and moreover I
will give you a son by her; I will bless her, and she
shall be a mother of nations; kings of peoples shall
come from her." 17Then Abraham fell on his face and
laughed, and said to himself, "Shall a child be born
to a man who is a hundred years old? Shall Sarah,
who is ninety years old, bear a child?" 18And Abraham said to God, "O that Ish'mael might live in your
sight!" 19God said, "No, but Sarah your wife shall
bear you a son, and you shall call his name Isaac.[z]
I will establish my covenant with him as an everlasting covenant for his descendants after him. 20As
for Ish'mael, I have heard you; behold, I will bless
him and make him fruitful and multiply him exceedingly; he shall be the father of twelve princes, and I
will make him a great nation. 21But I will establish
my covenant with Isaac, whom Sarah shall bear to
you at this season next year."
22 When he had finished talking with him, God
went up from Abraham. 23Then Abraham took
Ish'mael his son and all the slaves born in his house
or bought with his money, every male among the
men of Abraham's house, and he circumcised the
flesh of their foreskins that very day, as God had
said to him. 24Abraham was ninety-nine years old
when he was circumcised in the flesh of his foreskin. 25And Ish'mael his son was thirteen years
old when he was circumcised in the flesh of his
foreskin. 26That very day Abraham and his son
Ish'mael were circumcised; 27and all the men of his
house, those born in the house and those bought
with money from a foreigner, were circumcised
with him.

### A Son Promised to Abraham and Sarah

18 And the LORD appeared to him by the
Oaks[a] of Mamre, as he sat at the door of his
tent in the heat of the day. 2He lifted up his eyes and
looked, and behold, three men stood in front of him.
When he saw them, he ran from the tent door to meet
them, and bowed himself to the earth, 3and said, "My
lord, if I have found favor in your sight, do not pass
by your servant. 4Let a little water be brought, and
wash your feet, and rest yourselves under the tree,
5while I fetch a morsel of bread, that you may refresh
yourselves, and after that you may pass on—since
you have come to your servant." So they said, "Do as
you have said." 6And Abraham hastened into the tent
to Sarah, and said, "Make ready quickly three measures[b] of fine meal, knead it, and make cakes." 7And
Abraham ran to the herd, and took a calf, tender and
good, and gave it to the servant, who hastened to prepare it. 8Then he took curds, and milk, and the calf
which he had prepared, and set it before them; and he
stood by them under the tree while they ate.
9 They said to him, "Where is Sarah your
wife?" And he said, "She is in the tent." 10The LORD
said, "I will surely return to you in the spring, and
Sarah your wife shall have a son." And Sarah was
listening at the tent door behind him. 11Now Abraham and Sarah were old, advanced in age; it had
ceased to be with Sarah after the manner of women.
12So Sarah laughed to herself, saying, "After I have
grown old, and my husband is old, shall I have
pleasure?" 13The LORD said to Abraham, "Why did

**18:10:** Rom 9:9. **18:12:** 1 Pet 3:6. **18:14:** Mt 19:26; Mk 10:27; Lk 1:37; Rom 9:9.

prominent with the promise that Sarah will be a mother of "kings" (17:16).

**17:17 laughed:** The Hebrew *yitshaq* is identical in form to the name "Isaac" (17:19). Sarah has the same reaction to the news of his birth in 18:12. For a similar wordplay linking Abraham to Ishmael, see note on 16:2.

**17:21 covenant with Isaac:** The election of Isaac as the heir shuts Ishmael out of the divine plan for Abraham's family. This is further demonstrated in the Genesis narrative as Hagar and Ishmael are expelled from the camp of Abraham and disinherited (21:8–14). See topical essay: *Blessings and Birthrights* at Gen 48.

**17:25 thirteen:** Some evidence suggests that Egyptian boys were circumcised at puberty, around age 13. This would underscore that Ishmael was an Egyptian like his mother, Hagar (25:12).

**18:1–15** God, appearing as a traveler, comes to the tent of Abraham and Sarah to reaffirm his promise of a son (15:4; 17:19). Abraham welcomes him and his companions as an eager and attentive host, doing everything possible to ensure their comfort (18:4–8). • Abraham is probably one of the models of hospitality spoken of in Heb 13:2.

**18:1 the Oaks of Mamre:** Near the city of Hebron in southern Palestine, where Abraham has been living since his separation from Lot (13:18). **heat of the day:** When shade and refreshment are needed most.

**18:2 three men:** Identified in the context as Yahweh (18:1) and two of his angels (19:1). Following this encounter, the two angels are sent off to inspect Sodom (18:22; 19:13), while Abraham is left to haggle with the Lord over the fate of city (18:22–33). Christian tradition often saw the three visitors as an image of the Trinity. • Abraham saw three figures but worshiped only one, for there is one God, one Lord, and one Spirit. There is oneness of honor because there is oneness of power (St. Ambrose, *The Holy Spirit* 2, 4).

**18:3 My lord:** The Hebrew is *'adonay*, an address used exclusively for God in the Bible.

**18:6 three measures:** One for each guest, for a combined total of nearly a half bushel. • *Morally*, the three measures of flour are faith, hope, and love. These virtues contain all the fruits of the Church, so that if one possesses all three, he can receive the entire Trinity at the banquet of his heart (St. Caesarius of Arles, *Sermons* 83, 5).

**18:11 the manner of women:** At 90 years of age, Sarah has already passed through menopause (17:17).

**18:12 Sarah laughed:** A wordplay on Isaac's name, which means "he laughs". See note on 17:17.

**18:14 too hard for the LORD?:** The question is rhetorical, implying that nothing is impossible for God (Jer 32:17; CCC 269). • This verse, which prepares for the miraculous conception of Isaac, is later echoed when the angel Gabriel announces to Mary the virginal conception of Jesus (Lk 1:37; CCC 489).

[z] That is *he laughs.*
[a] Or *Terebinths.*
[b] Heb *seahs.*
[c] Or *wonderful.*

Sarah laugh, and say, 'Shall I indeed bear a child, now that I am old?' 14 Is anything too hard[c] for the LORD? At the appointed time I will return to you, in the spring, and Sarah shall have a son." 15 But Sarah denied, saying, "I did not laugh"; for she was afraid. He said, "No, but you did laugh."

### Abraham Intercedes for Sodom

16 Then the men set out from there, and they looked toward Sodom; and Abraham went with them to set them on their way. 17 The LORD said, "Shall I hide from Abraham what I am about to do, 18 seeing that Abraham shall become a great and mighty nation, and all the nations of the earth shall bless themselves by him?[d] 19 No, for I have chosen[e] him, that he may charge his children and his household after him to keep the way of the LORD by doing righteousness and justice; so that the LORD may bring to Abraham what he has promised him." 20 Then the LORD said, "Because the outcry against Sodom and Gomor'rah is great and their sin is very grave, 21 I will go down to see whether they have done altogether according to the outcry which has come to me; and if not, I will know."

22 So the men turned from there, and went toward Sodom; but Abraham still stood before the LORD. 23 Then Abraham drew near, and said, "Will you indeed destroy the righteous with the wicked? 24 Suppose there are fifty righteous within the city; will you then destroy the place and not spare it for the fifty righteous who are in it? 25 Far be it from you to do such a thing, to slay the righteous with the wicked, so that the righteous fare as the wicked! Far be that from you! Shall not the Judge of all the earth do right?" 26 And the LORD said, "If I find at Sodom fifty righteous in the city, I will spare the whole place for their sake." 27 Abraham answered, "Behold, I have taken upon myself to speak to the Lord, I who am but dust and ashes. 28 Suppose five of the fifty righteous are lacking? Will you destroy the whole city for lack of five?" And he said, "I will not destroy it if I find forty-five there." 29 Again he spoke to him, and said, "Suppose forty are found there." He answered, "For the sake of forty I will not do it." 30 Then he said, "Oh let not the Lord be angry, and I will speak. Suppose thirty are found there." He answered, "I will not do it, if I find thirty there." 31 He said, "Behold, I have taken upon myself to speak to the Lord. Suppose twenty are found there." He answered, "For the sake of twenty I will not destroy it." 32 Then he said, "Oh let not the Lord be angry, and I will speak again but this once. Suppose ten are found there." He answered, "For the sake of ten I will not destroy it." 33 And the LORD went his way, when he had finished speaking to Abraham; and Abraham returned to his place.

### The Immorality of Sodom

**19** The two angels came to Sodom in the evening; and Lot was sitting in the gate of Sodom. When Lot saw them, he rose to meet them, and bowed himself with his face to the earth, 2 and said, "My lords, turn aside, I pray you, to your servant's house and spend the night, and wash your feet; then you may rise up early and go on your way." They said, "No; we will spend the night in the street." 3 But he urged them strongly; so they turned aside to him and entered his house; and he made them a feast, and baked unleavened bread, and they ate. 4 But before they lay down, the men of the city, the men of Sodom, both young and old, all the people to the last man, surrounded the house; 5 and they called to Lot, "Where are the men who came to you tonight? Bring them out to us, that we may know them." 6 Lot went out of the door to the men, shut the door after him, 7 and said, "I beg you, my brothers, do not act so wickedly. 8 Behold, I have two daughters who have not known man; let me bring them out to you, and do to them as you please; only do nothing to these men, for they have come under the shelter of my roof." 9 But they said, "Stand back!" And they said, "This fellow came to sojourn, and he would play

**18:18:** Gen 12:3; Acts 3:25; Gal 3:8.

**18:19 way of the LORD:** In the time of the Patriarchs, the way of justice and righteousness was known through the dictates of the natural law inscribed on the heart (26:5; Rom 2:13–15).

**18:21 I will go down to see:** God is depicted in humanlike terms, as though he had to investigate Sodom and Gomorrah firsthand in order to confirm reports of their wickedness. See note on 6:6.

**18:22–33** Abraham intercedes for Sodom by bargaining with the Lord. The dialogue centers on the character of God, whose *justice* overlooks neither righteousness nor wickedness and whose *mercy* is willing to spare the wicked from mass destruction for the sake of the righteous. These themes play out in the following episode, when divine justice rains down upon Sodom (19:24) and divine mercy spares both Lot (19:16) and city to which he flees (19:21–22).

**19:1–23** Angels appearing as men come to inspect Sodom and evacuate Lot (CCC 332). They are sent to destroy several cities in the Dead Sea valley (19:29) infamous for their injustice (Is 3:9), disregard for the poor (Ezek 16:49), and unnatural lust (Jude 7).

**19:1 sitting in the gate:** May indicate that Lot is a respected elder of the city, i.e., someone who adjudicates civil disputes (Deut 21:18–21). **bowed himself:** Lot welcomes the visitors with the same gestures of Near Eastern hospitality shown by Abraham (18:2–8).

**19:5 that we may know them:** More than just a sin against hospitality, the mob presses in to abuse the visiting men in a perverted, homosexual way. This form of sexual depravity, which is a grievous offense against God and nature (Rom 1:26–27), was rampant among the peoples indigenous to Canaan (Lev 18:22–25). Homosexual sins were punished by death in ancient Israel (Lev 20:13) (CCC 1867, 2357–59).

**19:8 I have two daughters:** An unflattering depiction of Lot, who is willing to endanger his own daughters to ensure the protection of his guests. The rejection of his offer accentuates the Sodomites' disordered preference for men over women.

[d] Or *in him all the nations of the earth shall be blessed.*

[e] Heb *known.*

the judge! Now we will deal worse with you than with them." Then they pressed hard against the man Lot, and drew near to break the door. 10But the men put forth their hands and brought Lot into the house to them, and shut the door. 11And they struck with blindness the men who were at the door of the house, both small and great, so that they wearied themselves groping for the door.

**Sodom and Gomorrah Destroyed**

12 Then the men said to Lot, "Have you any one else here? Sons-in-law, sons, daughters, or any one you have in the city, bring them out of the place; 13for we are about to destroy this place, because the outcry against its people has become great before the LORD, and the LORD has sent us to destroy it." 14So Lot went out and said to his sons-in-law, who were to marry his daughters, "Up, get out of this place; for the LORD is about to destroy the city." But he seemed to his sons-in-law to be jesting.

15 When morning dawned, the angels urged Lot, saying, "Arise, take your wife and your two daughters who are here, lest you be consumed in the punishment of the city." 16But he lingered; so the men seized him and his wife and his two daughters by the hand, the LORD being merciful to him, and they brought him forth and set him outside the city. 17And when they had brought them forth, they[f] said, "Flee for your life; do not look back or stop anywhere in the valley; flee to the hills, lest you be consumed." 18And Lot said to them, "Oh, no, my lords; 19behold, your servant has found favor in your sight, and you have shown me great kindness in saving my life; but I cannot flee to the hills, lest the disaster overtake me, and I die. 20Behold, yonder city is near enough to flee to, and it is a little one. Let me escape there—is it not a little one? —and my life will be saved!" 21He said to him, "Behold, I grant you this favor also, that I will not overthrow the city of which you have spoken. 22Make haste, escape there; for I can do nothing till you arrive there." Therefore the name of the city was called Zoar.[g] 23The sun had risen on the earth when Lot came to Zoar.

24 Then the LORD rained on Sodom and Gomor'rah brimstone and fire from the LORD out of heaven; 25and he overthrew those cities, and all the valley, and all the inhabitants of the cities, and what grew on the ground. 26But Lot's wife behind him looked back, and she became a pillar of salt. 27And Abraham went early in the morning to the place where he had stood before the LORD; 28and he looked down toward Sodom and Gomor'rah and toward all the land of the valley, and beheld, and behold, the smoke of the land went up like the smoke of a furnace.

29 So it was that, when God destroyed the cities of the valley, God remembered Abraham, and sent Lot out of the midst of the overthrow, when he overthrew the cities in which Lot dwelt.

**The Shameful Origin of the Moabites and Ammonites**

30 Now Lot went up out of Zoar, and dwelt in the hills with his two daughters, for he was afraid to dwell in Zoar; so he dwelt in a cave with his two daughters. 31And the first-born said to the younger, "Our father is old, and there is not a man on earth to come in to us after the manner of all the earth. 32Come, let us make our father drink wine, and we will lie with him, that we may preserve offspring through our father." 33So they made their father drink wine that night; and the first-born went in, and lay with her father; he did not know when she lay down or when she arose. 34And on the next day, the first-born said to the younger, "Behold, I lay last night with my father; let us make him drink wine tonight also; then you go in and lie with him, that we may preserve offspring through our father." 35So they made their father drink wine that night

**19:24, 25:** Lk 17:29. **19:26:** Lk 17:32. **19:28:** Rev 9:2.

**19:11 struck with blindness:** A flash of angelic judgment buys enough time for Lot and his family to flee the city before its demise.

**19:16 he lingered:** Hesitation implies an attachment to Sodom. The same affections can be seen in Lot's wife when she gazes back on the burning city with longing (19:26).

**19:22 Zoar:** Originally slated for destruction along with the other cities of the valley (19:21). Zoar is spared at the last minute on account of righteous Lot (18:22–23; 2 Pet 2:7–8). Its name in Hebrew means "little", confirming the observation that the city is "a little one" (19:20).

**19:24–29** The Lord pulverizes the cities of the valley with flaming rocks of sulfur. The event brings death and destruction to the entire region, leaving it a scorched and smoking wasteland. The memory of this catastrophe serves as a warning to the wicked and stands as an illustration of God's judgment on sin (Deut 29:23; 2 Pet 2:6). Likewise, the destruction of an entire population of sinners, the rescue of a single family, and the account of a sexual sin in which the surviving father begets offspring that is hostile to Israel are all paralleled in the flood narrative and its aftermath (chaps. 6–9).

**19:26 pillar of salt:** Lot's wife becomes part of the landscape, resembling one of the natural salt formations in the southern Dead Sea basin.

**19:29 cities of the valley:** Sodom and Gomorrah as well as Admah and Zeboiim (14:2; Deut 29:23). **God remembered Abraham:** This is the second time Lot is rescued by the timely intervention of his uncle Abraham (14:12–16; 18:22–33).

**19:30–38** The shameful origin of Israel's eastern neighbors, the Moabites and the Ammonites. These nations showed themselves enemies of Israel during its Exodus journey (Num 22:1–6; 25:1–3; Deut 23:3–4). The episode recalls the drunkenness of Noah and what appears to be the incestuous origin of the Canaanites in 9:18–27.

**19:30 afraid to dwell in Zoar:** A reversal of Lot's original fear to dwell in the hills (19:17–20).

**19:31 not a man on earth:** The sisters seem to think the devastation of the region is a worldwide calamity. Some interpret the incest that follows as a case of poetic justice, i.e., Lot is made to pay the bitter penalty for recklessly offering his daughters to the perverted Sodomites (19:8).

[f] Gk Syr Vg: Heb *he*.
[g] That is *Little*.

also; and the younger arose, and lay with him; and he did not know when she lay down or when she arose. 36 Thus both the daughters of Lot were with child by their father. 37 The first-born bore a son, and called his name Moab; he is the father of the Moabites to this day. 38 The younger also bore a son, and called his name Ben-am′mi; he is the father of the Am′monites to this day.

### Abraham and Sarah at Gerar

20 From there Abraham journeyed toward the territory of the Neg′eb, and dwelt between Ka′desh and Shur; and he sojourned in Ge′rar. 2 And Abraham said of Sarah his wife, "She is my sister." And Abim′elech king of Ge′rar sent and took Sarah. 3 But God came to Abim′elech in a dream by night, and said to him, "Behold, you are a dead man, because of the woman whom you have taken; for she is a man's wife." 4 Now Abim′elech had not approached her; so he said, "Lord, will you slay an innocent people? 5 Did he not himself say to me, 'She is my sister'? And she herself said, 'He is my brother.' In the integrity of my heart and the innocence of my hands I have done this." 6 Then God said to him in the dream, "Yes, I know that you have done this in the integrity of your heart, and it was I who kept you from sinning against me; therefore I did not let you touch her. 7 Now then restore the man's wife; for he is a prophet, and he will pray for you, and you shall live. But if you do not restore her, know that you shall surely die, you, and all that are yours."

8 So Abim′elech rose early in the morning, and called all his servants, and told them all these things; and the men were very much afraid. 9 Then Abim′elech called Abraham, and said to him, "What have you done to us? And how have I sinned against you, that you have brought on me and my kingdom a great sin? You have done to me things that ought not to be done." 10 And Abim′elech said to Abraham, "What were you thinking of, that you did this thing?" 11 Abraham said, "I did it because I thought, There is no fear of God at all in this place, and they will kill me because of my wife. 12 Besides she is indeed my sister, the daughter of my father but not the daughter of my mother; and she became my wife. 13 And when God caused me to wander from my father's house, I said to her, 'This is the kindness you must do me: at every place to which we come, say of me, He is my brother.'" 14 Then Abim′elech took sheep and oxen, and male and female slaves, and gave them to Abraham, and restored Sarah his wife to him. 15 And Abim′elech said, "Behold, my land is before you; dwell where it pleases you." 16 To Sarah he said, "Behold, I have given your brother a thousand pieces of silver; it is your vindication in the eyes of all who are with you; and before every one you are righted." 17 Then Abraham prayed to God; and God healed Abim′elech, and also healed his wife and female slaves so that they bore children. 18 For the LORD had closed all the wombs of the house of Abim′elech because of Sarah, Abraham's wife.

### The Birth of Isaac

21 The LORD visited Sarah as he had said, and the LORD did to Sarah as he had promised. 2 And Sarah conceived, and bore Abraham a son in his old age at the time of which God had spoken to him. 3 Abraham called the name of his son who was born to him, whom Sarah bore him, Isaac. 4 And Abraham circumcised his son Isaac when he was eight days old, as God had commanded him. 5 Abraham was a hundred years old when his son Isaac was born to him. 6 And Sarah said, "God has made laughter for me; every one who hears will laugh over me." 7 And she said, "Who would have said to Abraham that Sarah would suckle children? Yet I have borne him a son in his old age."

### Hagar and Ishmael Sent Away

---

**21:4:** Acts 7:8.

---

**19:37 Moab:** Resembles the Hebrew expression "from a father".

**19:38 Ben-ammi:** Means "son of my people".

**20:1–18** Abraham's sojourn in Gerar. The episode shows God ensuring the fulfillment of his promises to Abraham by protecting his wife, Sarah, who will eventually bear him a son (21:1). Despite being taken into the royal harem (20:2), she is untouched by Abimelech (20:6) and delivered back safely to the patriarch (20:14). For similar accounts in Genesis, see 12:10–20 and 26:1–11.

**20:1 From there:** From the Oaks of Mamre in Hebron, where Abraham had moved his camp after parting with Lot (13:18; 14:13; 18:1). **Gerar:** In the arid Negeb region in southern Palestine.

**20:2 Abimelech:** The name means "my father is king." It may be a title or throne name of the local monarch. Isaac encounters another king of this name in the same city years later (26:1).

**20:3 dream:** Often a channel of divine instruction in the Bible. See word study: *Dream* at 37:5.

**20:7 prophet:** The first occurrence of this term in Scripture. In this context, it means, not that Abraham has a gift for predicting the future, but that he is a powerful intercessor and friend of God (cf. Num 14:19–20; 21:7; Deut 34:10).

**20:9 a great sin:** Adultery was widely acknowledged as a serious injustice in the ancient Near East, as it also was in Israel (Ex 20:14; Lev 18:20).

**20:12 my sister:** Abraham and Sarah have the same biological father but not the same mother. The patriarch plays up this family connection for his own protection. Prohibitions against marriages between close relatives did not arise until the Torah was given to Israel (Lev 18:11).

**20:18 closed all the wombs:** The royal house of Abimelech is temporarily stricken with infertility.

**21:1–14** The birth of Isaac and the banishment of Ishmael. These pivotal events ensure that Isaac alone will inherit the covenant promises made to Abraham (17:21; 21:12).

**21:3 Isaac:** The name means "he laughs", recalling how Abraham and Sarah burst into laughter when God promised them a child in their elderly years (17:17; 18:12). The same response is expected from all who hear of the miracle (21:6).

**21:4 eight days old:** As required by the Abrahamic covenant (17:12).

**21:8 weaned:** At about age three (2 Mac 7:27).

8 And the child grew, and was weaned; and Abraham made a great feast on the day that Isaac was weaned. [9]But Sarah saw the son of Hagar the Egyptian, whom she had borne to Abraham, playing with her son Isaac.[h] [10]So she said to Abraham, "Cast out this slave woman with her son; for the son of this slave woman shall not be heir with my son Isaac." [11]And the thing was very displeasing to Abraham on account of his son. [12]But God said to Abraham, "Be not displeased because of the lad and because of your slave woman; whatever Sarah says to you, do as she tells you, for through Isaac shall your descendants be named. [13]And I will make a nation of the son of the slave woman also, because he is your offspring." [14]So Abraham rose early in the morning, and took bread and a skin of water, and gave it to Hagar, putting it on her shoulder, along with the child, and sent her away. And she departed, and wandered in the wilderness of Be′er-she′ba.

15 When the water in the skin was gone, she cast the child under one of the bushes. [16]Then she went, and sat down over against him a good way off, about the distance of a bowshot; for she said, "Let me not look upon the death of the child." And as she sat over against him, the child lifted up his voice[i] and wept. [17]And God heard the voice of the lad; and the angel of God called to Hagar from heaven, and said to her, "What troubles you, Hagar? Fear not; for God has heard the voice of the lad where he is. [18]Arise, lift up the lad, and hold him fast with your hand; for I will make him a great nation." [19]Then God opened her eyes, and she saw a well of water; and she went, and filled the skin with water, and gave the lad a drink. [20]And God was with the lad, and he grew up; he lived in the wilderness, and became an expert with the bow. [21]He lived in the wilderness of Par′an; and his mother took a wife for him from the land of Egypt.

### Abraham and Abimelech Make a Covenant

22 At that time Abim′elech and Phi′col the commander of his army said to Abraham, "God is with you in all that you do; [23]now therefore swear to me here by God that you will not deal falsely with me or with my offspring or with my posterity, but as I have dealt loyally with you, you will deal with me and with the land where you have sojourned." [24]And Abraham said, "I will swear."

25 When Abraham complained to Abim′elech about a well of water which Abimelech's servants had seized, [26]Abim′elech said, "I do not know who has done this thing; you did not tell me, and I have not heard of it until today." [27]So Abraham took sheep and oxen and gave them to Abim′elech, and the two men made a covenant. [28]Abraham set seven ewe lambs of the flock apart. [29]And Abim′elech said to Abraham, "What is the meaning of these seven ewe lambs which you have set apart?" [30]He said, "These seven ewe lambs you will take from my hand, that you may be a witness for me that I dug this well." [31]Therefore that place was called Be′er-she′ba;[j] because there both of them swore an oath. [32]So they made a covenant at Be′er-she′ba. Then Abim′elech and Phi′col the commander of his army rose up and returned to the land of the Philis′tines. [33]Abraham planted a tamarisk tree in Be′er-she′ba, and called there on the name of the LORD, the Everlasting God. [34]And Abraham sojourned many days in the land of the Philis′tines.

### God Tests Abraham

22 After these things God tested Abraham, and said to him, "Abraham!" And he said, "Here am I." [2]He said, "Take your son, your only-

**21:10:** Gal 4:30. **21:12:** Rom 9:7; Heb 11:18. **21:31:** Gen 26:33. **22:1–18:** Heb 11:17–19.

**21:9 playing:** The Hebrew is "laughing", here in the negative sense of "laughing at". To the distress of Sarah, the teenager Ishmael is taunting or mocking the toddler Isaac. • Paul will later interpret this as an act of persecution (Gal 4:29).

**21:10 shall not be heir:** Sarah presses Abraham to disinherit Ishmael and expel him from the camp.

**21:17 the angel of God:** The same heavenly messenger who spoke to Hagar the first time she left Abraham's camp (16:7–14). See word study: *Angel of the LORD* at 16:7.

**21:21 wilderness of Paran:** Covers the northeastern expanse of the Sinai Peninsula.

**21:22–34** A covenant of mutual peace between Abraham and Abimelech. It follows the pattern of a Near Eastern kinship or parity covenant between equals. Both parties swear a solemn oath during the ratification ceremony (21:31), invoking God's name (21:23) and expressing their mutual commitments through a verbal declaration (21:30) and ritual action (21:28).

**21:31 Beer-sheba:** Translates "well of seven" or "well of the oath". The two meanings are related, since the number seven has the same root as the verb for swearing an oath in biblical Hebrew. In this episode, Abraham enacts his oath by giving "seven" lambs as a covenant witness (21:30) to his rightful ownership of the well seized by Abimelech's servants (21:25).

**21:33 tamarisk tree:** A sacred landmark, planted as a memorial of God's blessings to Abraham during his sojourn in Canaan. See note on 12:7.

**22:1–19** The binding of Isaac, recalling how Abraham "bound" his son for sacrifice (22:9). The event is sometimes called the Aqedah, the term for "binding" in Hebrew. For its significance, see topical essay: *The Sacrifice of Isaac*.

**22:1 Here am I:** The reply of someone ready and eager to accept God's will (Ex 3:4; 1 Sam 3:4; Is 6:8).

**22:2 only-begotten son:** Follows the reading of the Latin Vulgate. The Hebrew text states that Isaac is the "only son" of Abraham, with the added nuance that he is "unique" and "precious". The expulsion and disinheritance of Ishmael in the preceding chapter is presupposed (21:8–14). The Greek LXX translates the Hebrew "only son" as "beloved son" in all three of its occurrences (22:2, 12, 16). • The epithet "beloved son" is given to Jesus at his Baptism (Mt 3:17) and Transfiguration (Mt 17:5). • Isaac is a type of Christ, for he was a son as Christ was a Son, and he carried the wood of his sacrifice just as the Lord bore the wood of

[h] Gk Vg: Heb lacks *with her son Isaac.*

[i] Gk: Heb *she lifted up her voice.*

[j] That is *Well of seven* or *Well of the oath.*

begotten son Isaac, whom you love, and go to the land of Mori′ah, and offer him there as a burnt offering upon one of the mountains of which I shall tell you." 3So Abraham rose early in the morning, saddled his donkey, and took two of his young men with him, and his son Isaac; and he cut the wood for the burnt offering, and arose and went to the place of which God had told him. 4On the third day Abraham lifted up his eyes and saw the place afar off. 5Then Abraham said to his young men, "Stay here with the donkey; I and the lad will go yonder and worship, and come again to you." 6And Abraham took the wood of the burnt offering, and laid it on Isaac his son; and he took in his hand the fire and the knife. So they went both of them together. 7And Isaac said to his father Abraham, "My father!" And he said, "Here am I, my son." He said, "Behold, the fire and the wood; but where is the lamb for a burnt offering?" 8Abraham said, "God will provide himself the lamb for a burnt offering, my son." So they went both of them together.

9 When they came to the place of which God had told him, Abraham built an altar there, and laid the wood in order, and bound Isaac his son, and laid him on the altar, upon the wood. 10Then Abraham put forth his hand, and took the knife to slay his son. 11But the angel of the LORD called to him from heaven, and said, "Abraham, Abraham!" And he said, "Here am I." 12He said, "Do not lay your hand on the lad or do anything to him; for now I know that you fear God, seeing you have not withheld your son, your only-begotten son, from me." 13And Abraham lifted up his eyes and looked, and behold, behind him was a ram, caught in a thicket by his horns; and Abraham went and took the ram, and offered it up as a burnt offering instead of his son. 14So Abraham called the name of that place The LORD will provide;[k] as it is said to this day, "On the mount of the LORD it shall be provided."[l]

15 And the angel of the LORD called to Abraham a second time from heaven, 16and said, "By myself I have sworn, says the LORD, because you have done this, and have not withheld your son, your only-begotten son, 17I will indeed bless you, and I will multiply your descendants as the stars of heaven and as the sand which is on the seashore. And your descendants shall possess the gate of their enemies, 18and by your descendants shall all the nations of the earth bless themselves, because you have obeyed my voice." 19So Abraham returned

**22:9, 10, 12:** Jas 2:21. **22:16, 17:** Lk 1:73; Heb 6:13, 14; 11:12. **22:18:** Acts 3:25; Gal 3:16.

the Cross (St. Clement of Alexandria, *Christ the Educator* 1, 5, 23). The Lord carried his Cross as Isaac carried the wood; and the ram, caught by its horns in the thicket, prefigures Jesus crowned with thorns and then slain in sacrifice (St. Augustine, *City of God* 16, 32). **Moriah:** The future site of the Jerusalem Temple according to Scripture (2 Chron 3:1) and Jewish tradition (*Jubilees* 18, 13; Josephus, *Antiquities* 1, 226).

**22:5 come again:** By faith, Abraham anticipates the safe return of Isaac, if necessary, by a resurrection from the dead (Heb 11:17–19).

**22:9 bound Isaac:** The text does not specify Isaac's age, only that he is old enough to talk and carry firewood (22:6–7). Jewish tradition believed him to be a grown man, either 25 (Josephus, *Antiquities* 1, 227) or 37 years old (Targum *Neofiti* at Ex 12:42). This would suggest that Isaac gave consent to be tied up and sacrificed, a notion found in ancient Jewish and Christian writings (Josephus, *Antiquities* 1, 232; *4 Maccabees* 13, 12; St. Clement of Rome, *1 Clement* 31).

**22:11 angel of the LORD:** Sent to rescue Isaac and reward Abraham for his obedience (22:15–18). See word study: *Angel of the LORD* at 16:7.

**22:12 not withheld your son:** Abraham has learned the lesson of total surrender to God. • Paul alludes to this verse when he marvels that God the Father did not spare his own Son but surrendered him to be sacrificed for the world (Rom 8:32).

**22:14 The LORD will provide:** The Hebrew is *YHWH yir'eh*, "the LORD will see". The idea is that God will "see to" providing a lamb for sacrifice (22:8). • The announcement in Jn 1:29 that Jesus is the "Lamb of God" is connected partly with this prophecy.

**22:16–18** God swears an unconditional oath to bless the world through Abraham's offspring (CCC 706). • The divine oath of Gen 22 is central to Paul's discussion in Gal 3:6–18. It indicates that God assumed full responsibility for blessing Israel and the Gentiles in spite of their sins and the curses later imposed by the Mosaic covenant. For Paul, the act that elicits the oath (the binding of Isaac) prefigures the act that fulfills the oath (the Crucifixion of Jesus).

**22:16 By myself:** Men swear oaths by calling on the name of the Lord. God, who has no superior to invoke, must swear by his own name to guarantee the fulfillment of his pledge. For the significance of this, see Heb 6:13–18.

**22:18 bless themselves:** Or, "be blessed". See note on 12:3. **you have obeyed my voice:** Abraham's obedience is rewarded with *blessings* for his descendants and the world (26:4–5). This is in contrast to Adam, who obeyed the voice of his wife instead of the Lord (3:17) and brought *curses* upon his descendants and the world (Rom 5:12; 1 Cor 15:22).

### Word Study

*Descendants* (22:18)

*Zera'* (Heb.): A noun meaning "seed" or "offspring". It can refer to seed sown in a field (Ezek 17:5), the produce of a field (Deut 28:38), or male semen (Lev 15:12). Like the English word "deer", the Hebrew term can be used individually or collectively, referring to one or many. An individual seed is simply the child of his parents (Gen 4:25; 21:13); a collective seed can be a family or nation that stems from a common ancestor (Gen 46:6). Both of these possibilities are inherent in Gen 22:18, where the seed of Abraham (translated "your descendants") refers to his natural offspring, Isaac, but also envisions his national offspring, Israel. Through the former, the latter is elected to mediate divine blessings to the world (26:4; 28:14). Paul sees Isaac and Israel as types of Abraham's messianic offspring, Jesus Christ (Gal 3:16).

[k] Or *see*.
[l] Or *he will be seen*.

to his young men, and they arose and went together to Be'er-she'ba; and Abraham dwelt at Beer-sheba.

### The Children of Nahor

20 Now after these things it was told Abraham, "Behold, Milcah also has borne children to your brother Na'hor: 21Uz the first-born, Buz his brother, Ke'muel the father of Ar'am, 22Che'sed, Ha'zo, Pil-dash, Jidlaph, and Bethu'el." 23Bethu'el became the father of Rebekah. These eight Milcah bore to Na'hor, Abraham's brother. 24Moreover, his concubine, whose name was Reu'mah, bore Te'bah, Ga'ham, Ta'hash, and Ma'acah.

### Sarah's Death and Burial

23 Sarah lived a hundred and twenty-seven years; these were the years of the life of Sarah. 2And Sarah died at Kir'iath-ar'ba (that is, He'bron) in the land of Canaan; and Abraham went in to mourn for Sarah and to weep for her. 3And Abraham rose up from before his dead, and said to the Hittites, 4"I am a stranger and a sojourner among you; give me property among you for a burying place, that I may bury my dead out of my sight." 5The Hittites answered Abraham, 6"Hear us, my lord; you are a mighty prince among us. Bury your dead in the choicest of our sepulchres; none of us will withhold from you his sepulchre, or hinder you from burying your dead." 7Abraham rose and bowed to the Hittites, the people of the land. 8And he said to them, "If you are willing that I should bury my dead out of my sight, hear me, and entreat for me E'phron

**23:4:** Heb 11:9, 13.

**22:20–24** The sons of Abraham's younger brother, Nahor, living in upper Mesopotamia (11:27). This is the first introduction of Isaac's wife, **Rebekah**, in the Genesis narrative.

**23:1–20** Abraham buys land in southern Canaan as a burial plot for Sarah. The chapter details the negotiation and purchase of the property and stresses that Abraham declined to accept it as a gift. This field is the only portion of land that ever belongs to Abraham personally, but his purchase of the site anticipates the full acquisition of Canaan by his descendants (12:7; 17:8).

**23:3 the Hittites:** The descendants of "Heth" (10:15), one of the ten nations that occupied Canaan before its conquest by the Israelites (15:18–21).

**23:4 a stranger:** A foreigner living among natives but possessing no property.

**23:9 cave of Mach-pelah:** Abraham will be buried with Sarah in this same cave (25:9–10), as will Isaac and his wife, Rebekah, and Jacob and his first wife, Leah (49:29–32). Samaritan tradition locates the burial place of the Patriarchs, not in Hebron, but in Shechem in central Palestine. Stephen follows this Samaritan tradition in Acts 7:16.

## The Sacrifice of Isaac

The drama of the Book of Genesis reaches its greatest intensity in 22:1–19, the heart-wrenching story of Abraham offering his beloved son as a sacrifice on Mt. Moriah. So momentous is the event and its outcome that it stands as one of the defining moments of salvation history. Had Abraham shown anything less than heroic faith, there is no telling how the grand narrative of the Bible would have developed thereafter.

The question is how to interpret the significance of the episode. For some, the story is a protest against the rituals of child sacrifice that plagued the biblical world. By holding back the knife, the Lord shows that he rejects rather than requires this kind of savagery in the name of religion. For others, the story is a lesson in trusting God and obeying his word, even when life's circumstances seem to contradict his promises. Stretching our faith beyond comfortable limits is seen as the path to greater blessing that Abraham blazes for us by his example.

Both of these readings provide genuine insights into Genesis 22. But more can be said about the spiritual and theological dimensions of the episode. In the interpretive tradition of Judaism and Christianity, the sacrifice of Isaac is an event of monumental historic importance. It is one of the few events in Scripture that have a lasting effect on the shape of God's plans for the future and the world.

### SPIRITUAL SIGNIFICANCE

For Abraham personally, the sacrifice of Isaac marks the highpoint of his developing relationship with the Lord. Ever since his call in Genesis 12, Abraham's faith in God has been gradually deepening and maturing to the point where, in Genesis 22, God sees fit to test the strength of his commitment. Preceding chapters describe how the plot builds to reach this climactic moment. (**1**) Initially Abraham is asked to leave his *home* and set out for the land of Canaan at the Lord's direction (Gen 12:1–2). (**2**) Later he is asked to sacrifice animals from his *herds* (Gen 15:9–10) so that the Lord can put his lingering doubts to rest by the ratification of a covenant (Gen 15:18–20). (**3**) Then the patriarch is asked to sacrifice part of *himself* in a covenant of circumcision at the age of ninety-nine (Gen 17:1–21). (**4**) Finally, the Lord asks for the life of Isaac, Abraham's beloved *heir* (Gen 22:1–2). No greater sacrifice could be asked of a father than this, all the more so since God's promises to bless Abraham are literally bound up with Isaac on the altar (see Gen 17:19).

So it is that Abraham learns the lesson of trustful surrender to the Lord. At each stage in the process, more is asked of him than before, until all that Abraham holds dear is given over to God and nothing is held back. Each time he is summoned to sacrifice, he is asked to love the Creator more than his creatures and to esteem the divine Giver above his most precious gifts. Even when God's promises and credibility hang by a thread, the only acceptable course is to entrust ourselves to him in faith. Because Abraham followed this course, he shows himself to be one who fears God (Gen 22:12). This is significant because

the son of Zo'har, 9that he may give me the cave
of Mach-pe'lah, which he owns; it is at the end of
his field. For the full price let him give it to me in
your presence as a possession for a burying place."
10Now E'phron was sitting among the Hittites; and
Ephron the Hittite answered Abraham in the hearing of the Hittites, of all who went in at the gate of
his city, 11"No, my lord, hear me; I give you the field,
and I give you the cave that is in it; in the presence
of the sons of my people I give it to you; bury your
dead." 12Then Abraham bowed down before the
people of the land. 13And he said to E'phron in the
hearing of the people of the land, "But if you will,
hear me; I will give the price of the field; accept it
from me, that I may bury my dead there." 14E'phron
answered Abraham, 15"My lord, listen to me; a piece
of land worth four hundred shekels of silver, what is
that between you and me? Bury your dead." 16Abra-
ham agreed with E'phron; and Abraham weighed
out for Ephron the silver which he had named in
the hearing of the Hittites, four hundred shekels of
silver, according to the weights current among the
merchants.

17 So the field of E'phron in Mach-pe'lah, which
was to the east of Mamre, the field with the cave
which was in it and all the trees that were in the
field, throughout its whole area, was made over 18to
Abraham as a possession in the presence of the Hittites, before all who went in at the gate of his city.
19After this, Abraham buried Sarah his wife in the
cave of the field of Mach-pe'lah east of Mamre (that
is, He'bron) in the land of Canaan. 20The field and
the cave that is in it were made over to Abraham as
a possession for a burying place by the Hittites.

**The Marriage of Isaac and Rebekah**

**23:16, 17:** Acts 7:16.

**23:10 who went in at the gate:** Not passersby, but the elders or officials of the city that oversee legal transactions (cf. Ruth 4:1–2).

**23:15 four hundred shekels:** A very high price.

**24:1–67** Abraham commissions his head servant to find a bride for Isaac. The story details how God, in his Providence, oversees the process and ensures the success of the mission.

**24:2 hand under my thigh:** The loins or thighs represent the locus of man's procreative powers (Job 40:16; Heb 7:10). Putting the hand under the thigh is an oath gesture, signifying that the swearing party invokes a curse of sterility upon himself should he fail to uphold his pledge (Deut 33:11). Here the oath makes Abraham's last living request binding upon his servant should he die before Isaac is

the Bible extols "fear of the Lord" as the preeminent religious virtue, the very essence of what it means to possess wisdom and to live uprightly in the eyes of the Almighty (Ex 20:20; Job 1:1; 28:28; Ps 111:10; Prov 1:7).

**THEOLOGICAL SIGNIFICANCE**

In early Jewish theology, the sacrifice or "binding" of Isaac is an event that sends ripples down through the history of the covenant people. It is said, for example, that Isaac played an active role on Moriah by offering himself as a willing victim and that the merits of his action were stored up for the redemption of Israel in future days. Thus, saving events such as the Exodus from Egypt, the forgiveness of the people after the golden calf apostasy, and the crossing of the Jordan into the Promised Land were all made possible by the sacrifice of Isaac. Likewise, the cultic ministries of the Temple, especially the daily burnt offering and the yearly Passover sacrifice, were considered liturgical memorials of Isaac's offering. In these and other ways, the sacrifice of Isaac was believed to secure lasting benefits for the descendants of Abraham.

From a Christian perspective, the sacrifice of Isaac points forward to the salvation of the world by the Messiah. Anticipation of this rests on both a prophetical and typological reading of Genesis 22. *Prophetically*, the divine oath to bless the world through Abraham in Gen 22:16–19 is fulfilled in Jesus Christ as the messianic offspring of Abraham (Gal 3:16). Through him the blessings of God's covenant with Abraham, destined for all families and nations, are poured out for the salvation of Israel and the Gentiles alike (Mt 28:19; Acts 3:25–26; Gal 3:14). In this way, the curses of the Adamic covenant are surpassed and surmounted by the blessings of the Abrahamic covenant fulfilled by the Messiah (see Rom 5:12–21). *Typologically*, the offering of Isaac serves as a preview of how the world's redemption would be accomplished. Like Isaac, Jesus is an only beloved Son (Mt 3:17; Jn 3:16) who is not spared by his Father but is offered in sacrifice (Rom 8:32). So too, as Isaac is returned alive to the arms of his father, thanks to the intervention of God (Gen 22:12), Jesus is restored to life in his Resurrection (Heb 11:17–19). Building on this NT foundation, the Fathers of the Church went on to correlate Isaac carrying the firewood (Gen 22:6) with Jesus bearing his own Cross (Jn 19:17), to link the deliverance of Isaac on the third day after consignment to death (Gen 22:4) with the deliverance of Jesus from death on the third day (Mt 16:21), and to see the ram caught by its horns in the thicket (Gen 22:13) as a depiction of Jesus, the sacrificial Lamb (Jn 1:29), crowned with thorns (Jn 19:2). Finally, the sacrifice of Isaac is said to have taken place on Moriah (Gen 22:2), which is none other than the mountainous elevation of Jerusalem (2 Chron 3:1), the city where Jesus was called upon to offer his life in sacrifice. Given these remarkable prophetical and typological features, it is no surprise that Christian tradition places Genesis 22 alongside other OT passages such as Isaiah 53 that most clearly describe the work of the Messiah for our redemption. «

**24** Now Abraham was old, well advanced in years; and the LORD had blessed Abraham in all things. [2]And Abraham said to his servant, the oldest of his house, who had charge of all that he had, "Put your hand under my thigh, [3]and I will make you swear by the LORD, the God of heaven and of the earth, that you will not take a wife for my son from the daughters of the Canaanites, among whom I dwell, [4]but will go to my country and to my kindred, and take a wife for my son Isaac." [5]The servant said to him, "Perhaps the woman may not be willing to follow me to this land; must I then take your son back to the land from which you came?" [6]Abraham said to him, "See to it that you do not take my son back there. [7]The LORD, the God of heaven, who took me from my father's house and from the land of my birth, and who spoke to me and swore to me, 'To your descendants I will give this land,' he will send his angel before you, and you shall take a wife for my son from there. [8]But if the woman is not willing to follow you, then you will be free from this oath of mine; only you must not take my son back there." [9]So the servant put his hand under the thigh of Abraham his master, and swore to him concerning this matter.

10 Then the servant took ten of his master's camels and departed, taking all sorts of choice gifts from his master; and he arose, and went to Mesopota'mia, to the city of Na'hor. [11]And he made the camels kneel down outside the city by the well of water at the time of evening, the time when women go out to draw water. [12]And he said, "O LORD, God of my master Abraham, grant me success today, I beg you, and show mercy to my master Abraham. [13]Behold, I am standing by the spring of water, and the daughters of the men of the city are coming out to draw water. [14]Let the maiden to whom I shall say, 'Please let down your jar that I may drink,' and who shall say, 'Drink, and I will water your camels'—let her be the one whom you have appointed for your servant Isaac. By this I shall know that you have shown mercy to my master."

15 Before he had done speaking, behold, Rebekah, who was born to Bethu'el the son of Milcah, the wife of Na'hor, Abraham's brother, came out with her water jar upon her shoulder. [16]The maiden was very fair to look upon, a virgin, whom no man had known. She went down to the spring, and filled her jar, and came up. [17]Then the servant ran to meet her, and said, "Please give me a little water to drink from your jar." [18]She said, "Drink, my lord"; and she quickly let down her jar upon her hand, and gave him a drink. [19]When she had finished giving him a drink, she said, "I will draw for your camels also, until they have done drinking." [20]So she quickly emptied her jar into the trough and ran again to the well to draw, and she drew for all his camels. [21]The man gazed at her in silence to learn whether the LORD had prospered his journey or not.

22 When the camels had done drinking, the man took a gold ring weighing a half shekel, and two bracelets for her arms weighing ten gold shekels, [23]and said, "Tell me whose daughter you are. Is there room in your father's house for us to lodge in?" [24]She said to him, "I am the daughter of Bethu'el the son of Milcah, whom she bore to Na'hor." [25]She added, "We have both straw and food enough, and room to lodge in." [26]The man bowed his head and worshiped the LORD, [27]and said, "Blessed be the LORD, the God of my master Abraham, who has not forsaken his mercy and his faithfulness toward my master. As for me, the LORD has led me in the way to the house of my master's kinsmen."

28 Then the maiden ran and told her mother's household about these things. [29]Rebekah had a brother whose name was La'ban; and Laban ran out to the man, to the spring. [30]When he saw the ring, and the bracelets on his sister's arms, and when he heard the words of Rebekah his sister, "Thus the man spoke to me," he went to the man; and behold, he was standing by the camels at the spring. [31]He said, "Come in, O blessed of the LORD; why do you stand outside? For I have prepared the house and a place for the camels." [32]So the man came into the house; and La'ban ungirded the camels, and gave him straw and food for the camels, and water to wash his feet and the feet of the men who were with him. [33]Then food was set before him to eat; but he said, "I will not eat until I have told my errand." He said, "Speak on."

34 So he said, "I am Abraham's servant. [35]The LORD has greatly blessed my master, and he has become great; he has given him flocks and herds, silver and gold, menservants and maidservants, cam-

---

married. For a similar oath imposed by the aging Jacob, see 47:29-31.

**24:3 daughters of the Canaanites:** Anticipates the later Mosaic restriction that forbids Israelites to intermarry with Canaanites (9:25; Deut 7:1-4).

**24:7 his angel:** A heavenly scout will be sent ahead to prosper the mission. This appears to be the angel who will lead Israel to the Promised Land (Ex 23:20). See word study: *Angel of the LORD* at 16:7.

**24:10 ten ... camels:** Taken along to accommodate the entourage of Abraham's men (24:32) as well as Rebekah and her maids on the return trip (24:61). Though camels were not widely used as beasts of burden until after 1000 B.C., there is evidence from Egypt for a limited domestication of camels in the Near East dating back into the third millennium B.C. Egypt is precisely where Abraham's family is said to have acquired these animals in 12:16. **Nahor:** Located in upper Mesopotamia. A city of this name is mentioned in the Mari tablets of the 18th century B.C.

**24:11 well of water:** Also the setting where Jacob met his wife, Rachel (29:1-14), and where Moses found his wife, Zipporah (Ex 2:15-22). **evening:** After the heat of midday has passed.

**24:12 O LORD:** The story is punctuated with the prayers and pious actions of the servant (24:26-27, 42-44, 52).

**24:22 gold ring ... two bracelets:** Betrothal gifts.

els and donkeys. [36]And Sarah my master's wife bore a son to my master when she was old; and to him he has given all that he has. [37]My master made me swear, saying, 'You shall not take a wife for my son from the daughters of the Canaanites, in whose land I dwell; [38]but you shall go to my father's house and to my kindred, and take a wife for my son.' [39]I said to my master, 'Perhaps the woman will not follow me.' [40]But he said to me, 'The LORD, before whom I walk, will send his angel with you and prosper your way; and you shall take a wife for my son from my kindred and from my father's house; [41]then you will be free from my oath, when you come to my kindred; and if they will not give her to you, you will be free from my oath.'

42 "I came today to the spring, and said, 'O LORD, the God of my master Abraham, if now you will prosper the way which I go, [43]behold, I am standing by the spring of water; let the young woman who comes out to draw, to whom I shall say, "Please give me a little water from your jar to drink," [44]and who will say to me, "Drink, and I will draw for your camels also," let her be the woman whom the LORD has appointed for my master's son.'

45 "Before I had done speaking in my heart, behold, Rebekah came out with her water jar on her shoulder; and she went down to the spring, and drew. I said to her, 'Please let me drink.' [46]She quickly let down her jar from her shoulder, and said, 'Drink, and I will give your camels drink also.' So I drank, and she gave the camels drink also. [47]Then I asked her, 'Whose daughter are you?' She said, 'The daughter of Bethu'el, Na'hor's son, whom Milcah bore to him.' So I put the ring on her nose, and the bracelets on her arms. [48]Then I bowed my head and worshiped the LORD, and blessed the LORD, the God of my master Abraham, who had led me by the right way to take the daughter of my master's kinsman for his son. [49]Now then, if you will deal loyally and truly with my master, tell me; and if not, tell me; that I may turn to the right hand or to the left."

50 Then La'ban and Bethu'el answered, "The thing comes from the LORD; we cannot speak to you bad or good. [51]Behold, Rebekah is before you, take her and go, and let her be the wife of your master's son, as the LORD has spoken."

52 When Abraham's servant heard their words, he bowed himself to the earth before the LORD. [53]And the servant brought forth jewelry of silver and of gold, and raiment, and gave them to Rebekah; he also gave to her brother and to her mother costly ornaments. [54]And he and the men who were with him ate and drank, and they spent the night there. When they arose in the morning, he said, "Send me back to my master." [55]Her brother and her mother said, "Let the maiden remain with us a while, at least ten days; after that she may go." [56]But he said to them, "Do not delay me, since the LORD has prospered my way; let me go that I may go to my master." [57]They said, "We will call the maiden, and ask her." [58]And they called Rebekah, and said to her, "Will you go with this man?" She said, "I will go." [59]So they sent away Rebekah their sister and her nurse, and Abraham's servant and his men. [60]And they blessed Rebekah, and said to her, "Our sister, be the mother of thousands of ten thousands; and may your descendants possess the gate of those who hate them!" [61]Then Rebekah and her maids arose, and rode upon the camels and followed the man; thus the servant took Rebekah, and went his way.

62 Now Isaac had come from[n] Be'er-la'hai-roi, and was dwelling in the Neg'eb. [63]And Isaac went out to meditate in the field in the evening; and he lifted up his eyes and looked, and behold, there were camels coming. [64]And Rebekah lifted up her eyes, and when she saw Isaac, she alighted from the camel, [65]and said to the servant, "Who is the man yonder, walking in the field to meet us?" The servant said, "It is my master." So she took her veil and covered herself. [66]And the servant told Isaac all the things that he had done. [67]Then Isaac brought her into the tent,[o] and took Rebekah, and she became his wife; and he loved her. So Isaac was comforted after his mother's death.

### Abraham Marries Keturah

25 Abraham took another wife, whose name was Ketu'rah. [2]She bore him Zimran, Jokshan, Me'dan, Mid'ian, Ishbak, and Shuah. [3]Jokshan was the father of Sheba and De'dan. The sons of Dedan were Asshu'rim, Letu'shim, and Le-um'mim. [4]The sons of Mid'ian were E'phah, E'pher, Ha'noch,

**24:58 Will you go ...?:** The success of the mission hinges in part on Rebekah's consent (24:5, 8).

**24:62 Beer-lahai-roi:** In the Negeb region of southern Canaan, where the birth of Ishmael was first announced (16:14).

**24:63 went out to meditate:** Suggests that Isaac is a spiritual man who has developed a personal and prayerful relationship with Yahweh.

**24:65 my master:** A turning point in the narrative. Up until now, the servant has repeatedly acknowledged Abraham—not Isaac—as his master (24:9–10, 12, 14, etc.). But now that Isaac the heir has acquired a wife, he becomes the master of all his father's belongings (25:5). **covered herself:** Out of respect for her future husband, Rebekah dismounts her camel (24:64) and drapes herself with a bridal veil (Song 4:1).

**25:1–19** Rounding off the Abraham narrative is a genealogy of the patriarch's offspring: six sons by Keturah (25:1–6), one by Hagar (25:12–18), and one by Sarah (25:19). In between is a short account of his death and burial at 175 years of age (25:7–11).

**25:1 Keturah:** A concubine taken as Abraham's second wife after the death of Sarah (1 Chron 1:32). She bears additional sons for Abraham (25:2), although he eventually sends them away (25:6) as he did his first-born, Ishmael (21:1–14).

**25:5 all he had:** Confirms that Isaac has displaced the older Ishmael as the heir of the Abrahamic blessings. See topical essay: *Blessings and Birthrights* at Gen 48.

[n] Syr Tg: Heb *from coming to.*

[o] Heb adds *of Sarah his mother.*

Abi'da, and Elda'ah. All these were the children of Ketu'rah. [5]Abraham gave all he had to Isaac. [6]But to the sons of his concubines Abraham gave gifts, and while he was still living he sent them away from his son Isaac, eastward to the east country.

### The Death of Abraham

7 These are the days of the years of Abraham's life, a hundred and seventy-five years. [8]Abraham breathed his last and died in a good old age, an old man and full of years, and was gathered to his people. [9]Isaac and Ish'mael his sons buried him in the cave of Mach-pe'lah, in the field of E'phron the son of Zo'har the Hittite, east of Mamre, [10]the field which Abraham purchased from the Hittites. There Abraham was buried, with Sarah his wife. [11]After the death of Abraham God blessed Isaac his son. And Isaac dwelt at Be'er-la'hai-roi.

### The Descendants of Ishmael

12 These are the descendants of Ish'mael, Abraham's son, whom Hagar the Egyptian, Sarah's maid, bore to Abraham. [13]These are the names of the sons of Ish'mael, named in the order of their birth: Neba'ioth, the first-born of Ishmael; and Ke'dar, Ad'beel, Mibsam, [14]Mishma, Du'mah, Massa, [15]Ha'dad, Te'ma, Je'tur, Na'phish, and Ked'emah. [16]These are the sons of Ish'mael and these are their names, by their villages and by their encampments, twelve princes according to their tribes. [17](These are the years of the life of Ish'mael, a hundred and thirty-seven years; he breathed his last and died, and was gathered to his kindred.) [18]They dwelt from Hav'ilah to Shur, which is opposite Egypt in the direction of Assyria; he settled[p] over against all his people.

### The Birth of Esau and Jacob

19 These are the descendants of Isaac, Abraham's son: Abraham was the father of Isaac, [20]and Isaac was forty years old when he took to wife Rebekah, the daughter of Bethu'el the Arame'an of Pad'dan-ar'am, the sister of La'ban the Aramean. [21]And Isaac prayed to the LORD for his wife, because she was barren; and the LORD granted his prayer, and Rebekah his wife conceived. [22]The children struggled together within her; and she said, "If it is thus, why do I live?"[q] So she went to inquire of the LORD. [23]And the LORD said to her,

"Two nations are in your womb,
  and two peoples, born of you, shall be divided;
the one shall be stronger than the other,
  the elder shall serve the younger."

[24]When her days to be delivered were fulfilled, behold, there were twins in her womb. [25]The first came forth red, all his body like a hairy mantle; so they called his name Esau. [26]Afterward his brother came forth, and his hand had taken hold of Esau's heel; so his name was called Jacob.[r] Isaac was sixty years old when she bore them.

### Esau Sells His Birthright

27 When the boys grew up, Esau was a skilful hunter, a man of the field, while Jacob was a quiet man, dwelling in tents. [28]Isaac loved Esau, because he ate of his game; but Rebekah loved Jacob.

29 Once when Jacob was boiling pottage, Esau

---

**25:13–16:** 1 Chron 1:29–31.

---

**25:8 gathered to his people:** An idiom meaning Abraham has entered the realm of the dead to rest with his deceased ancestors (35:29; 49:29).

**25:9 cave of Mach-pelah:** The burial place of Sarah on the plot of land that Abraham purchased from the Hittites in Hebron. See note on 23:9.

**25:12–18** The genealogy of Ishmael. His 12 sons, born of an Egyptian wife (21:21), spread across northern Arabia (25:18). Ishmael is traditionally considered the father of the Arabs in Jewish tradition (*Jubilees* 20, 12–13; Josephus, *Antiquities* 1, 220–21).

**25:16 twelve princes:** In fulfillment of God's promise to Abraham (17:20).

**25:19—36:43** Stories of Isaac and Jacob, the grandfather and father of tribal Israel. Less attention is given to Isaac than to Jacob in these narratives, although he is an important link in the genealogical chain of Genesis because he passes the "blessing of Abraham" down to Jacob (28:4), who in turn passes the blessing to his 12 sons, who make up the family of Israel (49:2–28).

**25:19 These are the descendants:** A formula that introduces new phases of history and narrative in Genesis. See introduction: *Structure.*

**25:20 Paddan-aram:** Upper Mesopotamia, the home of Abraham's relatives living in Haran (11:31; 24:10; 28:2).

**25:21 Isaac prayed:** Isaac is a powerful intercessor like his father (20:7). This is because he is a righteous and spiritual man (24:63; Jas 5:16). **she was barren:** Rebekah carries the burden of childlessness like Sarah before her (11:30) and Rachel after her (30:2).

**25:22 struggled:** The unborn twins are already wrestling for primogeniture (first-born status). This anticipates the fraternal rivalry between Jacob and Esau, which comes to a head when the younger Jacob usurps the blessing and birthright from the first-born Esau (25:33; 27:36). Beyond the horizon of Genesis, the "elder" will serve the "younger" (25:23) when the Israelites (descended from Jacob) make vassals of the Edomites (descended from Esau) under the leadership of David (2 Sam 8:13–14). • Paul sees in these events the drama of divine election played out in history (Rom 9:10–13).

**25:25 red:** The Hebrew term resembles the word "Edom", which is another name for Esau (25:30). **hairy:** The Hebrew term resembles the word "Seir", which is the mountainous region of southeast Palestine where the descendents of Esau settled (36:8).

**25:26 Jacob:** The Hebrew name *ya'aqob* resembles the "heel" (*'aqeb*) that Jacob grasped as an infant, foreshadowing how he later "supplanted" (*'aqab*) Esau as the rightful recipient of the first-born blessing (27:36).

**25:27–34** As with Isaac and Ishmael, the younger Jacob is elevated over the first-born Esau and becomes the heir to the promises of the Abrahamic covenant.

**25:30 pottage:** A type of boiled lentil stew (25:34). Its **red** color involves another play on Esau's name, similar to the one at 25:25.

---

[p] Heb *fell.*

[q] Syr: Heb obscure.

[r] That is *He takes by the heel* or *He supplants.*

came in from the field, and he was famished. [30]And Esau said to Jacob, "Let me eat some of that red pottage, for I am famished!" (Therefore his name was called E'dom.)[s] [31]Jacob said, "First sell me your birthright." [32]Esau said, "I am about to die; of what use is a birthright to me?" [33]Jacob said, "Swear to me first."[t] So he swore to him, and sold his birthright to Jacob. [34]Then Jacob gave Esau bread and pottage of lentils, and he ate and drank, and rose and went his way. Thus Esau despised his birthright.

### Isaac and Abimelech

26 Now there was a famine in the land, besides the former famine that was in the days of Abraham. And Isaac went to Ge'rar, to Abim'elech king of the Philis'tines. [2]And the LORD appeared to him, and said, "Do not go down to Egypt; dwell in the land of which I shall tell you. [3]Sojourn in this land, and I will be with you, and will bless you; for to you and to your descendants I will give all these lands, and I will fulfil the oath which I swore to Abraham your father. [4]I will multiply your descendants as the stars of heaven, and will give to your descendants all these lands; and by your descendants all the nations of the earth shall bless themselves: [5]because Abraham obeyed my voice and kept my charge, my commandments, my statutes, and my laws."

6 So Isaac dwelt in Ge'rar. [7]When the men of the place asked him about his wife, he said, "She is my sister"; for he feared to say, "My wife," thinking, "lest the men of the place should kill me for the sake of Rebekah"; because she was fair to look upon. [8]When he had been there a long time, Abim'elech king of the Philis'tines looked out of a window and saw Isaac fondling Rebekah his wife. [9]So Abim'elech called Isaac, and said, "Behold, she is your wife; how then could you say, 'She is my sister'?" Isaac said to him, "Because I thought, 'Lest I die because of her.'" [10]Abim'elech said, "What is this you have done to us? One of the people might easily have lain with your wife, and you would have brought guilt upon us." [11]So Abim'elech warned all the people, saying, "Whoever touches this man or his wife shall be put to death."

12 And Isaac sowed in that land, and reaped in the same year a hundredfold. The LORD blessed him, [13]and the man became rich, and gained more and more until he became very wealthy. [14]He had possessions of flocks and herds, and a great household, so that the Philis'tines envied him. [15](Now the Philis'tines had stopped and filled with earth all the wells which his father's servants had dug in the days of Abraham his father.) [16]And Abim'elech said to Isaac, "Go away from us; for you are much mightier than we."

17 So Isaac departed from there, and encamped in the valley of Ge'rar and dwelt there. [18]And Isaac dug again the wells of water which had been dug in the days of Abraham his father; for the Philis'tines had stopped them after the death of Abraham; and he gave them the names which his father had given them. [19]But when Isaac's servants dug in the valley and found there a well of springing water, [20]the herdsmen of Ge'rar quarreled with Isaac's herdsmen, saying, "The water is ours." So he called the name of the well E'sek,[u] because they contended with him. [21]Then they dug another well, and they quarreled over that also; so he called its name Sitnah.[v] [22]And he moved from there and dug another well, and over that they did not quarrel; so he called its name Reho'both,[w] saying, "For now the LORD has made room for us, and we shall be fruitful in the land."

23 From there he went up to Be'er-she'ba. [24]And the LORD appeared to him the same night and said, "I am the God of Abraham your father; fear not, for I am with you and will bless you and multiply your descendants for my servant Abraham's sake." [25]So

---

**26:1–35** The only memories of Isaac in the prime of his life preserved in Genesis. They concern his dealings with the Philistines (26:6–11, 17–33) and highlight the divine blessings showered upon him (26:3–5, 12–16, 28).

**26:1 famine:** All three of the Patriarchs faced such a food shortage during their sojourn in Canaan (12:10; 42:1–5). **Gerar:** In the arid Negeb region in southern Palestine. **Abimelech:** Earlier a king of this name or title made a covenant with Abraham (21:22–34).

**26:3–5** A renewal of the divine oaths sworn to Abraham. God had pledged to give him **land** (15:18), multiple **descendants** (22:17), and blessings for **all the nations** (22:18). Isaac is thus confirmed as the heir of the covenant promises (17:21).

**26:5 because Abraham obeyed:** The benefits promised to Abraham (land, descendants, worldwide blessing) were pledged as a reward for his loyalty to Yahweh. See note on 22:18. **my charge, my commandments, my statutes:** The precepts of the natural moral law inscribed on the heart (Rom 2:14–15). These precepts are later made explicit in the Torah revealed to Israel (Deut 11:1).

**26:6–11** Isaac's sojourn in Gerar parallels Abraham's sojourns in Egypt (12:10–20) and Gerar (20:1–18). All three episodes have the patriarch passing the matriarch off as his sister instead of his spouse. Apparently it was hazardous at this time to travel abroad with a beautiful wife (12:11; 20:11; 26:7).

**26:8 fondling:** Or, "caressing". The Hebrew *tsaḥaq* is a play on the name "Isaac" (*yitsḥaq*).

**26:12 hundredfold:** An extraordinary harvest for the first year. It is evidence of the Lord's blessings on Isaac.

**26:17–33** A series of disputes over wells dug and redug by the Patriarchs. Isaac stands out amidst the quarreling as a man of patience, waiting for the Lord to give him "room" to claim a well of his own (26:22).

**26:17 valley of Gerar:** Isaac moves to another location within the same region where he has already chosen to make his residence (26:6).

**26:25 built an altar:** Isaac continues the priestly legacy of his father, Abraham, who consecrated several sites in Canaan with sacrificial altars (12:7–8; 13:18; 22:9).

---

[s] That is *Red.*
[t] Heb *today.*
[u] That is *Contention.*
[v] That is *Enmity.*
[w] That is *Broad places* or *Room.*

he built an altar there and called upon the name of the LORD, and pitched his tent there. And there Isaac's servants dug a well.

26 Then Abim'elech went to him from Ge'rar with Ahuz'zath his adviser and Phi'col the commander of his army. [27]Isaac said to them, "Why have you come to me, seeing that you hate me and have sent me away from you?" [28]They said, "We see plainly that the LORD is with you; so we say, let there be an oath between you and us, and let us make a covenant with you, [29]that you will do us no harm, just as we have not touched you and have done to you nothing but good and have sent you away in peace. You are now the blessed of the LORD." [30]So he made them a feast, and they ate and drank. [31]In the morning they rose early and took oath with one another; and Isaac set them on their way, and they departed from him in peace. [32]That same day Isaac's servants came and told him about the well which they had dug, and said to him, "We have found water." [33]He called it Shi'bah; therefore the name of the city is Be'er-she'ba to this day.

### Esau's Hittite Wives

34 When Esau was forty years old, he took to wife Judith the daughter of Bee'ri the Hittite, and Bas'emath the daughter of E'lon the Hittite; [35]and they made life bitter for Isaac and Rebekah.

### Isaac Blesses Jacob

27 When Isaac was old and his eyes were dim so that he could not see, he called Esau his older son, and said to him, "My son"; and he answered, "Here I am." [2]He said, "Behold, I am old; I do not know the day of my death. [3]Now then, take your weapons, your quiver and your bow, and go out to the field, and hunt game for me, [4]and prepare for me savory food, such as I love, and bring it to me that I may eat; that I may bless you before I die."

5 Now Rebekah was listening when Isaac spoke to his son Esau. So when Esau went to the field to hunt for game and bring it, [6]Rebekah said to her son Jacob, "I heard your father speak to your brother Esau, [7]'Bring me game, and prepare for me savory food, that I may eat it, and bless you before the LORD before I die.' [8]Now therefore, my son, obey my word as I command you. [9]Go to the flock, and fetch me two good kids, that I may prepare from them savory food for your father, such as he loves; [10]and you shall bring it to your father to eat, so that he may bless you before he dies." [11]But Jacob said to Rebekah his mother, "Behold, my brother Esau is a hairy man, and I am a smooth man. [12]Perhaps my father will feel me, and I shall seem to be mocking him, and bring a curse upon myself and not a blessing." [13]His mother said to him, "Upon me be your curse, my son; only obey my word, and go, fetch them to me." [14]So he went and took them and brought them to his mother; and his mother prepared savory food, such as his father loved. [15]Then Rebekah took the best garments of Esau her older son, which were with her in the house, and put them on Jacob her younger son; [16]and the skins of the kids she put upon his hands and upon the smooth part of his neck; [17]and she gave the savory food and the bread, which she had prepared, into the hand of her son Jacob.

18 So he went in to his father, and said, "My father"; and he said, "Here I am; who are you, my son?" [19]Jacob said to his father, "I am Esau your first-born. I have done as you told me; now sit up and eat of my game, that you may bless me." [20]But Isaac said to his son, "How is it that you have found it so quickly, my son?" He answered, "Because the LORD your God granted me success." [21]Then Isaac said to Jacob, "Come near, that I may feel you, my son, to know whether you are really my son Esau or not." [22]So Jacob went near to Isaac his father, who felt him and said, "The voice is Jacob's voice, but the hands are the hands of Esau." [23]And he did not recognize him, because his hands were hairy like his brother Esau's hands; so he blessed him. [24]He said, "Are you really my son Esau?" He answered, "I am." [25]Then he said, "Bring it to me, that I may eat of my son's game and bless you." So he brought it to him, and he

---

**26:33:** Gen 21:31. **27:5:** Gen 12:3; Num 24:9.

---

**26:28 covenant with you:** Abimelech seeks a covenant of mutual peace with Isaac, like the one made with Abraham years earlier. See note on 21:22–34.

**26:33 Shibah:** The Hebrew means "seven" and resembles the word for "oath" (*shebu'ah*). **Beer-sheba:** Means "well of seven" or "well of the oath". It was remembered as the place where Abraham and Isaac made covenants with their neighbors (21:22–34).

**26:34 took to wife:** Unlike Isaac and Jacob, who married Semitic women, the disinherited sons of the Patriarchs, Ishmael and Esau, marry Hamitic women outside the elect family of Abraham (Egyptian, 21:21; Hittite, 26:34; Hivite, 36:2).

**27:1–46** Jacob intercepts the blessing intended for Esau and cheats him out of the inheritance of the first-born. His mother, Rebekah, is the mastermind behind the ruse, guiding him at each crucial step. The Genesis narrative is not blind to their underhanded ways; rather, it frowns upon Jacob the deceiver and almost pities Esau the victim. It is just as aware, however, that Esau shamefully despised his natural birthright (25:29–34). The story thus illustrates how God can further his plan despite the failings of his people. God had already elected Jacob over Esau to bear the blessings of the Abrahamic covenant (25:23; Rom 9:10–13). See topical essay: *Blessings and Birthrights* at Gen 48.

**27:4 before I die:** Blessings are given on the eve of family separation, either when the death of the father draws near (49:1–33; Deut 33:1–29) or when his children are about to go away (24:60–61; 28:1–5; 31:55).

**27:13 Upon me be your curse:** Rebekah pays a bitter price for her cunning when her beloved Jacob is forced to flee Canaan, never to return again during her lifetime.

**27:21 Esau or not:** Suggests that Isaac was suspicious from the beginning, heightening the drama and suspense of the whole episode.

**27:22–27** Isaac is deceived by three of the four senses he has left. Already blind (27:1), his sense of touch (27:22), taste (27:25), and smell (27:27) fail to detect the scam unfolding before him. Only his hearing proves to be reliable (27:22).

ate; and he brought him wine, and he drank. [26]Then
his father Isaac said to him, "Come near and kiss me,
my son." [27]So he came near and kissed him; and he
smelled the smell of his garments, and blessed him,
and said,

"See, the smell of my son
is as the smell of a field which the LORD has
blessed!
[28]May God give you of the dew of heaven,
and of the fatness of the earth,
and plenty of grain and wine.
[29]Let peoples serve you,
and nations bow down to you.
Be lord over your brothers,
and may your mother's sons bow down to you.
Cursed be every one who curses you,
and blessed be every one who blesses you!"

**Esau's Lost Blessing**

30 As soon as Isaac had finished blessing
Jacob, when Jacob had scarcely gone out from
the presence of Isaac his father, Esau his brother
came in from his hunting. [31]He also prepared
savory food, and brought it to his father. And he
said to his father, "Let my father arise, and eat
of his son's game, that you may bless me."
[32]His father Isaac said to him, "Who are you?" He
answered, "I am your son, your first-born, Esau."
[33]Then Isaac trembled violently, and said, "Who was
it then that hunted game and brought it to me, and I
ate it all[x] before you came, and I have blessed him?—
yes, and he shall be blessed." [34]When Esau heard the
words of his father, he cried out with an exceedingly
great and bitter cry, and said to his father, "Bless
me, even me also, O my father!" [35]But he said, "Your
brother came with guile, and he has taken away your
blessing." [36]Esau said, "Is he not rightly named Jacob?
For he has supplanted me these two times. He took
away my birthright; and behold, now he has taken
away my blessing." Then he said, "Have you not
reserved a blessing for me?" [37]Isaac answered Esau,
"Behold, I have made him your lord, and all his brothers I have given to him for servants, and with grain
and wine I have sustained him. What then can I do
for you, my son?" [38]Esau said to his father, "Have you
but one blessing, my father? Bless me, even me also,
O my father." And Esau lifted up his voice and wept.

39 Then Isaac his father answered him:
"Behold, away from[y] the fatness of the earth shall
your dwelling be,
and away from[y] the dew of heaven on high.
[40]By your sword you shall live,
and you shall serve your brother;
but when you break loose
you shall break his yoke from your neck."

**Jacob Escapes Esau's Fury**

41 Now Esau hated Jacob because of the blessing with which his father had blessed him, and
Esau said to himself, "The days of mourning for my
father are approaching; then I will kill my brother
Jacob." [42]But the words of Esau her older son were
told to Rebekah; so she sent and called Jacob her
younger son, and said to him, "Behold, your brother
Esau comforts himself by planning to kill you.
[43]Now therefore, my son, obey my voice; arise, flee
to La'ban my brother in Haran, [44]and stay with him
a while, until your brother's fury turns away; [45]until
your brother's anger turns away, and he forgets
what you have done to him; then I will send, and
fetch you from there. Why should I be bereft of you
both in one day?"

46 Then Rebekah said to Isaac, "I am weary of
my life because of the Hittite women. If Jacob marries one of the Hittite women such as these, one of
the women of the land, what good will my life be to
me?"

28 Then Isaac called Jacob and blessed him,
and charged him, "You shall not marry
one of the Canaanite women. [2]Arise, go to Pad'-
dan-ar'am to the house of Bethu'el your mother's
father; and take as wife from there one of the
daughters of La'ban your mother's brother. [3]God
Almighty[z] bless you and make you fruitful and
multiply you, that you may become a company
of peoples. [4]May he give the blessing of Abraham
to you and to your descendants with you, that
you may take possession of the land of your

**27:28 the fatness of the earth:** The blessings of prosperity and abundance reserved for Israel in the Promised Land (Deut 7:13; 33:28).

**27:29 lord over your brothers:** Looks ahead to the subjugation of the Edomites (descended from Esau) under the lordship of the Israelites (descended from Jacob) in the days of King David (2 Sam 8:13–14).

**27:33 he shall be blessed:** Isaac insists that the fatherly blessing cannot be retrieved once it has gone forth (Heb 12:16–17).

**27:36 supplanted:** A wordplay on the name Jacob. See note on 25:26.

**27:39 away from the fatness:** Esau is barred from the blessed and fertile land promised to Jacob (27:28). Historically, the Edomites lived outside the borders of Israel in the rugged highlands south of the Dead Sea.

**27:40 when you break loose:** Foresees the Edomite revolt against the divided kingdom of Israel several centuries later (2 Kings 8:20–22).

**27:43 flee to Laban:** Jacob is urged to find safety in Haran in upper Mesopotamia. This is where Rebekah's family lives under the headship of her brother, Laban (24:29).

**27:45 bereft of you both:** Rebekah fears that Esau, too, will be slain in vengeance if he manages to kill Jacob as planned (27:41).

**27:46 the Hittite women:** Esau's wives (26:34).

**28:1 Canaanite women:** Recalls how Abraham forbade Isaac to intermarry with the foreign peoples of Canaan (24:3). Jacob, like Isaac, is to seek a wife among his Semitic kinsfolk (see 24:4, 10).

**28:2 Paddan-aram:** Upper Mesopotamia, the homeland of Jacob's mother, Rebekah (25:20).

[x] Cn: Heb *of all.*
[y] Or *of.*
[z] Heb *El Shaddai.*

sojournings which God gave to Abraham!" [5]Thus
Isaac sent Jacob away; and he went to Pad'-
danar'am to La'ban, the son of Bethu'el the
Arame'an, the brother of Rebekah, Jacob's and Esau's
mother.

### Esau Marries Ishmael's Daughter

6 Now Esau saw that Isaac had blessed Jacob and
sent him away to Pad'dan-ar'am to take a wife from
there, and that as he blessed him he charged him,
"You shall not marry one of the Canaanite women,"
[7]and that Jacob had obeyed his father and his mother
and gone to Pad'dan-ar'am. [8]So when Esau saw that
the Canaanite women did not please Isaac his father,
[9]Esau went to Ish'mael and took to wife, besides the
wives he had, Maha'lath the daughter of Ishmael
Abraham's son, the sister of Neba'ioth.

### Jacob's Dream at Bethel

10 Jacob left Be'er-she'ba, and went toward
Haran. [11]And he came to a certain place, and stayed
there that night, because the sun had set. Taking
one of the stones of the place, he put it under his
head and lay down in that place to sleep. [12]And he
dreamed that there was a ladder set up on the earth,
and the top of it reached to heaven; and behold, the
angels of God were ascending and descending on it!
[13]And behold, the LORD stood above it[a] and said, "I
am the LORD, the God of Abraham your father and
the God of Isaac; the land on which you lie I will
give to you and to your descendants; [14]and your
descendants shall be like the dust of the earth, and
you shall spread abroad to the west and to the east
and to the north and to the south; and by you and
your descendants shall all the families of the earth
bless themselves.[b] [15]Behold, I am with you and will
keep you wherever you go, and will bring you back
to this land; for I will not leave you until I have done
that of which I have spoken to you." [16]Then Jacob
awoke from his sleep and said, "Surely the LORD is
in this place; and I did not know it." [17]And he was
afraid, and said, "How awesome is this place! This
is none other than the house of God, and this is the
gate of heaven."

18 So Jacob rose early in the morning, and he
took the stone which he had put under his head and
set it up for a pillar and poured oil on the top of it.
[19]He called the name of that place Bethel;[c] but the
name of the city was Luz at the first. [20]Then Jacob
made a vow, saying, "If God will be with me, and
will keep me in this way that I go, and will give me
bread to eat and clothing to wear, [21]so that I come
again to my father's house in peace, then the LORD
shall be my God, [22]and this stone, which I have set
up for a pillar, shall be God's house; and of all that
you give me I will give the tenth to you."

### Jacob Meets Rachel

29 Then Jacob went on his journey, and came
to the land of the people of the east. [2]As he
looked, he saw a well in the field, and behold, three
flocks of sheep lying beside it; for out of that well
the flocks were watered. The stone on the well's
mouth was large, [3]and when all the flocks were
gathered there, the shepherds would roll the stone
from the mouth of the well, and water the sheep,
and put the stone back in its place upon the mouth
of the well.

4 Jacob said to them, "My brothers, where do
you come from?" They said, "We are from Haran."
[5]He said to them, "Do you know La'ban the son of
Na'hor?" They said, "We know him." [6]He said to
them, "Is it well with him?" They said, "It is well; and
see, Rachel his daughter is coming with the sheep!"
[7]He said, "Behold, it is still high day, it is not time
for the animals to be gathered together; water the
sheep, and go, pasture them." [8]But they said, "We

---

**28:12 ladder:** The Hebrew envisions, not a ladder with rungs, but an ascending stairway. It is used by a host of angels, walking up and down, ministering to the will of Yahweh. The dream convinces Jacob that he is lying near the "gate" where heaven touches down to earth (28:17). • Jacob's ladder is a prophetic image of Christ, who bridges heaven and earth by the union of his divine and human natures (Jn 1:51). This makes him the one, perfect mediator between God and man (1 Tim 2:5). **reached to heaven:** Recalls the plans for the Tower of Babel in 11:4.

**28:13–14** Reiterates the promises made to Abraham by divine oath. The gifts of the covenant include **land** (15:18), multiple **descendants** (22:17), and blessings for **all the families** of the world (22:18). Jacob is thus confirmed as the heir of the covenant promises, just as Isaac was in 26:3–5.

**28:14 your descendants:** The tribal family of Israel (Ex 1:1–7).

**28:15 I am with you:** The Lord promises to stay with Jacob on his travels and to prosper his way wherever he goes.

**28:18 pillar:** Jacob anoints the stone headrest and props it up as a landmark and memorial of Yahweh's presence in the land. The practice of erecting such religious monuments was well known in pre-Israelite Canaan. Moses later instructed Israel to demolish every pillar dedicated to a Canaanite god (Ex 23:24; Deut 12:1–3).

**28:19 Bethel:** Means "house of God", alluding to Jacob's description in 28:17. Bethel has been a sacred site since the time of Abraham, who built an altar nearby (12:8).

**28:20 If:** Jacob's vow is conditional, suggesting he is mildly skeptical of the extraordinary blessings promised to him in the dream (28:13–14). He thus makes a deal with the Lord to test his faithfulness.

**28:22 I will give the tenth:** A vow to give 10 percent of his earnings to the Lord (14:20). Tithing was later mandated for Israel in the Torah (Num 18:21–24).

**29:1–30** The betrothal and marriages of Jacob. In the first episode, divine *Providence* arranges the encounter between Jacob and Rachel, inspires the love between them, and stirs the enthusiasm of Laban for their union (29:1–14). In the second, divine *justice* catches up with Jacob the deceiver and gives him his first taste of the cruelty of deception (29:15–30).

**29:1 people of the east:** The Semitic peoples of Mesopotamia. Jacob is searching for Haran (29:4), where Abraham had moved with his family before venturing into Canaan (11:31).

**29:2 a well:** Also the setting where brides are found for Isaac (24:11–27) and Moses (Ex 2:15–21).

---

[a]Or *beside him.*

[b]Or *be blessed.*

[c]That is *The house of God.*

cannot until all the flocks are gathered together, and
the stone is rolled from the mouth of the well; then
we water the sheep."
9 While he was still speaking with them,
Rachel came with her father's sheep; for she kept
them. 10 Now when Jacob saw Rachel the daughter
of La'ban his mother's brother, and the sheep of
Laban his mother's brother, Jacob went up and
rolled the stone from the well's mouth, and watered
the flock of Laban his mother's brother. 11 Then
Jacob kissed Rachel, and wept aloud. 12 And Jacob
told Rachel that he was her father's kinsman, and
that he was Rebekah's son; and she ran and told
her father.
13 When La'ban heard the tidings of Jacob his
sister's son, he ran to meet him, and embraced him
and kissed him, and brought him to his house. Jacob
told Laban all these things, 14 and La'ban said to
him, "Surely you are my bone and my flesh!" And he
stayed with him a month.

**Jacob Marries Laban's Daughters**

15 Then La'ban said to Jacob, "Because you
are my kinsman, should you therefore serve me
for nothing? Tell me, what shall your wages be?"
16 Now La'ban had two daughters; the name of the
older was Leah, and the name of the younger was
Rachel. 17 Leah's eyes were weak, but Rachel was
beautiful and lovely. 18 Jacob loved Rachel; and
he said, "I will serve you seven years for your
younger daughter Rachel." 19 La'ban said, "It is
better that I give her to you than that I should give
her to any other man; stay with me." 20 So Jacob
served seven years for Rachel, and they seemed
to him but a few days because of the love he had
for her.
21 Then Jacob said to La'ban, "Give me my wife
that I may go in to her, for my time is completed."
22 So La'ban gathered together all the men of the
place, and made a feast. 23 But in the evening he took
his daughter Leah and brought her to Jacob; and he
went in to her. 24 (La'ban gave his maid Zilpah to his
daughter Leah to be her maid.) 25 And in the morning, behold, it was Leah; and Jacob said to La'ban,
"What is this you have done to me? Did I not serve
with you for Rachel? Why then have you deceived
me?" 26 La'ban said, "It is not so done in our country,
to give the younger before the first-born. 27 Complete
the week of this one, and we will give you the other
also in return for serving me another seven years."
28 Jacob did so, and completed her week; then La'ban
gave him his daughter Rachel to wife. 29 (La'ban
gave his maid Bilhah to his daughter Rachel to be
her maid.) 30 So Jacob went in to Rachel also, and he
loved Rachel more than Leah, and served La'ban for
another seven years.
31 When the LORD saw that Leah was hated, he
opened her womb; but Rachel was barren. 32 And
Leah conceived and bore a son, and she called his
name Reuben;[d] for she said, "Because the LORD has
looked upon my affliction; surely now my husband
will love me." 33 She conceived again and bore a son,
and said, "Because the LORD has heard[e] that I am
hated, he has given me this son also"; and she called
his name Simeon. 34 Again she conceived and bore a
son, and said, "Now this time my husband will be
joined[f] to me, because I have borne him three sons";
therefore his name was called Levi. 35 And she conceived again and bore a son, and said, "This time I
will praise[g] the LORD"; therefore she called his name
Judah; then she ceased bearing.
30 When Rachel saw that she bore Jacob no
children, she envied her sister; and she said

**29:10 rolled the stone:** An impressive feat for one man. Normally it took several shepherds working together to heave aside the well cover (29:2–3).

**29:11 kissed ... wept:** Expressions linked with the joys of a family reunion (33:4; 45:15).

**29:14 my bone and my flesh:** An acknowledgment of kinship (Judg 9:2; 2 Sam 5:1).

**29:16 two daughters:** Leah, the less attractive first-born (29:26), and Rachel, the younger and more beautiful one (29:17). In Hebrew, Leah means "wild cow" and Rachel means "ewe lamb". Destined to marry the same man, the sisters are forced to compete for Jacob's time and attention. Later law forbade an Israelite to marry sisters (Lev 18:18).

**29:17 beautiful:** Like the other matriarchs in Genesis, Sarah (12:11) and Rebekah (24:16).

**29:25 you deceived me:** Brides were customarily veiled until the wedding night (24:65). This, combined with the darkness of his tent, explains why Jacob is blind to the scheming of his uncle until the morning after. One senses that Jacob is paying the just penalty for deceiving his blind father, Isaac (27:1–19). That Jacob is tricked into marrying the first-born (29:26) likewise recalls how he himself used trickery to steal the first-born blessing from his older brother, Esau (27:36).

**29:27 Complete the week:** Wedding festivities often ran for several days in biblical antiquity (Judg 14:12; Tob 11:19), a tradition that continued in Judaism well into the post-biblical period (Mishnah, *Negaim* 3, 2).

**29:31 Leah was hated:** Not despised, but "less favored and loved", as indicated by the preceding verse (29:30). **opened her womb:** Hints that God does not endorse Jacob's preferential love for Rachel over the neglected Leah. **Rachel was barren:** Like the other matriarchs in Genesis, Sarah (11:30) and Rebekah (25:21).

**29:32—30:24** The eleven sons born to Jacob outside the Promised Land. Each of their names involves a wordplay related to the circumstances of their birth. By Leah, Jacob fathered **Reuben** ("he saw my distress"), **Simeon** ("he has heard"), **Levi** ("he will cling"), **Judah** ("I will praise"), and later **Issachar** ("he has hired"), and **Zebulun** ("he will honor me"). By Rachel's maid, Bilhah, he fathered **Dan** ("he has judged") and **Naphtali** ("my struggle"). By Leah's maid, Zilpah, he fathered **Gad** ("good fortune") and **Asher** ("my happiness"). By Rachel, he fathered **Joseph** ("may he add"). Jacob's twelfth son, **Benjamin** ("son of the right hand"), was born years later near Bethlehem in Palestine (35:16–20).

**30:2 the place of God:** The blessing of fertility depends entirely upon the Lord, who is able to grant or withhold it according to his purpose (1:28; 25:21; 30:22) (CCC 2374).

[d] That is *See, a son.*
[e] Heb *shama.*
[f] Heb *lawah.*
[g] Heb *hodah.*

to Jacob, "Give me children, or I shall die!" [2]Jacob's anger was kindled against Rachel, and he said, "Am I in the place of God, who has withheld from you the fruit of the womb?" [3]Then she said, "Here is my maid Bilhah; go in to her, that she may bear upon my knees, and even I may have children through her." [4]So she gave him her maid Bilhah as a wife; and Jacob went in to her. [5]And Bilhah conceived and bore Jacob a son. [6]Then Rachel said, "God has judged me, and has also heard my voice and given me a son"; therefore she called his name Dan.[h] [7]Rachel's maid Bilhah conceived again and bore Jacob a second son. [8]Then Rachel said, "With mighty wrestlings I have wrestled[i] with my sister, and have prevailed"; so she called his name Naph'tali.

9 When Leah saw that she had ceased bearing children, she took her maid Zilpah and gave her to Jacob as a wife. [10]Then Leah's maid Zilpah bore Jacob a son. [11]And Leah said, "Good fortune!" so she called his name Gad.[j] [12]Leah's maid Zilpah bore Jacob a second son. [13]And Leah said, "Blessed am I! For the women will call me blessed"; so she called his name Asher.[k]

14 In the days of wheat harvest Reuben went and found mandrakes in the field, and brought them to his mother Leah. Then Rachel said to Leah, "Give me, I pray, some of your son's mandrakes." [15]But she said to her, "Is it a small matter that you have taken away my husband? Would you take away my son's mandrakes also?" Rachel said, "Then he may lie with you tonight for your son's mandrakes." [16]When Jacob came from the field in the evening, Leah went out to meet him, and said, "You must come in to me; for I have hired you with my son's mandrakes." So he lay with her that night. [17]And God hearkened to Leah, and she conceived and bore Jacob a fifth son. [18]Leah said, "God has given me my hire[l] because I gave my maid to my husband"; so she called his name Is'sachar. [19]And Leah conceived again, and she bore Jacob a sixth son. [20]Then Leah said, "God has endowed me with a good dowry; now my husband will honor[m] me, because I have borne him six sons"; so she called his name Zeb'ulun. [21]Afterwards she bore a daughter, and called her name Dinah. [22]Then God remembered Rachel, and God hearkened to her and opened her womb. [23]She conceived and bore a son, and said, "God has taken away my reproach"; [24]and she called his name Joseph,[n] saying, "May the LORD add to me another son!"

### Jacob Prospers

25 When Rachel had borne Joseph, Jacob said to La'ban, "Send me away, that I may go to my own home and country. [26]Give me my wives and my children for whom I have served you, and let me go; for you know the service which I have given you." [27]But La'ban said to him, "If you will allow me to say so, I have learned by divination that the LORD has blessed me because of you; [28]name your wages, and I will give it." [29]Jacob said to him, "You yourself know how I have served you, and how your cattle have fared with me. [30]For you had little before I came, and it has increased abundantly; and the LORD has blessed you wherever I turned. But now when shall I provide for my own household also?" [31]He said, "What shall I give you?" Jacob said, "You shall not give me anything; if you will do this for me, I will again feed your flock and keep it: [32]let me pass through all your flock today, removing from it every speckled and spotted sheep and every black lamb, and the spotted and speckled among the goats; and such shall be my wages. [33]So my honesty will answer for me later, when you come to look into my wages with you. Every one that is not speckled and spotted among the goats and black among the lambs, if found with me, shall be counted stolen." [34]La'ban said, "Good! Let it be as you have said." [35]But that day La'ban removed the he-goats that were striped and spotted, and all the she-goats that were speckled and spotted, every one that had white on it, and every lamb that was black, and put them in charge of his sons; [36]and he set a distance of three days' journey between himself and Jacob; and Jacob fed the rest of La'ban's flock.

37 Then Jacob took fresh rods of poplar and almond and plane, and peeled white streaks in them, exposing the white of the rods. [38]He set the rods which he had peeled in front of the flocks in the runnels, that is, the watering troughs, where the flocks came to drink. And since they bred when they

---

**30:3 bear upon my knees:** Alludes to an ancient adoption rite where a newborn is placed in the lap of the legal parent soon after delivery. For the Near Eastern custom of surrogate motherhood, see note on 16:1–6.

**30:14 mandrakes:** Herbal roots thought to enhance fertility. The ancients knew them as a natural aphrodisiac. Ironically, Leah barters away her mandrakes in exchange for a night with Jacob, only to conceive her fifth son without them (30:17).

**30:25–43** After years of loyal service, Jacob is ready to move his family back to Canaan, but Laban, a sly opportunist, tries to manipulate him into staying. The story unfolds as a game of wits between the two men, with Jacob outsmarting Laban and gaining the upper hand.

**30:27 divination:** The occultic art of predicting future events. Scripture condemns this superstition as evil (Deut 18:10).

**30:32 speckled ... spotted ... black:** Abnormal colorations. Sheep are usually all white and goats are all black or dark brown.

**30:37–43** Ancient herdsmen believed that visual stimuli could affect the offspring of breeding animals. Jacob resorts to this measure with great success: he has the goats stare at the streaked rods while mating and has the sheep stare at the dark-colored goats while mating.

---

[h] That is *He judged.*
[i] Heb *niphtal.*
[j] That is *Fortune.*
[k] That is *Blessed.*
[l] Heb *sakar.*
[m] Heb *zabal.*
[n] That is *He adds.*

came to drink, [39]the flocks bred in front of the rods and so the flocks brought forth striped, speckled, and spotted. [40]And Jacob separated the lambs, and set the faces of the flocks toward the striped and all the black in the flock of La'ban; and he put his own droves apart, and did not put them with Laban's flock. [41]Whenever the stronger of the flock were breeding Jacob laid the rods in the runnels before the eyes of the flock, that they might breed among the rods, [42]but for the feebler of the flock he did not lay them there; so the feebler were La'ban's, and the stronger Jacob's. [43]Thus the man grew exceedingly rich, and had large flocks, maidservants and menservants, and camels and donkeys.

### Jacob Flees with His Family and Flocks

31 Now Jacob heard that the sons of La'ban were saying, "Jacob has taken all that was our father's; and from what was our father's he has gained all this wealth." [2]And Jacob saw that La'ban did not regard him with favor as before. [3]Then the LORD said to Jacob, "Return to the land of your fathers and to your kindred, and I will be with you." [4]So Jacob sent and called Rachel and Leah into the field where his flock was, [5]and said to them, "I see that your father does not regard me with favor as he did before. But the God of my father has been with me. [6]You know that I have served your father with all my strength; [7]yet your father has cheated me and changed my wages ten times, but God did not permit him to harm me. [8]If he said, 'The spotted shall be your wages,' then all the flock bore spotted; and if he said, 'The striped shall be your wages,' then all the flock bore striped. [9]Thus God has taken away the cattle of your father, and given them to me. [10]In the mating season of the flock I lifted up my eyes, and saw in a dream that the he-goats which leaped upon the flock were striped, spotted, and mottled. [11]Then the angel of God said to me in the dream, 'Jacob,' and I said, 'Here I am!' [12]And he said, 'Lift up your eyes and see, all the goats that leap upon the flock are striped, spotted, and mottled; for I have seen all that La'ban is doing to you. [13]I am the God of Bethel, where you anointed a pillar and made a vow to me. Now arise, go forth from this land, and return to the land of your birth.'" [14]Then Rachel and Leah answered him, "Is there any portion or inheritance left to us in our father's house? [15]Are we not regarded by him as foreigners? For he has sold us, and he has been using up the money given for us. [16]All the property which God has taken away from our father belongs to us and to our children; now then, whatever God has said to you, do."

17 So Jacob arose, and set his sons and his wives on camels; [18]and he drove away all his cattle, all his livestock which he had gained, the cattle in his possession which he had acquired in Pad'dan-ar'am, to go to the land of Canaan to his father Isaac. [19]La'ban had gone to shear his sheep, and Rachel stole her father's household gods. [20]And Jacob outwitted La'ban the Arame'an, in that he did not tell him that he intended to flee. [21]He fled with all that he had, and arose and crossed the Euphra'tes, and set his face toward the hill country of Gilead.

### Laban Overtakes Jacob

22 When it was told La'ban on the third day that Jacob had fled, [23]he took his kinsmen with him and pursued him for seven days and followed close after him into the hill country of Gilead. [24]But God came to La'ban the Arame'an in a dream by night, and said to him, "Take heed that you say not a word to Jacob, either good or bad."

25 And La'ban overtook Jacob. Now Jacob had pitched his tent in the hill country, and Laban with his kinsmen encamped in the hill country of Gilead. [26]And La'ban said to Jacob, "What have you done, that you have cheated me, and carried away my daughters like captives of the sword? [27]Why did you flee secretly, and cheat me, and did not tell me, so that I might have sent you away with mirth and songs, with tambourine and lyre? [28]And why did you not permit me to kiss my sons and my daughters farewell? Now you have done foolishly. [29]It is in my power to do you harm; but the God of your father spoke to me last night, saying, 'Take heed that you speak to Jacob neither good nor bad.' [30]And now you have gone away because you longed greatly for your father's house, but why did you steal my gods?" [31]Jacob answered La'ban, "Because I was afraid, for I thought that you would take your daughters from me by force. [32]Any one with whom you find your gods shall not live. In the presence of our kinsmen point out what I have that is yours, and take it." Now Jacob did not know that Rachel had stolen them.

33 So La'ban went into Jacob's tent, and into

---

**30:43 exceedingly rich:** Jacob finds himself enriched far beyond the basic provisions of food and clothing he has asked of the Lord (28:20–21).

**31:1–16** Building on the preceding narrative, which emphasizes the human element of Jacob's cleverness (30:25–43), the story is retold to stress the divine element, stating that God is ultimately responsible for Jacob's protection and prosperity during his years in Paddan-aram (31:5, 7, 9).

**31:19 household gods:** Cultic figurines, or "teraphim", used for divination (Ezek 21:21; Zech 10:2). That Rachel smuggled them out may suggest a lingering attachment to pagan religion. If so, she will be forced to renounce her idolatrous ways when the caravan reaches Bethel (35:1–4).

**31:21 Gilead:** The highlands east of the Jordan River.

**31:24 not a word to Jacob:** The Lord cautions Laban against a hostile confrontation with his fleeing family. Jacob takes this to be a "rebuke" (31:42).

**31:27 mirth and songs:** It is doubtful Laban would have celebrated Jacob's departure in such grand fashion. He has been fighting all along against the prospect of Jacob leaving (30:25–36).

**31:31 Because I was afraid:** Does not answer the accusation of stealing (31:30), but states the reason why he fled in secret (31:27). Jacob does not even know the idols have been stolen; otherwise, he would not have promised death to the culprit (31:32), endangering his beloved Rachel (31:19).

Leah's tent, and into the tent of the two maidservants, but he did not find them. And he went out
of Leah's tent, and entered Rachel's. [34]Now Rachel
had taken the household gods and put them in the
camel's saddle, and sat upon them. La'ban felt all
about the tent, but did not find them. [35]And she said
to her father, "Let not my lord be angry that I cannot
rise before you, for the way of women is upon me."
So he searched, but did not find the household gods.
36 Then Jacob became angry, and upbraided
La'ban; Jacob said to Laban, "What is my offense?
What is my sin, that you have hotly pursued me?
[37]Although you have felt through all my goods, what
have you found of all your household goods? Set it
here before my kinsmen and your kinsmen, that
they may decide between us two. [38]These twenty
years I have been with you; your ewes and your she-
goats have not miscarried, and I have not eaten the
rams of your flocks. [39]That which was torn by wild
beasts I did not bring to you; I bore the loss of it
myself; of my hand you required it, whether stolen
by day or stolen by night. [40]Thus I was; by day the
heat consumed me, and the cold by night, and my
sleep fled from my eyes. [41]These twenty years I have
been in your house; I served you fourteen years for
your two daughters, and six years for your flock,
and you have changed my wages ten times. [42]If
the God of my father, the God of Abraham and the
Fear of Isaac, had not been on my side, surely now
you would have sent me away empty-handed. God
saw my affliction and the labor of my hands, and
rebuked you last night."

### Laban and Jacob Make a Covenant

43 Then La'ban answered and said to Jacob,
"The daughters are my daughters, the children are
my children, the flocks are my flocks, and all that
you see is mine. But what can I do this day to these
my daughters, or to their children whom they have
borne? [44]Come now, let us make a covenant, you and
I; and let it be a witness between you and me." [45]So
Jacob took a stone, and set it up as a pillar. [46]And
Jacob said to his kinsmen, "Gather stones," and they
took stones, and made a heap; and they ate there by
the heap. [47]La'ban called it Je'gar-sahadu'tha:[o] but
Jacob called it Gale'ed.[p] [48]La'ban said, "This heap is
a witness between you and me today." Therefore he
named it Gale'ed, [49]and the pillar[q] Mizpah,[r] for he
said, "The LORD watch between you and me, when
we are absent one from the other. [50]If you ill-treat my
daughters, or if you take wives besides my daughters, although no man is with us, remember, God is
witness between you and me."
51 Then La'ban said to Jacob, "See this heap and
the pillar, which I have set between you and me.
[52]This heap is a witness, and the pillar is a witness,
that I will not pass over this heap to you, and you
will not pass over this heap and this pillar to me,
for harm. [53]The God of Abraham and the God of
Na'hor, the God of their father, judge between us."
So Jacob swore by the Fear of his father Isaac, [54]and
Jacob offered a sacrifice on the mountain and called
his kinsmen to eat bread; and they ate bread and tar-
ried all night on the mountain.
55 [s]Early in the morning La'ban arose, and
kissed his grandchildren and his daughters and
blessed them; then he departed and returned home.

32 Jacob went on his way and the angels of
God met him; [2]and when Jacob saw them he
said, "This is God's army!" So he called the name of
that place Ma"hana'im.[t]

### Jacob Sends Gifts to Appease Esau

3 And Jacob sent messengers before him to
Esau his brother in the land of Se'ir, the country
of Edom, [4]instructing them, "Thus you shall say

---

**31:35 the way of women:** Rachel pretends to be menstrually "unclean" and so excuses herself from climbing off the camel (cf. Lev 15:19–20).

**31:39 torn by wild beasts:** In the ancient Near East, a shepherd was bound to make restitution for a stolen animal, but he was usually exempt from this obligation if the animal was mauled to death by a predator and its remains could be shown to the owner. Jacob went beyond the call of duty by making up for such losses anyway. This legal background is evident in both biblical (Ex 22:12–13) and Babylonian texts (*Code of Hammurabi* 266).

**31:42 the Fear of Isaac:** A title for Yahweh, the God of the Patriarchs (31:53).

**31:43–55** Jacob and Laban seal a covenant by invoking witnesses (31:48–50), swearing oaths (31:53), and sharing a meal (31:54). In the presence of God, they pledge to live as allies instead of enemies. Covenants of this type were made to establish bonds of legal kinship or strengthen bonds of biological kinship. For parallel examples of a covenant peace treaty in Genesis, see 21:22–34 and 26:26–33.

**31:47 Jegar-sahadutha ... Galeed:** Both expressions mean "heap of witness", the first in Aramaic and the second in Hebrew. This bilingual tradition mirrors the genealogical distinction between Laban the Aramean (31:20) and Jacob, the grandson of "Abram the Hebrew" (14:13).

**31:49 Mizpah:** The Hebrew *mitspah* resembles the saying "The LORD watch" (*yitsep YHWH*). It was an ancient settlement in Gilead (Judg 10:17), presumably where the covenant between Jacob and Laban was ratified (31:25).

**32:1 the angels of God:** A vision of angels greets Jacob on his return home, just as a vision of angels had sent him off 20 years earlier (28:10–17).

**32:2 God's army:** Or, "God's camp". **Mahanaim:** The Hebrew means "two camps", referring either to two camps of angels or to Jacob's camp (32:21) and a second angelic one. There was an ancient settlement of this name in Gilead, east of the Jordan (Josh 21:38).

**32:3 land of Seir:** The hill country south of the Dead Sea. This is the homeland of Esau and his descendants, the Edomites (36:8).

**32:4 my lord ... your servant:** These titles, used several times in the following narrative (32:18, 20; 33:5, 8, 13, 15), imply that Jacob is surrendering his authority to his angry older brother. In effect, this reverses the fraternal relation-

---

[o] In Aramaic *The heap of witness.*
[p] In Hebrew *The heap of witness.*
[q] Compare Sam: Heb lacks *the pillar.*
[r] That is *Watchpost.*
[s] Ch 32:1 in Heb.
[t] Here taken to mean *Two armies.*

to my lord Esau: Thus says your servant Jacob, 'I
have sojourned with La'ban, and stayed until now;
5and I have oxen, donkeys, flocks, menservants, and
maidservants; and I have sent to tell my lord, in
order that I may find favor in your sight.'"

6 And the messengers returned to Jacob, saying, "We came to your brother Esau, and he is coming to meet you, and four hundred men with him."
7Then Jacob was greatly afraid and distressed; and
he divided the people that were with him, and the
flocks and herds and camels, into two companies,
8thinking, "If Esau comes to the one company and
destroys it, then the company which is left will
escape."

9 And Jacob said, "O God of my father Abraham
and God of my father Isaac, O LORD who said to me,
'Return to your country and to your kindred, and
I will do you good,' 10I am not worthy of the least
of all the mercy and all the faithfulness which you
have shown to your servant, for with only my staff
I crossed this Jordan; and now I have become two
companies. 11Deliver me, I beg you, from the hand
of my brother, from the hand of Esau, for I fear him,
lest he come and slay us all, the mothers with the
children. 12But you said, 'I will do you good, and
make your descendants as the sand of the sea, which
cannot be numbered for multitude.'"

13 So he lodged there that night, and took from
what he had with him a present for his brother Esau,
14two hundred she-goats and twenty he-goats, two
hundred ewes and twenty rams, 15thirty milch camels and their colts, forty cows and ten bulls, twenty
she-donkeys and ten he-donkeys. 16These he delivered into the hand of his servants, every drove by
itself, and said to his servants, "Pass on before me,
and put a space between drove and drove." 17He
instructed the foremost, "When Esau my brother
meets you, and asks you, 'To whom do you belong?
Where are you going? And whose are these before
you?' 18then you shall say, 'They belong to your
servant Jacob; they are a present sent to my lord
Esau; and moreover he is behind us.'" 19He likewise
instructed the second and the third and all who followed the droves, "You shall say the same thing
to Esau when you meet him, 20and you shall say,
'Moreover your servant Jacob is behind us.'" For he
thought, "I may appease him with the present that
goes before me, and afterwards I shall see his face;
perhaps he will accept me." 21So the present passed
on before him; and he himself lodged that night in
the camp.

### Jacob Wrestles at Peniel

22 The same night he arose and took his two
wives, his two maids, and his eleven children, and
crossed the ford of the Jabbok. 23He took them and
sent them across the stream, and likewise everything that he had. 24And Jacob was left alone; and a
man wrestled with him until the breaking of the day.
25When the man saw that he did not prevail against
Jacob, he touched the hollow of his thigh; and Jacob's
thigh was put out of joint as he wrestled with him.
26Then he said, "Let me go, for the day is breaking." But Jacob said, "I will not let you go, unless
you bless me." 27And he said to him, "What is your

---

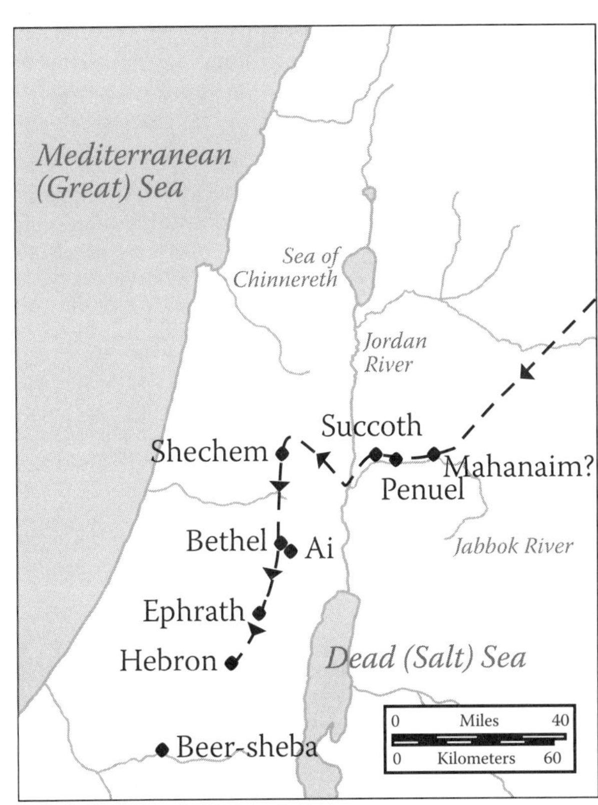


**Jacob Returns to Canaan**

ship set out in the blessing of Isaac, which made Jacob the "lord" over Esau (27:29, 37) and the one whom Esau must "serve" (27:40). Coupled with other factors, this strategy helps to pave the way for Esau's unexpectedly warm welcome of Jacob in 33:4.

**32:6 four hundred men:** To the fearful Jacob, who parted with his brother on bitter terms, this sounds like an approaching army.

**32:9–12** Jacob calls upon the Lord and pleads for deliverance from Esau. In the wider context of Genesis, it is evident that Jacob returns home a more humble and prayerful man than when he left.

**32:13 a present:** A gift of more than 550 animals is unusually extravagant (32:14–15). It is calculated to "appease" an embittered Esau (32:20).

**32:22–32** A mysterious contest between Jacob and a nameless angel (Hos 12:4). After a night of outwrestling his opponent, Jacob is renamed "Israel" and limps away from the scene with a blessing and a bad hip. • *Allegorically*, the angel is a type of Christ, and his defeat points to the Passion of Christ, who allowed his own people to prevail over him. And just as the victorious Jacob was blessed and injured at the same time, so with the people of Israel: some are blessed to believe in Christ, while others are crippled in unbelief (St. Augustine, *City of God* 16, 39). *Morally*, to wrestle with God is to struggle for virtue (St. Ambrose, *On Jacob and the Blessed Life* 7, 30) (CCC 2573).

**32:22 the Jabbok:** A tributary that flows into the Jordan from the east.

---

[u] That is *He who strives with God* or *God strives.*

name?" And he said, "Jacob." 28Then he said, "Your
name shall no more be called Jacob, but Israel,[u] for
you have striven with God and with men, and have
prevailed." 29Then Jacob asked him, "Tell me, I pray,
your name." But he said, "Why is it that you ask my
name?" And there he blessed him. 30So Jacob called
the name of the place Peni'el,[v] saying, "For I have
seen God face to face, and yet my life is preserved."
31The sun rose upon him as he passed Penu'el, limp-
ing because of his thigh. 32Therefore to this day the
Israelites do not eat the sinew of the hip which is
upon the hollow of the thigh, because he touched the
hollow of Jacob's thigh on the sinew of the hip.

### Jacob and Esau Meet

33 And Jacob lifted up his eyes and looked,
and behold, Esau was coming, and four
hundred men with him. So he divided the children
among Leah and Rachel and the two maids. 2And he
put the maids with their children in front, then Leah
with her children, and Rachel and Joseph last of all.
3He himself went on before them, bowing himself to
the ground seven times, until he came near to his
brother.

4 But Esau ran to meet him, and embraced him,
and fell on his neck and kissed him, and they wept.
5And when Esau raised his eyes and saw the women
and children, he said, "Who are these with you?"
Jacob said, "The children whom God has graciously
given your servant." 6Then the maids drew near,
they and their children, and bowed down; 7Leah
likewise and her children drew near and bowed
down; and last Joseph and Rachel drew near, and
they bowed down. 8Esau said, "What do you mean
by all this company which I met?" Jacob answered,
"To find favor in the sight of my lord." 9But Esau
said, "I have enough, my brother; keep what you
have for yourself." 10Jacob said, "No, I beg you, if
I have found favor in your sight, then accept my
present from my hand; for truly to see your face is
like seeing the face of God, with such favor have
you received me. 11Accept, I beg you, my gift that
is brought to you, because God has dealt graciously
with me, and because I have enough." Thus he urged
him, and he took it.

12 Then Esau said, "Let us journey on our way,
and I will go before you." 13But Jacob said to him,
"My lord knows that the children are frail, and that
the flocks and herds giving suck are a care to me;
and if they are overdriven for one day, all the flocks
will die. 14Let my lord pass on before his servant,
and I will lead on slowly, according to the pace of the
cattle which are before me and according to the pace
of the children, until I come to my lord in Se'ir."

15 So Esau said, "Let me leave with you some of
the men who are with me." But he said, "What need
is there? Let me find favor in the sight of my lord."
16So Esau returned that day on his way to Se'ir.
17But Jacob journeyed to Succoth,[w] and built himself
a house, and made booths for his cattle; therefore the
name of the place is called Succoth.

---

**32:30 face to face:** God is seen, not directly, but refracted through the face of the angel (e.g., Judg 13:21–22). A direct or unmediated vision of God is not granted in this life but is a blessing reserved for heaven (1 Cor 13:12). See note on 16:13 and word study: *Angel of the* L*ORD* at 16:7. **Peniel:** An alternative spelling of "Penuel", both meaning "face of God" (32:31). It was an ancient settlement in Gilead, east of the Jordan (Judg 8:8).

**32:32 Israelites do not eat:** A food restriction mentioned only here in the OT.

**33:1–14** The fateful reunion of Jacob and Esau after 20 years of separation. The encounter is unexpectedly cordial, given the murderous intentions of Esau years earlier (27:41). Henceforth in Genesis the brothers live on distant but reconciled terms (35:29).

**33:2 Rachel and Joseph last:** Jacob's favored wife and son are given a more protected position in the caravan.

**33:3 bowing himself:** Like vassals before a king, Jacob and his family prostrate themselves before Esau (33:6–7) and lavish gifts on him (33:11). For the significance of this, see note on 32:4.

**33:8 all this company:** Refers, not to Jacob's wives and children (33:5–7), but to the gift of flocks and herds sent ahead to win Esau's good favor (32:13–21).

**33:10 like seeing ... God:** Recalls the preceding episode at Peniel, where Jacob was surprised to see God's face and live to tell about it (32:30). Here, too, he is relieved to see Esau's face again and to walk away unharmed.

**33:14 until I come:** Seems to be a diversion, since Jacob never continues south to Seir but immediately turns west into Canaan.

**33:17 Succoth:** On the bank of the Jabbok stream where it flows into the Jordan (Josh 13:27). The settlement is named after the "booths" (Heb. *sukkot*) that Jacob set up to shelter his cattle.

**33:18 Shechem:** A city in central Palestine about 15 miles west of the Jordan. It is named after one of the sons of Hamor, a local chieftain, landowner, and spokesman for the city. Notice that Jacob is retracing the footsteps of Abraham on his return to Canaan from Mesopotamia: both made

---

[v] That is *The face of God.*
[w] That is *Booths.*

### Word Study

*Israel* (32:28)

*Yisra'el* (Heb.): Translates "Israel" and consists of a wordplay on the verb *sarah* ("strive, struggle, contend") coupled with the noun *'el* ("God"). Though compound names such as this are common in Hebrew and related Semitic languages, it is unusual for the divine name suffix to represent the object rather than the subject of the verbal element. But in Scripture the name Israel is taken to mean "he who strives with God" rather than the expected "God strives" (Hos 12:3). This is the new name given to Jacob after wrestling with God's angel (Gen 32:28; 35:10) and the national name given to the twelve tribes descended from Jacob (Gen 47:27; Deut 1:1). In later biblical history, the name Israel can also stand for the Northern Kingdom that broke away from Southern Kingdom of Judah in the tenth century B.C. (1 Kings 12:20; Amos 1:1).

### Jacob Comes to Shechem

18 And Jacob came safely to the city of She'chem,
which is in the land of Canaan, on his way from
Pad'dan-ar'am; and he camped before the city.
19And from the sons of Ha'mor, She'chem's father, he
bought for a hundred pieces of money[x] the piece of
land on which he had pitched his tent. 20There he
erected an altar and called it El-El'ohe-Israel.[y]

### Shechem Defiles Dinah

34 Now Dinah the daughter of Leah, whom
she had borne to Jacob, went out to visit the
women of the land; 2and when She'chem the son of
Ha'mor the Hi'vite, the prince of the land, saw her,
he seized her and lay with her and humbled her.
3And his soul was drawn to Dinah the daughter of
Jacob; he loved the maiden and spoke tenderly to
her. 4So She'chem spoke to his father Ha'mor, saying, "Get me this maiden for my wife." 5Now Jacob
heard that he had defiled his daughter Dinah; but
his sons were with his cattle in the field, so Jacob
held his peace until they came. 6And Ha'mor the
father of She'chem went out to Jacob to speak with
him. 7The sons of Jacob came in from the field when
they heard of it; and the men were indignant and
very angry, because he had wrought folly in Israel
by lying with Jacob's daughter, for such a thing
ought not to be done.

8 But Ha'mor spoke with them, saying, "The soul
of my son She'chem longs for your daughter; I beg
you, give her to him in marriage. 9Make marriages
with us; give your daughters to us, and take our
daughters for yourselves. 10You shall dwell with us;
and the land shall be open to you; dwell and trade in
it, and get property in it." 11She'chem also said to her
father and to her brothers, "Let me find favor in your
eyes, and whatever you say to me I will give. 12Ask
of me ever so much as marriage present and gift,
and I will give according as you say to me; only give
me the maiden to be my wife."

13 The sons of Jacob answered She'chem and his
father Ha'mor deceitfully, because he had defiled
their sister Dinah. 14They said to them, "We cannot do this thing, to give our sister to one who is
uncircumcised, for that would be a disgrace to us.
15Only on this condition will we consent to you: that
you will become as we are and every male of you be
circumcised. 16Then we will give our daughters to
you, and we will take your daughters to ourselves,
and we will dwell with you and become one people.
17But if you will not listen to us and be circumcised,
then we will take our daughter, and we will be
gone."

18 Their words pleased Ha'mor and Hamor's
son She'chem. 19And the young man did not delay
to do the thing, because he had delight in Jacob's
daughter. Now he was the most honored of all his
family. 20So Ha'mor and his son She'chem came
to the gate of their city and spoke to the men of their
city, saying, 21"These men are friendly with us; let
them dwell in the land and trade in it, for behold,
the land is large enough for them; let us take their
daughters in marriage, and let us give them our
daughters. 22Only on this condition will the men
agree to dwell with us, to become one people: that
every male among us be circumcised as they are circumcised. 23Will not their cattle, their property and
all their beasts be ours? Only let us agree with them,
and they will dwell with us." 24And all who went out
of the gate of his city hearkened to Ha'mor and his
son She'chem; and every male was circumcised, all
who went out of the gate of his city.

### Dinah Is Avenged by Her Brothers

25 On the third day, when they were sore, two of
the sons of Jacob, Simeon and Levi, Dinah's brothers,
took their swords and came upon the city unawares,
and killed all the males. 26They slew Ha'mor and
his son She'chem with the sword, and took Dinah
out of Shechem's house, and went away. 27And the
sons of Jacob came upon the slain, and plundered
the city, because their sister had been defiled; 28they
took their flocks and their herds, their donkeys, and
whatever was in the city and in the field; 29all their
wealth, all their little ones and their wives, all that
was in the houses, they captured and made their
prey. 30Then Jacob said to Simeon and Levi, "You
have brought trouble on me by making me odious
to the inhabitants of the land, the Canaanites and
the Per'izzites; my numbers are few, and if they

---

their first stop in Shechem, where they built an altar (12:5–7; 33:20), and then both turned south to Bethel, where they built another altar (12:8; 35:1, 6–7).

**33:19 the piece of land:** The eventual burial site of the patriarch Joseph (Josh 24:32). For the Samaritan version of this tradition, see note on 23:9.

**34:1–31** The rape of Jacob's daughter, Dinah, which triggers a violent response against Shechem and disturbs the balance of peace in the region. Jacob, who neither conceived nor condoned the plan to attack the city, is left fearful of reprisals from local Canaanites (34:30).

**34:2 the Hivite:** One of the Canaanite peoples (10:17) that occupied Palestine before its conquest by the Israelites (Deut 7:1).

**34:9 marriages with us:** Hamor negotiates a peaceful alliance between Israel and Shechem with the hope of intermarriage. He sells the idea to the men of the city as an opportunity for gain (34:20–23). The offer is savagely refused by Jacob's sons, anticipating later Deuteronomic law, which forbade intermarriage between Israelites and Canaanites—even singling out the Hivites—and called instead for their destruction (Deut 7:1–3).

**34:15 circumcised:** Circumcision is proposed as a condition for intermarriage. But to Jacob's sons, it is a cunning means to disable the defensive manpower of Shechem.

**34:24 all who went out:** All the men of military age who could "go out" to war. Once the entire Shechemite army is temporarily crippled by the wounds of circumcision, the city is left vulnerable to attack (34:25).

**34:25 Simeon and Levi:** Two of Dinah's older brothers, all three of them being children of Leah (29:31–34; 30:21). Jacob will later curse their burning rage (49:5–7).

---

[x] Heb *a hundred qesitah.*

[y] That is *God, the God of Israel.*

gather themselves against me and attack me, I shall
be destroyed, both I and my household." [31]But they
said, "Should he treat our sister as a harlot?"

### Jacob Returns to Bethel

35 God said to Jacob, "Arise, go up to Bethel,
and dwell there; and make there an altar to
the God who appeared to you when you fled from
your brother Esau." [2]So Jacob said to his household
and to all who were with him, "Put away the foreign
gods that are among you, and purify yourselves,
and change your garments; [3]then let us arise and go
up to Bethel, that I may make there an altar to the
God who answered me in the day of my distress and
has been with me wherever I have gone." [4]So they
gave to Jacob all the foreign gods that they had, and
the rings that were in their ears; and Jacob hid them
under the oak which was near She'chem.

5 And as they journeyed, a terror from God fell
upon the cities that were round about them, so that
they did not pursue the sons of Jacob. [6]And Jacob
came to Luz (that is, Bethel), which is in the land of
Canaan, he and all the people who were with him,
[7]and there he built an altar, and called the place
El-beth'el,[z] because there God had revealed himself
to him when he fled from his brother. [8]And Deborah,
Rebekah's nurse, died, and she was buried under
an oak below Bethel; so the name of it was called
Al'lon-bac'uth.[a]

9 God appeared to Jacob again, when he came
from Pad'dan-ar'am, and blessed him. [10]And God
said to him, "Your name is Jacob; no longer shall
your name be called Jacob, but Israel shall be your
name." So his name was called Israel. [11]And God
said to him, "I am God Almighty:[b] be fruitful and
multiply; a nation and a company of nations shall
come from you, and kings shall spring from you.
[12]The land which I gave to Abraham and Isaac
I will give to you, and I will give the land to your
descendants after you." [13]Then God went up from
him in the place where he had spoken with him.
[14]And Jacob set up a pillar in the place where he had
spoken with him, a pillar of stone; and he poured out
a drink offering on it, and poured oil on it. [15]So Jacob
called the name of the place where God had spoken
with him, Bethel.

### The Birth of Benjamin and the Death of Rachel

16 Then they journeyed from Bethel; and when
they were still some distance from Eph'rath, Rachel
went into labor, and she had hard labor. [17]And when
she was in her hard labor, the midwife said to her,
"Fear not; for now you will have another son." [18]And
as her soul was departing (for she died), she called
his name Ben-o'ni;[c] but his father called his name
Benjamin.[d] [19]So Rachel died, and she was buried on
the way to Eph'rath (that is, Bethlehem), [20]and Jacob
set up a pillar upon her grave; it is the pillar of Rachel's
tomb, which is there to this day. [21]Israel journeyed on,
and pitched his tent beyond the tower of E'der.

22 While Israel dwelt in that land Reuben went
and lay with Bilhah his father's concubine; and
Israel heard of it.

---

**35:1–15** Jacob returns to Bethel to fulfill his vow to the Lord (28:18–22). He expresses his full allegiance to God by building an altar (35:7), erecting a memorial pillar (35:14), and ridding his household of idols and other gods (35:2–4). The intervening narratives between his departure (chap. 28) and return to Bethel (chap. 35) amply attest to the faithfulness of God in providing for his needs, protecting his life, and prospering his way.

**35:2 Put away the foreign gods:** A call to renounce and discard the idol images that made the trip from Paddan-aram (31:19, 33–35). In this way, Jacob's entourage readies itself to worship the true God at Bethel. For another act of idol renunciation at Shechem, see Josh 24:14–25.

**35:4 the rings:** Superstitious amulets. **the oak:** Possibly the Oak of Moreh, where God first appeared to Abraham in Canaan (12:6–7).

**35:5 terror from God:** Panic seizes the region as news of Shechem's demise begins to spread (34:30). The Lord incites this fear to ensure the safety of the elect family of Jacob. For a similar protection given to the Israelites entering Canaan, see Ex 23:27 and Josh 2:9.

**35:9–12** Jacob is again confirmed as the heir of the Abrahamic covenant at Bethel (also in 28:13–14). The words spoken to Jacob parallel the divine discourse with Abraham in 17:1–8, where God changes the *name* of the patriarch (17:5; 35:10), introduces himself as *God Almighty* (17:1; 35:11), promises to make him *fruitful* (17:2, 6; 35:11), appoints him the father of *nations* (17:4–5; 35:11), pledges to raise up *kings* from his line (17:6; 35:11), and grants him a *land* inheritance (17:8; 35:12).

**35:14 pillar of stone:** This is the second memorial stele that Jacob erects in Bethel (28:18–19).

**35:15 Bethel:** Means "house of God". See note on 28:19.

**35:18 she died:** Rachel dies as she delivers her second son to Jacob. Her prayer for another child after Joseph has been answered (30:24). **Ben-oni:** Rachel names the infant "Son of my sorrow". **Benjamin:** Jacob renames the infant "Son of the right hand" or "Son of the south". The latter meaning brings out what is unique to the child: Jacob's 11 older sons were born in Paddan-aram, northeast of Palestine, whereas Benjamin alone was born after Jacob moved his family south into Canaan. Later biblical narratives also indicate that the tribe of Benjamin was assigned a land inheritance in the southern half of Palestine (Josh 18:11–28), and in the days of the divided monarchy, the Benjaminites attached themselves to the Southern Kingdom of Judah (1 Kings 12:21).

**35:20 Rachel's tomb:** Her traditional resting place is still memorialized in Bethlehem today. • The evangelist Matthew assumes knowledge of this tradition when he speaks of Rachel weeping over the slaughtered infants of Bethlehem (Mt 2:16–18).

**35:21 tower of Eder:** South of Bethlehem on the way to Hebron.

**35:22 Reuben ... lay with Bilhah:** An aggressive move to ensure his first-born authority over Jacob's other children. Ironically, this sinful bid for power will deprive Reuben of the blessing and inheritance he was entitled to receive by virtue of his place in the birth order. Angered and offended by this treachery, Jacob will pass Reuben's birthright over to Joseph, the first-born of Rachel (49:3–4; 1 Chron 5:1–2). See topical essay: *Blessings and Birthrights* at Gen 48.

---

[z] That is *God of Bethel.*
[a] That is *Oak of weeping.*
[b] Heb *El Shaddai.*
[c] That is *Son of my sorrow.*
[d] That is *Son of the right hand* or *Son of the South.*

Now the sons of Jacob were twelve. 23 The sons
of Leah: Reuben (Jacob's first-born), Simeon, Levi,
Judah, Is'sachar, and Zeb'ulun. 24 The sons of Rachel:
Joseph and Benjamin. 25 The sons of Bilhah, Rachel's
maid: Dan and Naph'tali. 26 The sons of Zilpah,
Leah's maid: Gad and Asher. These were the sons of
Jacob who were born to him in Pad'dan-ar'am.

### The Death of Isaac

27 And Jacob came to his father Isaac at Mamre,
or Kir'iath-ar'ba (that is, He'bron), where Abraham
and Isaac had sojourned. 28 Now the days of Isaac
were a hundred and eighty years. 29 And Isaac
breathed his last; and he died and was gathered to
his people, old and full of days; and his sons Esau
and Jacob buried him.

### Esau's Descendants

36 These are the descendants of Esau (that
is, E'dom). 2 Esau took his wives from the
Canaanites: A'dah the daughter of E'lon the Hittite, Oholiba'mah the daughter of An'ah the son[e]
of Zib'eon the Hi'vite, 3 and Bas'emath, Ish'mael's
daughter, the sister of Neba'ioth. 4 And A'dah bore
to Esau, Eli'phaz; Bas'emath bore Reu'el; 5 and
Oholiba'mah bore Je'ush, Ja'lam, and Ko'rah. These
are the sons of Esau who were born to him in the
land of Canaan.

6 Then Esau took his wives, his sons, his daughters, and all the members of his household, his cattle, all his beasts, and all his property which he had
acquired in the land of Canaan; and he went into a
land away from his brother Jacob. 7 For their possessions were too great for them to dwell together; the
land of their sojournings could not support them
because of their cattle. 8 So Esau dwelt in the hill
country of Se'ir; Esau is E'dom.

9 These are the descendants of Esau the father
of the E'domites in the hill country of Se'ir. 10 These
are the names of Esau's sons: Eli'phaz the son of
A'dah the wife of Esau, Reu'el the son of Bas'emath
the wife of Esau. 11 The sons of Eli'phaz were Te'man,
Omar, Ze'pho, Ga'tam, and Ke'naz. 12 (Timna was a
concubine of Eli'phaz, Esau's son; she bore Am'alek
to Eliphaz.) These are the sons of A'dah, Esau's wife.
13 These are the sons of Reu'el: Na'hath, Ze'rah, Shammah, and Mizzah. These are the sons of Bas'emath,
Esau's wife. 14 These are the sons of Oholiba'mah the
daughter of An'ah the son[f] of Zib'eon, Esau's wife:
she bore to Esau Je'ush, Ja'lam, and Ko'rah.

### Chiefs and Kings of Edom

15 These are the chiefs of the sons of Esau.
The sons of Eli'phaz the first-born of Esau: the
chiefs Te'man, Omar, Ze'pho, Ke'naz, 16 Ko'rah,
Ga'tam, and Am'alek; these are the chiefs of
Eli'phaz in the land of E'dom; they are the sons
of A'dah. 17 These are the sons of Reu'el, Esau's son:
the chiefs Na'hath, Ze'rah, Shammah, and Mizzah;
these are the chiefs of Reu'el in the land of
E'dom; they are the sons of Bas'emath, Esau's wife.
18 These are the sons of Oholiba'mah, Esau's wife:
the chiefs Je'ush, Ja'lam, and Ko'rah; these are the
chiefs born of Oholiba'mah the daughter of An'ah,
Esau's wife. 19 These are the sons of Esau (that is,
E'dom), and these are their chiefs.

20 These are the sons of Se'ir the Horite, the
inhabitants of the land: Lo'tan, Sho'bal, Zib'eon,
An'ah, 21 Di'shon, E'zer, and Di'shan; these are the
chiefs of the Horites, the sons of Se'ir in the land of
E'dom. 22 The sons of Lo'tan were Ho'ri and He'man;
and Lo'tan's sister was Timna. 23 These are the sons
of Sho'bal: Alvan, Man'ahath, E'bal, She'pho, and
Onam. 24 These are the sons of Zib'eon: A'iah and
An'ah; he is the Anah who found the hot springs
in the wilderness, as he pastured the donkeys of
Zibeon his father. 25 These are the children of An'ah:
Di'shon and Oholiba'mah the daughter of Anah.
26 These are the sons of Di'shon: Hemdan, Eshban,
Ithran, and Che'ran. 27 These are the sons of E'zer:
Bilhan, Za'avan, and A'kan. 28 These are the sons of
Di'shan: Uz and Ar'an. 29 These are the chiefs of the
Horites: the chiefs Lo'tan, Sho'bal, Zib'eon, An'ah,
30 Di'shon, E'zer, and Di'shan; these are the chiefs of
the Horites, according to their clans in the land of

---

**36:2:** Gen 26:34; 28:9. **36:20–28:** 1 Chron 1:38–42. **36:31–43:** 1 Chron 1:43–53.

---

**35:29 Isaac breathed his last:** The impression is that Isaac dies after a final reunion with Jacob. It is possible, however, that the account of his death and burial is not in the correct chronological order, i.e., it is moved here to conclude the primary Isaac and Jacob stories before turning to a detailed account of the Joseph story (37:1—50:26). Recall that Isaac was already on his deathbed in 27:1-2, some 20 years before Jacob's return to Canaan. **Esau and Jacob buried him:** Recalls how the feuding brothers, Isaac and Ishmael, reunited to bury their father, Abraham (25:9).

**36:1-43** Chap. 36 is a genealogical record of the Edomites and the Horites. The first part groups together Esau's wives (36:1-5), his sons and grandsons (36:6-14), and his chiefs (36: 15-19), and the second includes a roster of Horite clans (36:20-30), an Edomite king list (36:31-39), and another table of Edomite chieftains (36:40-43).

**36:1 These are the descendants:** A formula that introduces new phases of history and narrative in Genesis. See introduction: *Structure*.

**36:7 their possessions:** Overcrowding pressures Jacob and Esau to separate their tribes, just as it forced Abraham and Lot to part company and settle their families and flocks in different lands (13:2-18). The parallel is theologically significant: in both cases, the elect patriarch stays behind in Canaan (Abraham, Jacob) while his kinsmen venture outside its borders, excluding themselves from the blessings of the Promised Land (Lot, Esau).

**36:20 Horite:** One of the indigenous peoples of Seir, south of the Dead Sea (14:6). The Horites were eventually overrun by the Edomites, to whom God had given their land as an inheritance (Deut 2:12; Josh 24:4).

**36:31 before any king:** Perhaps an editorial comment inserted into Genesis sometime after the rise of the Israelite monarchy at the beginning of the first millennium B.C.

---

[e] Sam Gk Syr: Heb *daughter.*

[f] Gk Syr: Heb *daughter.*

Se'ir.
31 These are the kings who reigned in the land
of E'dom, before any king reigned over the Israelites. 32Be'la the son of Beor reigned in E'dom, the
name of his city being Din'habah. 33Be'la died, and
Jo'bab the son of Ze'rah of Bozrah reigned in his
stead. 34Jo'bab died, and Hu'sham of the land of the
Te'manites reigned in his stead. 35Hu'sham died, and
Ha'dad the son of Be'dad, who defeated Mid'ian in
the country of Moab, reigned in his stead, the name
of his city being A'vith. 36Ha'dad died, and Samlah
of Masre'kah reigned in his stead. 37Samlah died, and
Sha'ul of Reho'both on the Euphra'tes reigned in his
stead. 38Sha'ul died, and Ba'al-ha'nan the son of Ach-
bor reigned in his stead. 39Ba'al-ha'nan the son of Ach-
bor died, and Hadar reigned in his stead, the name of
his city being Pa'u; his wife's name was Mehet'abel,
the daughter of Ma'tred, daughter of Me'zahab.
40 These are the names of the chiefs of Esau,
according to their families and their dwelling places,
by their names: the chiefs Timna, Alvah, Je'theth,
41Oholiba'mah, E'lah, Pi'non, 42Ke'naz, Te'man,
Mibzar, 43Mag'diel, and I'ram; these are the chiefs
of E'dom (that is, Esau, the father of Edom), according to their dwelling places in the land of their
possession.

### Joseph Dreams of Greatness

37 Jacob dwelt in the land of his father's
sojournings, in the land of Canaan. 2This is
the history of the family of Jacob.
Joseph, being seventeen years old, was shepherding the flock with his brothers; he was a lad with
the sons of Bilhah and Zilpah, his father's wives; and
Joseph brought an ill report of them to their father.
3Now Israel loved Joseph more than any other of his
children, because he was the son of his old age; and
he made him a long robe with sleeves. 4But when his
brothers saw that their father loved him more than
all his brothers, they hated him, and could not speak
peaceably to him.
5 Now Joseph had a dream, and when he told
it to his brothers they only hated him the more.
6He said to them, "Hear this dream which I have
dreamed: 7behold, we were binding sheaves in
the field, and behold, my sheaf arose and stood
upright; and behold, your sheaves gathered round
it, and bowed down to my sheaf." 8His brothers
said to him, "Are you indeed to reign over us? Or
are you indeed to have dominion over us?" So
they hated him yet more for his dreams and for
his words. 9Then he dreamed another dream, and
told it to his brothers, and said, "Behold, I have
dreamed another dream; and behold, the sun, the
moon, and eleven stars were bowing down to me."
10But when he told it to his father and to his brothers,
his father rebuked him, and said to him, "What is
this dream that you have dreamed? Shall I and your
mother and your brothers indeed come to bow ourselves to the ground before you?" 11And his brothers
were jealous of him, but his father kept the saying

**37:11, 28:** Acts 7:9.

**37:1—50:26** The final storyline in Genesis is devoted to Jacob's sons, especially Joseph and, to a lesser extent, Judah. This material builds a bridge from the patriarchal narratives to the Book of Exodus, explaining how the family of Israel came to reside in Egypt. Several details in this section pertaining to Egyptian names, customs, funerary practices, and state administration have been verified as historically authentic.

**37:2 This is the history:** A formula that introduces new phases of history and narrative in Genesis. See introduction: *Structure*.

**37:3 loved Joseph more:** Preferential love again sows division in the family, just as it had with Jacob's own parents (25:28). **his old age:** Joseph was the last son born to Jacob during his sojourn in Paddan-aram (30:22–24). **long robe with sleeves:** A visible sign of Jacob's favor. The Greek LXX suggests the tunic was striped or multicolored. • *Allegorically*, the multicolored robe prefigures the glory with which the Father clothed the Son at his coming. And just as the sons of Jacob become enraged with their father's beloved Joseph, so the Pharisees would flame with anger against Christ, though he was destined to be their superior (St. Cyril of Alexandria, *Glaphyra on Genesis* 6, 4).

**37:8 reign over us?:** Fulfilled when Joseph is appointed prime minister over Egypt (41:39–43) and his brothers fall prostrate before him (42:6). • *Allegorically*, the dream of Joseph reveals the King who is to come, for the standing sheaf is the resurrected Lord, and the sheaves turned down are the saints on bended knee (St. Ambrose, *On Joseph* 2, 7).

**37:11 kept the saying in mind:** Jacob ponders the alleged visions, aware that God has revealed the plan for his own life in this way (28:12–15). Perhaps these dreams influenced his deathbed decision to give Joseph the blessing of the firstborn (49:22–26; 1 Chron 5:1–3).

### Word Study

*Dream* (37:5)

*Ḥalom* (Heb.): A "dream" experienced while sleeping. It was widely believed in the ancient Near East that visions of the night contained meaningful messages, often encrypted in bizarre symbols and storylines. In the biblical tradition, dreams are important channels of divine communication. Through them the Lord issues warnings and instructions (Gen 20:3–7; 31:24), reveals his glory and blessings (Gen 28:12–15; 1 Kings 3:5–15), and gives prophetic insights into the future (Num 12:6; Dan 2:1–45). Dreams play an especially important role in the life of Joseph, who dreams of his own preeminence in the family of Jacob (37:5–11) and interprets the symbolic visions of Pharaoh (Gen 41:1–32) and his royal servants (Gen 40:5–19). As Joseph recognizes, his ability to understand dreams is a gift from God (Gen 40:8; 41:16). Daniel will likewise possess the gift of dream interpretation many centuries later (Dan 1:17; 2:47).

in mind.

### Joseph Is Sold by His Brothers

12 Now his brothers went to pasture their
father's flock near She'chem. 13And Israel said to
Joseph, "Are not your brothers pasturing the flock
at She'chem? Come, I will send you to them." And
he said to him, "Here I am." 14So he said to him,
"Go now, see if it is well with your brothers, and
with the flock; and bring me word again." So he
sent him from the valley of He'bron, and he came to
She'chem. 15And a man found him wandering in the
fields; and the man asked him, "What are you seeking?" 16"I am seeking my brothers," he said, "tell
me, I beg you, where they are pasturing the flock."
17And the man said, "They have gone away, for I
heard them say, 'Let us go to Do'than.'" So Joseph
went after his brothers, and found them at Dothan.
18They saw him afar off, and before he came near to
them they conspired against him to kill him. 19They
said to one another, "Here comes this dreamer.
20Come now, let us kill him and throw him into one
of the pits; then we shall say that a wild beast has
devoured him, and we shall see what will become of
his dreams." 21But when Reuben heard it, he delivered him out of their hands, saying, "Let us not take
his life." 22And Reuben said to them, "Shed no blood;
cast him into this pit here in the wilderness, but lay
no hand upon him"—that he might rescue him out
of their hand, to restore him to his father. 23So when
Joseph came to his brothers, they stripped him of
his robe, the long robe with sleeves that he wore;
24and they took him and cast him into a pit. The pit
was empty, there was no water in it.

25 Then they sat down to eat; and looking up
they saw a caravan of Ish'maelites coming from
Gilead, with their camels bearing gum, balm, and
myrrh, on their way to carry it down to Egypt.
26Then Judah said to his brothers, "What profit
is it if we slay our brother and conceal his blood?
27Come, let us sell him to the Ish'maelites, and let
not our hand be upon him, for he is our brother, our
own flesh." And his brothers heeded him. 28Then
Mid'ianite traders passed by; and they drew Joseph
up and lifted him out of the pit, and sold him to the
Ish'maelites for twenty shekels of silver; and they
took Joseph to Egypt.

29 When Reuben returned to the pit and saw
that Joseph was not in the pit, he tore his clothes
30and returned to his brothers, and said, "The
lad is gone; and I, where shall I go?" 31Then they
took Joseph's robe, and killed a goat, and dipped
the robe in the blood; 32and they sent the long
robe with sleeves and brought it to their father,
and said, "This we have found; see now whether
it is your son's robe or not." 33And he recognized
it, and said, "It is my son's robe; a wild beast has
devoured him; Joseph is without doubt torn to
pieces." 34Then Jacob tore his garments, and put
sackcloth upon his loins, and mourned for his son
many days. 35All his sons and all his daughters
rose up to comfort him; but he refused to be comforted, and said, "No, I shall go down to Sheol

**37:15 a man:** The mysterious stranger may be an angel, like the visitors who came to Abraham (18:2) and the heavenly man who wrestled with Jacob (32:24).

**37:17 Dothan:** Not far from Shechem to the northwest.

**37:18–28** The conspiracy against Joseph by his resentful older brothers. His murder is barely averted by **Reuben**, the oldest, who persuades them to lower him into a pit, and **Judah**, the fourth-born, who advises they sell him to Arabian traders headed for Egypt.

**37:28 Midianite traders ... Ishmaelites:** Tribal groups descended from Abraham but outside the elect line of Isaac (25:1–2, 12–18). Some see the disparity of names in this verse as an indicator that two different traditions about Joseph have been combined without being harmonized. More likely, the designations Midianite/Ishmaelite were functionally synonymous, both referring to desert traders from Arabia with a common descent from Abraham (as appears to be the case also in Judg 8:22–24). **twenty shekels of silver:** An authentic detail reflective of the early second millennium B.C. The price for a slave climbed to 30 silver pieces by the middle of the second millennium (as in Ex 21:32) and rose much higher in first millennium B.C.

**37:29 tore his clothes:** A sign of extreme distress and sorrow (37:34; 44:13).

**37:31 robe in the blood:** The plan to deceive Jacob is soaked with irony. Just as Jacob tricked his own father with goat skins and Esau's garments (27:15–16), so he himself is deceived with goat blood and Joseph's garment (37:31–33). For other indications that Jacob's cunning in chap. 27 comes back to haunt him in later life, see note on 29:25.

**37:35 Sheol:** The realm of the dead. Biblical descriptions picture it as a dark and dreary land in the heart of the earth (42:38). See word study: *Sheol* at Num 16:30.

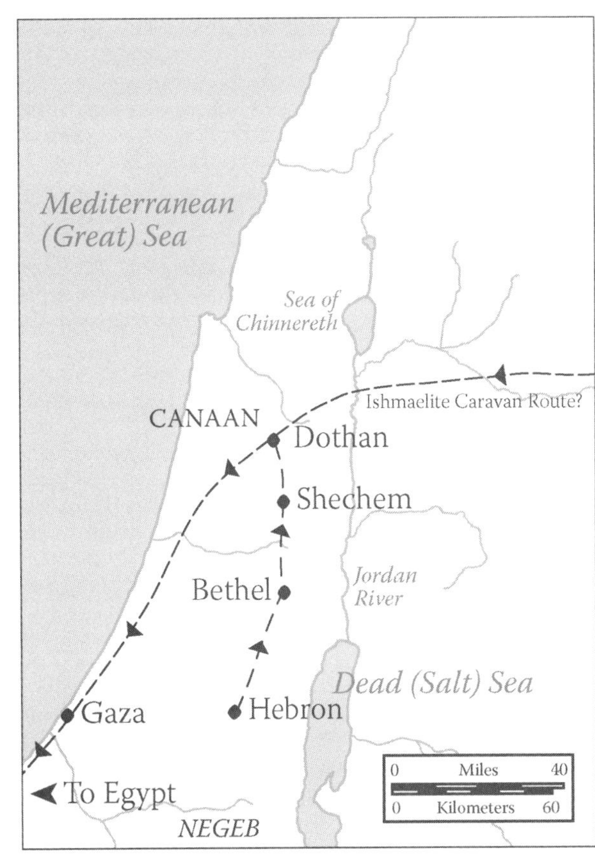


**Joseph and His Brothers**

to my son, mourning." Thus his father wept for him. 36Meanwhile the Mid'ianites had sold him in Egypt to Pot'iphar, an officer of Pharaoh, the captain of the guard.

### Judah and Tamar

38 It happened at that time that Judah went down from his brothers, and turned in to a certain Adul'lamite, whose name was Hi'rah. 2There Judah saw the daughter of a certain Canaanite whose name was Shua; he married her and went in to her, 3and she conceived and bore a son, and he called his name Er. 4Again she conceived and bore a son, and she called his name O'nan. 5Yet again she bore a son, and she called his name She'lah. She[g] was in Che'zib when she bore him. 6And Judah took a wife for Er his first-born, and her name was Ta'mar. 7But Er, Judah's first-born, was wicked in the sight of the LORD; and the LORD slew him. 8Then Judah said to O'nan, "Go in to your brother's wife, and perform the duty of a brother-in-law to her, and raise up offspring for your brother." 9But O'nan knew that the offspring would not be his; so when he went in to his brother's wife he spilled the semen on the ground, lest he should give offspring to his brother. 10And what he did was displeasing in the sight of the LORD, and he slew him also. 11Then Judah said to Ta'mar his daughter-in-law, "Remain a widow in your father's house, till She'lah my son grows up"—for he feared that he would die, like his brothers. So Ta'mar went and dwelt in her father's house.

12 In course of time the wife of Judah, Shua's daughter, died; and when Judah was comforted, he went up to Timnah to his sheepshearers, he and his friend Hi'rah the Adul'lamite. 13And when Tamar was told, "Your father-in-law is going up to Timnah to shear his sheep," 14she put off her widow's garments, and put on a veil, wrapping herself up, and sat at the entrance to Enaim, which is on the road to Timnah; for she saw that She'lah was grown up, and she had not been given to him in marriage. 15When Judah saw her, he thought her to be a harlot, for she had covered her face. 16He went over to her at the road side, and said, "Come, let me come in to you," for he did not know that she was his daughter-in-law. She said, "What will you give me, that you may come in to me?" 17He answered, "I will send you a kid from the flock." And she said, "Will you give me a pledge, till you send it?" 18He said, "What pledge shall I give you?" She replied, "Your signet and your cord, and your staff that is in your hand." So he gave them to her, and went in to her, and she conceived by him. 19Then she arose and went away, and taking off her veil she put on the garments of her widowhood.

20 When Judah sent the kid by his friend the Adul'lamite, to receive the pledge from the woman's hand, he could not find her. 21And he asked the men of the place, "Where is the harlot[h] who was at Ena'im by the wayside?" And they said, "No harlot[h] has been here." 22So he returned to Judah, and said, "I have not found her; and also the men of the

---

**38:1–30** The spotlight turns briefly from Joseph to Judah. Besides hinting that Israel is beginning to be assimilated into its Canaanite surroundings, the chapter explains how Judah became the father of Perez, the genealogical ancestor of King David (Ruth 4:18–22) and ultimately of Jesus the Messiah (Mt 1:3–16).

**38:1 Adullamite:** A resident of the Canaanite city of Adullam (Josh 12:15), which is later part of the tribal territory of Judah (Josh 15:35).

**38:2 a certain Canaanite:** Judah disregards the standards of his father (Jacob) and grandfather (Isaac), both of whom went to great lengths to avoid intermarriage with the Canaanites (24:3–4; 27:46—28:2).

**38:8 the duty:** The custom of levirate marriage (*levir* is "brother-in-law" in Latin). In ancient Semitic society, if a married man died without fathering a son, one of his brothers was expected to marry his widow in the hope that the second marriage would produce a legal heir who could inherit the deceased brother's name and estate. Technically, the obligation that fell upon the brother-in-law could be declined, but this was considered shameful. The duty of levirate marriage was later made into law (Deut 25:5–10).

**38:9 spilled:** The Hebrew could also be rendered "wasted" (Judg 6:5; Prov 23:8) or "destroyed" (6:17; 2 Sam 1:14). **semen on the ground:** Onan commits grave sin when he withdraws from sexual intercourse just before insemination. This was "displeasing" to the Lord (38:10), as was Onan's dishonorable intention to retain possession of his brother's property instead of providing him with a legal heir. Still, the seriousness of his sin is bound up with his action (*what* he did) and cannot be exclusively tied to his intention (*why* he did it). The reason for this conclusion is twofold. (**1**) If Onan's sin consisted simply in his disregard for a cultural custom (see note on 38:8), there would be no reason to spell out the lewd details of his bedroom behavior, especially given the delicacy with which the Bible normally describes sexual activity. At the very least, it would seem that Onan was guilty of lust; otherwise, refusal to have marital intercourse would have sufficed to deny offspring to his brother. (**2**) Disregard for the levirate marriage custom, however much it was frowned upon in ancient times, was never considered a capital crime. In its codified form, the levirate law prescribes only a ritual of public humiliation for one who declines to fulfill the duty of fathering an heir for his deceased brother (Deut 25:7–10). But since the Lord "slew" Onan, it is clear that his action was a serious transgression, on a par with sexual sins such as adultery, homosexual activity, and bestiality, all of which merit the death penalty in biblical law (Lev 20:10, 13, 15–16). In Catholic moral theology, the sin of "Onanism" covers contraceptive intercourse (including but not restricted to interrupted intercourse) as well as masturbation (CCC 2352, 2370).

**38:15 a harlot:** Disguised as a prostitute, Tamar is actually a grieving widow in search of the protection of marriage she was entitled to by Judah's third son, Shelah (38:14).

**38:18 signet:** A small cylinder with personal insignia used to sign contracts and other legal documents by rolling it across wax or clay.

**38:21 the harlot:** Not the same word used for a roadside prostitute in 38:15, but the Hebrew term for a cultic priestess who engages in ritual prostitution in the Canaanite religion. This subtle shift in terminology suggests the Adullamite is straining to dignify the impropriety of Judah.

---

[g] Gk: Heb *He*.

[h] Or *cult prostitute*.

place said, 'No harlot[h] has been here.'" 23And Judah replied, "Let her keep the things as her own, lest we be laughed at; you see, I sent this kid, and you could not find her."

24 About three months later Judah was told, "Ta'mar your daughter-in-law has played the harlot; and moreover she is with child by harlotry." And Judah said, "Bring her out, and let her be burned." 25As she was being brought out, she sent word to her father-in-law, "By the man to whom these belong, I am with child." And she said, "Mark, I beg you, whose these are, the signet and the cord and the staff." 26Then Judah acknowledged them and said, "She is more righteous than I, inasmuch as I did not give her to my son She'lah." And he did not lie with her again.

27 When the time of her delivery came, there were twins in her womb. 28And when she was in labor, one put out a hand; and the midwife took and bound on his hand a scarlet thread, saying, "This came out first." 29But as he drew back his hand, behold, his brother came out; and she said, "What a breach you have made for yourself!" Therefore his name was called Per'ez.[i] 30Afterward his brother came out with the scarlet thread upon his hand; and his name was called Ze'rah.

### Joseph and Potiphar's Wife

39 Now Joseph was taken down to Egypt, and Pot'iphar, an officer of Pharaoh, the captain of the guard, an Egyptian, bought him from the Ish'maelites who had brought him down there. 2The LORD was with Joseph, and he became a successful man; and he was in the house of his master the Egyptian, 3and his master saw that the LORD was with him, and that the LORD caused all that he did to prosper in his hands. 4So Joseph found favor in his sight and attended him, and he made him overseer of his house and put him in charge of all that he had. 5From the time that he made him overseer in his house and over all that he had the LORD blessed the Egyptian's house for Joseph's sake; the blessing of the LORD was upon all that he had, in house and field. 6So he left all that he had in Joseph's charge; and having him he had no concern for anything but the food which he ate.

Now Joseph was handsome and good-looking. 7And after a time his master's wife cast her eyes upon Joseph, and said, "Lie with me." 8But he refused and said to his master's wife, "Behold, having me my master has no concern about anything in the house, and he has put everything that he has in my hand; 9he is not greater in this house than I am; nor has he kept back anything from me except yourself, because you are his wife; how then can I do this great wickedness, and sin against God?" 10And although she spoke to Joseph day after day, he would not listen to her, to lie with her or to be with her. 11But one day, when he went into the house to do his work and none of the men of the house was there in the house, 12she caught him by his garment, saying, "Lie with me." But he left his garment in her hand, and fled and got out of the house. 13And when she saw that he had left his garment in her hand, and had fled out of the house, 14she called to the men of her household and said to them, "See, he has brought among us a Hebrew to insult us; he came in to me to lie with me, and I cried out with a loud voice; 15and when he heard that I lifted up my voice and cried, he left his garment with me, and fled and got out of the house." 16Then she laid up his garment by her until his master came home, 17and she told him the same story, saying, "The Hebrew servant, whom you have brought among us, came in to me to insult me; 18but as soon as I lifted up my voice and cried, he left his garment with me, and fled out of the house."

19 When his master heard the words which his wife spoke to him, "This is the way your servant treated me," his anger was kindled. 20And Joseph's master took him and put him into the prison, the place where the king's prisoners were confined, and he was there in prison. 21But the LORD was with Joseph and showed him mercy, and gave him favor in the sight of the keeper of the prison. 22And the keeper of the prison committed to Joseph's care all the prisoners who were in the prison; and whatever

**39:1, 2, 21:** Acts 7:9.

**38:24 let her be burned:** A punishment later applied to the promiscuous daughter of a Levitical priest (Lev 21:9).

**38:26 more righteous:** The point is not that Tamar's tactics were in all respects honorable, but that she was more in the right than Judah for acting in the interests of her family and future when Judah persisted in withholding his son from her unjustly.

**38:29 Perez:** The Hebrew means "breach". See topical essay: *Blessings and Birthrights* at Gen 48.

**39:1 Potiphar:** Chief officer of Pharaoh's elite guard unit. His name, alluding to the Egyptian deity Re, means "one whom Re gave". **Pharaoh:** A title for the ruling king of Egypt.

**39:2 the LORD was with Joseph:** The hand of God brings success to Joseph in Egypt and prospers all of his undertakings (39:3, 21, 23). The Lord is shaping Joseph into an effective leader and administrator so that he can be a mediator of blessing to others (39:5; 50:20).

**39:4 overseer:** Joseph's authority over the palace and possessions of Potiphar anticipates his oversight of the royal prison (39:22) and ultimately his exaltation over the kingdom of Egypt (41:39–44).

**39:6–18** Joseph resists the advances of Potiphar's wife with the armor of chastity and wise thinking. Aware of his own weaknesses, he refuses to reason with his passions, and he avoids even the near occasion of sin by refusing to work in the presence of the temptress (39:10; Prov 5:3–8). Fleeing the palace naked, Joseph runs away with his purity even as he leaves his robe and honored position behind.

**39:14 a Hebrew:** A Semite descended from "Eber" (10:21, 25; 11:16).

**39:20 prison:** A mild punishment considering that Joseph is a foreign slave charged with the attempted rape of an Egyptian noblewoman. That he is confined rather than killed may suggest that Potiphar had his doubts about the allegations of his wife.

[i] That is *A breach.*

was done there, he was the doer of it; 23the keeper
of the prison paid no heed to anything that was in
Joseph's care, because the LORD was with him; and
whatever he did, the LORD made it prosper.

### The Dreams of Two Prisoners

40 Some time after this, the butler of the king
of Egypt and his baker offended their lord
the king of Egypt. 2And Pharaoh was angry with
his two officers, the chief butler and the chief baker,
3and he put them in custody in the house of the captain of the guard, in the prison where Joseph was
confined. 4The captain of the guard charged Joseph
with them, and he waited on them; and they continued for some time in custody. 5And one night they
both dreamed—the butler and the baker of the
king of Egypt, who were confined in the prison—
each his own dream, and each dream with its own
meaning. 6When Joseph came to them in the morning and saw them, they were troubled. 7So he asked
Pharaoh's officers who were with him in custody in
his master's house, "Why are your faces downcast
today?" 8They said to him, "We have had dreams,
and there is no one to interpret them." And Joseph
said to them, "Do not interpretations belong to God?
Tell them to me, I beg you."

9 So the chief butler told his dream to Joseph, and
said to him, "In my dream there was a vine before
me, 10and on the vine there were three branches; as
soon as it budded, its blossoms shot forth, and the
clusters ripened into grapes. 11Pharaoh's cup was in
my hand; and I took the grapes and pressed them
into Pharaoh's cup, and placed the cup in Pharaoh's
hand." 12Then Joseph said to him, "This is its interpretation: the three branches are three days; 13within
three days Pharaoh will lift up your head and restore
you to your office; and you shall place Pharaoh's cup
in his hand as formerly, when you were his butler.
14But remember me, when it is well with you, and do
me the kindness, I beg you, to make mention of me
to Pharaoh, and so get me out of this house. 15For I
was indeed stolen out of the land of the Hebrews;
and here also I have done nothing that they should
put me into the dungeon."

16 When the chief baker saw that the interpretation was favorable, he said to Joseph, "I also had a
dream: there were three cake baskets on my head,
17and in the uppermost basket there were all sorts
of baked food for Pharaoh, but the birds were eating it out of the basket on my head." 18And Joseph
answered, "This is its interpretation: the three baskets are three days; 19within three days Pharaoh
will lift up your head—from you!—and hang you
on a tree; and the birds will eat the flesh from you."

20 On the third day, which was Pharaoh's birth-
day, he made a feast for all his servants, and lifted
up the head of the chief butler and the head of the
chief baker among his servants. 21He restored the
chief butler to his butlership, and he placed the cup
in Pharaoh's hand; 22but he hanged the chief baker,
as Joseph had interpreted to them. 23Yet the chief
butler did not remember Joseph, but forgot him.

### Joseph Interprets Pharaoh's Dream

41 After two whole years, Pharaoh dreamed
that he was standing by the Nile, 2and
behold, there came up out of the Nile seven cows
sleek and fat, and they fed in the reed grass. 3And
behold, seven other cows, gaunt and thin, came up
out of the Nile after them, and stood by the other
cows on the bank of the Nile. 4And the gaunt and
thin cows ate up the seven sleek and fat cows. And
Pharaoh awoke. 5And he fell asleep and dreamed a
second time; and behold, seven ears of grain, plump
and good, were growing on one stalk. 6And behold,
after them sprouted seven ears, thin and blighted by
the east wind. 7And the thin ears swallowed up the
seven plump and full ears. And Pharaoh awoke, and
behold, it was a dream. 8So in the morning his spirit
was troubled; and he sent and called for all the magicians of Egypt and all its wise men; and Pharaoh
told them his dream, but there was none who could
interpret it[j] to Pharaoh.

9 Then the chief butler said to Pharaoh, "I remem-

---

**40:8 interpretations belong to God:** Also recognized by the prophet Daniel (Dan 2:26–28). See word study: *Dream* at 37:5.

**40:13 lift up your head:** The subject of a wordplay. For the butler, the expression means that Pharaoh will restore him to service by an act of clemency. For the baker, it means that Pharaoh will sever his head from his body by a gruesome act of execution (40:19).

**40:15 dungeon:** The same Hebrew term is rendered "pit" in 37:24, hinting that Joseph finds himself back where he started, again cast into confinement as the victim of another's cruelty.

**40:19 hang you:** Not a public hanging by a noose around the neck, but the public exhibition of his corpse tied or impaled to a tree (cf. Deut 21:22).

**41:1–57** A pivotal chapter in the Joseph story, when he rises from the depths of a dungeon to the heights of royal power over Egypt. God has arranged for this elevation by endowing Joseph with the wisdom to interpret dreams and the foresight to prepare Egypt for a coming famine. • Gen 41 displays notable parallels with chap. 2 of the Book of Daniel: in both, a Near Eastern monarch has bizarre dreams about the future (Pharaoh, Nebuchadnezzar), and when his court magicians cannot explain its meaning, the king turns to a Hebrew slave living in exile (Joseph, Daniel), who interprets the visions with divine help and is made a royal overseer in the kingdom (Dan 2:1–49).

**41:2 the reed grass:** The word for "reeds" is an Egyptian term.

**41:6 the east wind:** A hot and dry wind that had a scorching effect on field crops.

**41:8 magicians . . . wise men:** The Pharaohs of the ancient world typically surrounded themselves with such royal advisers (Ex 7:11; Is 19:11–13). **his dream:** Pharaoh's visions of the night are given by God as visions of the future (41:32). See word study: *Dream* at 37:5.

**41:9 I remember my faults:** Only now, after the passing of two years (41:1), does the butler remember the kind service Joseph rendered to him in prison and the request he made to inform the Pharaoh of it (40:14, 23).

---

[j] Gk: Heb *them*.

ber my faults today. [10]When Pharaoh was angry with his servants, and put me and the chief baker in custody in the house of the captain of the guard, [11]we dreamed on the same night, he and I, each having a dream with its own meaning. [12]A young Hebrew was there with us, a servant of the captain of the guard; and when we told him, he interpreted our dreams to us, giving an interpretation to each man according to his dream. [13]And as he interpreted to us, so it came to pass; I was restored to my office, and the baker was hanged."

14 Then Pharaoh sent and called Joseph, and they brought him hastily out of the dungeon; and when he had shaved himself and changed his clothes, he came in before Pharaoh. [15]And Pharaoh said to Joseph, "I have had a dream, and there is no one who can interpret it; and I have heard it said of you that when you hear a dream you can interpret it." [16]Joseph answered Pharaoh, "It is not in me; God will give Pharaoh a favorable answer." [17]Then Pharaoh said to Joseph, "Behold, in my dream I was standing on the banks of the Nile; [18]and seven cows, fat and sleek, came up out of the Nile and fed in the reed grass; [19]and seven other cows came up after them, poor and very gaunt and thin, such as I had never seen in all the land of Egypt. [20]And the thin and gaunt cows ate up the first seven fat cows, [21]but when they had eaten them no one would have known that they had eaten them, for they were still as gaunt as at the beginning. Then I awoke. [22]I also saw in my dream seven ears growing on one stalk, full and good; [23]and seven ears, withered, thin, and blighted by the east wind, sprouted after them, [24]and the thin ears swallowed up the seven good ears. And I told it to the magicians, but there was no one who could explain it to me."

25 Then Joseph said to Pharaoh, "The dream of Pharaoh is one; God has revealed to Pharaoh what he is about to do. [26]The seven good cows are seven years, and the seven good ears are seven years; the dream is one. [27]The seven lean and gaunt cows that came up after them are seven years, and the seven empty ears blighted by the east wind are also seven years of famine. [28]It is as I told Pharaoh, God has shown to Pharaoh what he is about to do. [29]There will come seven years of great plenty throughout all the land of Egypt, [30]but after them there will arise seven years of famine, and all the plenty will be forgotten in the land of Egypt; the famine will consume the land, [31]and the plenty will be unknown in the land by reason of that famine which will follow, for it will be very grievous. [32]And the doubling of Pharaoh's dream means that the thing is fixed by God, and God will shortly bring it to pass. [33]Now therefore let Pharaoh select a man discreet and wise, and set him over the land of Egypt. [34]Let Pharaoh proceed to appoint overseers over the land, and take the fifth part of the produce of the land of Egypt during the seven plenteous years. [35]And let them gather all the food of these good years that are coming, and lay up grain under the authority of Pharaoh for food in the cities, and let them keep it. [36]That food shall be a reserve for the land against the seven years of famine which are to befall the land of Egypt, so that the land may not perish through the famine."

### Joseph's Rise to Power in Egypt

37 This proposal seemed good to Pharaoh and to all his servants. [38]And Pharaoh said to his servants, "Can we find such a man as this, in whom is the Spirit of God?" [39]So Pharaoh said to Joseph, "Since God has shown you all this, there is none so discreet and wise as you are; [40]you shall be over my house, and all my people shall order themselves as you command; only as regards the throne will I be greater than you." [41]And Pharaoh said to Joseph, "Behold, I have set you over all the land of Egypt." [42]Then Pharaoh took his signet ring from his hand and put it on Joseph's hand, and arrayed him in garments of fine linen, and put a gold chain about his neck; [43]and he made him to ride in his second chariot; and they cried before him, "Bow the knee!"[k] Thus he set him over all the land of Egypt. [44]Moreover Pharaoh said to Joseph, "I am Pharaoh, and without your consent no man shall lift up hand or foot in all the land of Egypt." [45]And Pharaoh called Joseph's name Zaph'enath-pane'ah; and he gave him in marriage

**41:14 shaved himself:** Unlike Semitic men, who normally wore beards, Egyptian men shaved their faces regularly and their heads occasionally.

**41:32 the doubling:** The two dreams, which tell one and the same story, are fixed in the divine plan. Within the wider context of Genesis, this statement implies that Joseph's own dreams, doubly attested, are also doubly certain (37:5–11).

**41:39–44** Joseph is promoted to the position of vizier or prime minister of Egypt, i.e., the one who is given authority **over** the royal **house** (41:40; Ps 105:21). This makes him the highest official in the land, second only to the Pharaoh. Entrusted with the Pharaoh's **signet ring**, he is given authority to promulgate royal decrees (47:26); and clothed in **linen** and **gold**, he is entitled to the honor and submission of the Egyptian people. The prestige of the vizier was widely recognized in the ancient Near East, where similar government positions were held in the kingdoms of Babylon (Dan 2:48), Persia (Esther 8:2, 15; 10:3), and Israel (Is 22:15–23). See word study: *Over the Household* at 1 Kings 16:9.

**41:45 Zaphenath-paneah:** An Egyptian name of uncertain meaning. Proposals include "the god speaks and he lives" and "he who is called Ip-ankh" (Ip-ankh being a common name in the second millennium B.C.). **Asenath:** An Egyptian name probably meaning, "belonging to the goddess Neith". **Potiphera:** Thought to be a slight variation of the name "Potiphar" borne by Joseph's former master (39:1). **On:** Ten miles north of modern Cairo. The city was also known by its Greek name, "Heliopolis" (Jer 43:13), meaning, "City of the Sun" (Is 19:18). It was a hub of learning in ancient times and a center of sun-god worship. That Joseph marries into the priestly caste at On means that he joins the ranks of the Egyptian nobility.

**41:46 thirty years old:** A full 13 years after Joseph first dreamed of greatness (37:2–11) and was sold into Egypt (37:25–36).

[k] *Abrek*, probably an Egyptian word similar in sound to the Hebrew word meaning *to kneel*.

As'enath, the daughter of Poti'phera priest of On. So Joseph went out over the land of Egypt.

46 Joseph was thirty years old when he entered the service of Pharaoh king of Egypt. And Joseph went out from the presence of Pharaoh, and went through all the land of Egypt. 47 During the seven plenteous years the earth brought forth abundantly, 48 and he gathered up all the food of the seven years when there was plenty[l] in the land of Egypt, and stored up food in the cities; he stored up in every city the food from the fields around it. 49 And Joseph stored up grain in great abundance, like the sand of the sea, until he ceased to measure it, for it could not be measured.

50 Before the year of famine came, Joseph had two sons, whom As'enath, the daughter of Poti'phera priest of On, bore to him. 51 Joseph called the name of the first-born Manas'seh,[m] "For," he said, "God has made me forget all my hardship and all my father's house." 52 The name of the second he called E'phraim,[n] "For God has made me fruitful in the land of my affliction."

53 The seven years of plenty that prevailed in the land of Egypt came to an end; 54 and the seven years of famine began to come, as Joseph had said. There was famine in all lands; but in all the land of Egypt there was bread. 55 When all the land of Egypt was famished, the people cried to Pharaoh for bread; and Pharaoh said to all the Egyptians, "Go to Joseph; what he says to you, do." 56 So when the famine had spread over all the land, Joseph opened all the storehouses,[o] and sold to the Egyptians, for the famine was severe in the land of Egypt. 57 Moreover, all the earth came to Egypt to Joseph to buy grain, because the famine was severe over all the earth.

### Joseph's Brothers Go to Egypt

42 When Jacob learned that there was grain in Egypt, he said to his sons, "Why do you look at one another?" 2 And he said, "Behold, I have heard that there is grain in Egypt; go down and buy grain for us there, that we may live, and not die." 3 So ten of Joseph's brothers went down to buy grain in Egypt. 4 But Jacob did not send Benjamin, Joseph's brother, with his brothers, for he feared that harm might befall him. 5 Thus the sons of Israel came to buy among the others who came, for the famine was in the land of Canaan.

6 Now Joseph was governor over the land; he it was who sold to all the people of the land. And Joseph's brothers came, and bowed themselves before him with their faces to the ground. 7 Joseph saw his brothers, and knew them, but he treated them like strangers and spoke roughly to them. "Where do you come from?" he said. They said, "From the land of Canaan, to buy food." 8 Thus Joseph knew his brothers, but they did not know him. 9 And Joseph remembered the dreams which he had dreamed of them; and he said to them, "You are spies, you have come to see the weakness of the land." 10 They said to him, "No, my lord, but to buy food have your servants come. 11 We are all sons of one man, we are honest men, your servants are not spies." 12 He said to them, "No, it is the weakness of the land that you have come to see." 13 And they said, "We, your servants, are twelve brothers, the sons of one man in the land of Canaan; and behold, the youngest is this day with our father, and one is no more." 14 But Joseph said to them, "It is as I said to you, you are spies. 15 By this you shall be tested: by the life of Pharaoh, you shall not go from this place unless your youngest brother comes here. 16 Send one of you, and let him bring your brother, while you remain in prison, that your words may be tested, whether there is truth in you; or else, by the life of Pharaoh, surely you are spies." 17 And he put them all together in prison for three days.

18 On the third day Joseph said to them, "Do this and you will live, for I fear God: 19 if you are honest men, let one of your brothers remain confined in your prison, and let the rest go and carry grain for the famine of your households, 20 and bring your youngest brother to me; so your words will be verified, and you shall not die." And they did so. 21 Then they said to one another, "In truth we are guilty concerning our brother, in that we saw the distress of his soul, when he begged us and we would not listen;

**41:38–45:** Acts 7:10. **41:54:** Acts 7:11. **42:2:** Acts 7:12. **42:5:** Acts 7:11.

**41:51–52** Joseph fathered two sons by his Egyptian wife: **Manasseh**, whose name is similar to the Hebrew expression "God has made me forget", and **Ephraim**, whose name resembles the statement "God has made me fruitful." These sons embody the joy and contentment of Joseph's new life in Egypt.

**41:57 came to Egypt:** Also a place of refuge from famine in the days of Abraham (12:10).

**42:4 did not send Benjamin:** Jacob is especially protective of Benjamin because (**1**) he is the youngest of his sons and (**2**) because Benjamin is presumed to be the last living son of his beloved wife Rachel (44:20). Joseph, who is Benjamin's only full brother, was similarly favored by Jacob (37:3) before his death was faked by his brothers (37:31–35).

**42:6 bowed themselves:** A fulfillment of Joseph's dreams (37:7, 9).

**42:9 You are spies:** A false accusation that Joseph uses to gather information about Benjamin and to effect a larger plan to reunite his family in Egypt. It proves successful on both counts (42:31; 43:7; 46:1–7).

**42:21 we are guilty:** After three days in prison (42:17), the brothers are haunted by memories of their cruelty toward Joseph. With heavy and remorseful hearts, they begin to sense that divine justice is catching up with them (42:22).

**42:22 Did I not tell you:** It was Reuben who first intervened to rescue Joseph from the murderous plans of his brothers (37:21).

**42:23 Joseph understood:** Only pretending to need an interpreter, Joseph follows everything his brothers are saying as they converse in their native Semitic dialect.

[l] Sam Gk: Heb *which were.*
[m] That is *Making to forget.*
[n] From a Hebrew word meaning *to be fruitful.*
[o] Gk Vg Compare Syr: Heb *all that was in them.*

therefore is this distress come upon us." [22]And Reuben answered them, "Did I not tell you not to sin
against the lad? But you would not listen. So now
there comes a reckoning for his blood." [23]They did
not know that Joseph understood them, for there
was an interpreter between them. [24]Then he
turned away from them and wept; and he returned
to them and spoke to them. And he took Simeon
from them and bound him before their eyes. [25]And
Joseph gave orders to fill their bags with grain,
and to replace every man's money in his sack, and
to give them provisions for the journey. This was
done for them.

### Joseph's Brothers Return to Canaan

26 Then they loaded their donkeys with their
grain, and departed. [27]And as one of them opened
his sack to give his donkey food at the lodging place,
he saw his money in the mouth of his sack; [28]and
he said to his brothers, "My money has been put
back; here it is in the mouth of my sack!" At this
their hearts failed them, and they turned trembling
to one another, saying, "What is this that God has
done to us?"

29 When they came to Jacob their father in the
land of Canaan, they told him all that had befallen
them, saying, [30]"The man, the lord of the land, spoke
roughly to us, and took us to be spies of the land.
[31]But we said to him, 'We are honest men, we are not
spies; [32]we are twelve brothers, sons of our father;
one is no more, and the youngest is this day with
our father in the land of Canaan.' [33]Then the man,
the lord of the land, said to us, 'By this I shall know
that you are honest men: leave one of your brothers with me, and take grain for the famine of your
households, and go your way. [34]Bring your youngest
brother to me; then I shall know that you are not
spies but honest men, and I will deliver to you your
brother, and you shall trade in the land.'"

35 As they emptied their sacks, behold, every
man's bundle of money was in his sack; and when
they and their father saw their bundles of money,
they were dismayed. [36]And Jacob their father said
to them, "You have bereaved me of my children:
Joseph is no more, and Simeon is no more, and now
you would take Benjamin; all this has come upon
me." [37]Then Reuben said to his father, "Slay my two
sons if I do not bring him back to you; put him in
my hands, and I will bring him back to you." [38]But
he said, "My son shall not go down with you, for his
brother is dead, and he only is left. If harm should
befall him on the journey that you are to make, you
would bring down my gray hairs with sorrow to
Sheol."

### Joseph's Brothers Bring Benjamin to Egypt

43 Now the famine was severe in the land.
[2]And when they had eaten the grain which
they had brought from Egypt, their father said to
them, "Go again, buy us a little food." [3]But Judah
said to him, "The man solemnly warned us, saying,
'You shall not see my face, unless your brother is
with you.' [4]If you will send our brother with us, we
will go down and buy you food; [5]but if you will not
send him, we will not go down, for the man said to
us, 'You shall not see my face, unless your brother
is with you.'" [6]Israel said, "Why did you treat me so
ill as to tell the man that you had another brother?"
[7]They replied, "The man questioned us carefully
about ourselves and our kindred, saying, 'Is your
father still alive? Have you another brother?' What
we told him was in answer to these questions; could
we in any way know that he would say, 'Bring your
brother down'?" [8]And Judah said to Israel his father,
"Send the lad with me, and we will arise and go, that
we may live and not die, both we and you and also
our little ones. [9]I will be surety for him; of my hand
you shall require him. If I do not bring him back to
you and set him before you, then let me bear the
blame for ever; [10]for if we had not delayed, we would
now have returned twice."

11 Then their father Israel said to them, "If it
must be so, then do this: take some of the choice
fruits of the land in your bags, and carry down to
the man a present, a little balm and a little honey,
gum, myrrh, pistachio nuts, and almonds. [12]Take
double the money with you; carry back with you
the money that was returned in the mouth of your
sacks; perhaps it was an oversight. [13]Take also your
brother, and arise, go again to the man; [14]may God
Almighty[p] grant you mercy before the man, that he
may send back your other brother and Benjamin. If
I am bereaved of my children, I am bereaved." [15]So
the men took the present, and they took double the
money with them, and Benjamin; and they arose
and went down to Egypt, and stood before Joseph.

16 When Joseph saw Benjamin with them, he
said to the steward of his house, "Bring the men into
the house, and slaughter an animal and make ready,
for the men are to dine with me at noon." [17]The man

---

**42:34 you shall trade:** The brothers hide from Jacob the fact that Joseph threatened them with death should they return to Egypt without Benjamin (42:18–19).

**42:37 Slay my two sons:** Just as Reuben, followed by Judah, intervened to save Joseph's life (37:21, 26), so Reuben, followed by Judah, volunteers to guard Benjamin's life (43:8–9).

**42:38 shall not go:** Jacob flatly refuses to send Benjamin to Egypt at this first proposal. It is only after the famine drags on and the food supply runs low that he agrees to let him go (43:1–14). **Sheol:** The realm of the dead. See note on 37:35.

**43:1–34** The sons of Jacob make a second trip to Egypt in search of grain. This time they bring Benjamin, under the personal protection of Judah, along with a goodwill gift for Joseph.

**43:9 I will be surety:** Judah vows to take personal responsibility for Benjamin's welfare on the trip. As a living guarantor, he volunteers to sacrifice himself for the sake of his youngest brother and to bear the consequences of nonfulfillment should anything go wrong (44:32; Sir 29:15).

**43:14 your other brother:** Simeon, who is still locked up in Joseph's prison (42:19, 24).

[p] Heb *El Shaddai.*

did as Joseph bade him, and brought the men to Joseph's house. 18And the men were afraid because they were brought to Joseph's house, and they said, "It is because of the money, which was replaced in our sacks the first time, that we are brought in, so that he may seek occasion against us and fall upon us, to make slaves of us and seize our donkeys." 19So they went up to the steward of Joseph's house, and spoke with him at the door of the house, 20and said, "Oh, my lord, we came down the first time to buy food; 21and when we came to the lodging place we opened our sacks, and there was every man's money in the mouth of his sack, our money in full weight; so we have brought it again with us, 22and we have brought other money down in our hand to buy food. We do not know who put our money in our sacks." 23He replied, "Rest assured, do not be afraid; your God and the God of your father must have put treasure in your sacks for you; I received your money." Then he brought Simeon out to them. 24And when the man had brought the men into Joseph's house, and given them water, and they had washed their feet, and when he had given their donkeys food, 25they made ready the present for Joseph's coming at noon, for they heard that they should eat bread there.

26 When Joseph came home, they brought into the house to him the present which they had with them, and bowed down to him to the ground. 27And he inquired about their welfare, and said, "Is your father well, the old man of whom you spoke? Is he still alive?" 28They said, "Your servant our father is well, he is still alive." And they bowed their heads and made obeisance. 29And he lifted up his eyes, and saw his brother Benjamin, his mother's son, and said, "Is this your youngest brother, of whom you spoke to me? God be gracious to you, my son!" 30Then Joseph made haste, for his heart yearned for his brother, and he sought a place to weep. And he entered his chamber and wept there. 31Then he washed his face and came out; and controlling himself he said, "Let food be served." 32They served him by himself, and them by themselves, and the Egyptians who ate with him by themselves, because the Egyptians might not eat bread with the Hebrews, for that is an abomination to the Egyptians. 33And they sat before him, the first-born according to his birthright and the youngest according to his youth; and the men looked at one another in amazement. 34Portions were taken to them from Joseph's table, but Benjamin's portion was five times as much as any of theirs. So they drank and were merry with him.

### Joseph Detains Benjamin

44 Then he commanded the steward of his house, "Fill the men's sacks with food, as much as they can carry, and put each man's money in the mouth of his sack, 2and put my cup, the silver cup, in the mouth of the sack of the youngest, with his money for the grain." And he did as Joseph told him. 3As soon as the morning was light, the men were sent away with their donkeys. 4When they had gone but a short distance from the city, Joseph said to his steward, "Up, follow after the men; and when you overtake them, say to them, 'Why have you returned evil for good? Why have you stolen my silver cup?[a] 5Is it not from this that my lord drinks, and by this that he divines? You have done wrong in so doing.'"

6 When he overtook them, he spoke to them these words. 7They said to him, "Why does my lord speak such words as these? Far be it from your servants that they should do such a thing! 8Behold, the money which we found in the mouth of our sacks, we brought back to you from the land of Canaan; how then should we steal silver or gold from your lord's house? 9With whomever of your servants it be found, let him die, and we also will be my lord's slaves." 10He said, "Let it be as you say: he with whom it is found shall be my slave, and the rest of you shall be blameless." 11Then every man quickly lowered his sack to the ground, and every man opened his sack. 12And he searched, beginning with the eldest and ending with the youngest; and the cup was found in Benja-

---

**43:26 bowed down:** The second time his brothers bow in homage (42:6), again in fulfillment of Joseph's dreams (as in 37:7, 9).

**43:29 my son!:** Benjamin is so addressed because he is much younger than Joseph.

**43:32 by himself ... by themselves:** Separate seating arrangements for the meal are a reflection of different ranks and races among the participants. The reason why Egyptians refuse table-fellowship with Hebrews is obscure, though it may be linked with the Hebrews' occupation as shepherds who engaged in animal sacrifice. This interpretation is supported by the fact that what is abominable to the Egyptians is mentioned elsewhere in the Pentateuch only in connection with shepherding (46:34) and ritual sacrifice (Ex 8:26). See note on 46:34.

**43:33 amazement:** The brothers are astonished when Joseph seats them at the table in the exact order of their birth.

**43:34 five times:** The heaping portions are evidence of Joseph's preferential love for Benjamin. This fivefold favoritism is also shown in 45:22.

**44:1–13** Joseph stages a final test to ascertain his brothers' love for Benjamin as well as their loyalty to Jacob. Planting his silver cup in Benjamin's grain sack succeeds in bringing both of these relational issues into the spotlight.

**44:5 he divines:** The royal drinking cup is also a divination cup. When liquids, oils, and other objects are poured into the vessel, the resulting formations were thought to reveal information about the future in symbolic ways. The practice was commonplace in the ancient Near East, and the detail adds a touch of authenticity to the account. However, there is no clear indication that Joseph is a practitioner of these superstitious arts; every indication up to this point suggests that he receives revelation directly from God (40:8; 41:16, 25, 32).

**44:9 let him die:** Recalls how Rachel stole her father's household gods (31:19) and Jacob, unaware of her scheme, promised death to the thief (31:32).

**44:13 tore their clothes:** A sign of extreme distress (37:29, 34).

[a] Gk Compare Vg: Heb lacks *Why have you stolen my silver cup?*

min's sack. [13]Then they tore their clothes, and every
man loaded his donkey, and they returned to the city.
14 When Judah and his brothers came to Joseph's
house, he was still there; and they fell before him
to the ground. [15]Joseph said to them, "What deed
is this that you have done? Do you not know that
such a man as I can indeed divine?" [16]And Judah
said, "What shall we say to my lord? What shall
we speak? Or how can we clear ourselves? God has
found out the guilt of your servants; behold, we are
my lord's slaves, both we and he also in whose hand
the cup has been found." [17]But he said, "Far be it
from me that I should do so! Only the man in whose
hand the cup was found shall be my slave; but as for
you, go up in peace to your father."

### Judah Pleads for Benjamin's Release

18 Then Judah went up to him and said, "O my
lord, let your servant, I beg you, speak a word in
my lord's ears, and let not your anger burn against
your servant; for you are like Pharaoh himself. [19]My
lord asked his servants, saying, 'Have you a father,
or a brother?' [20]And we said to my lord, 'We have a
father, an old man, and a young brother, the child
of his old age; and his brother is dead, and he alone
is left of his mother's children; and his father loves
him.' [21]Then you said to your servants, 'Bring him
down to me, that I may set my eyes upon him.' [22]We
said to my lord, 'The lad cannot leave his father, for
if he should leave his father, his father would die.'
[23]Then you said to your servants, 'Unless your
youngest brother comes down with you, you shall
see my face no more.' [24]When we went back to your
servant my father we told him the words of my lord.
[25]And when our father said, 'Go again, buy us a little
food,' [26]we said, 'We cannot go down. If our youngest brother goes with us, then we will go down; for
we cannot see the man's face unless our youngest
brother is with us.' [27]Then your servant my father
said to us, 'You know that my wife bore me two
sons; [28]one left me, and I said, Surely he has been
torn to pieces; and I have never seen him since. [29]If
you take this one also from me, and harm befalls
him, you will bring down my gray hairs in sorrow to
Sheol.' [30]Now therefore, when I come to your servant
my father, and the lad is not with us, then, as his life
is bound up in the lad's life, [31]when he sees that the
lad is not with us, he will die; and your servants will
bring down the gray hairs of your servant our father
with sorrow to Sheol. [32]For your servant became
surety for the lad to my father, saying, 'If I do not
bring him back to you, then I shall bear the blame
in the sight of my father all my life.' [33]Now therefore,
let your servant, I beg you, remain instead of the lad
as a slave to my lord; and let the lad go back with his
brothers. [34]For how can I go back to my father if the
lad is not with me? I fear to see the evil that would
come upon my father."

### Joseph Makes Himself Known to His Brothers

45 Then Joseph could not control himself
before all those who stood by him; and he
cried, "Make every one go out from me." So no one
stayed with him when Joseph made himself known
to his brothers. [2]And he wept aloud, so that the
Egyptians heard it, and the household of Pharaoh
heard it. [3]And Joseph said to his brothers, "I am
Joseph; is my father still alive?" But his brothers
could not answer him, for they were dismayed at his
presence.
4 So Joseph said to his brothers, "Come near to
me, I beg you." And they came near. And he said, "I
am your brother, Joseph, whom you sold into Egypt.
[5]And now do not be distressed, or angry with yourselves, because you sold me here; for God sent me
before you to preserve life. [6]For the famine has been
in the land these two years; and there are yet five
years in which there will be neither plowing nor harvest. [7]And God sent me before you to preserve for
you a remnant on earth, and to keep alive for you
many survivors. [8]So it was not you who sent me
here, but God; and he has made me a father to Pharaoh, and lord of all his house and ruler over all the

---

**45:1:** Acts 7:13.

---

**44:16 the guilt:** The guilt of disowning Joseph and deceiving Jacob about his fate. Judah senses that divine punishment for this iniquity has finally overtaken them. Note the similar statement by Reuben in 42:22. **my lord's slaves:** An ironic role reversal. Joseph, once sold into slavery by his brothers, is now in a position to enslave those same brothers in Egypt.

**44:18–34** Judah steps forward to deliver an emotional speech before Joseph. He is pleading for mercy, not just for Benjamin and the brothers generally, but for the elderly Jacob, who is sure to die in grief if his youngest son does not return to him. Judah is even willing to substitute himself for Benjamin and accept the shackles of slavery to avoid this. His desperate appeal leaves Joseph in tears (45:1–3). See note on 43:9.

**44:31 Sheol:** The realm of the dead. See note on 37:35.

**45:1–15** The highpoint of the Joseph story, when he reveals his identity, reconciles with his brothers, and reflects on the saving plan of God.

**45:2 wept aloud:** The third and final time that Joseph is overcome with emotion in the struggle to conceal his identity from his family (42:24; 43:30).

**45:5 do not be distressed:** Implies that Joseph has forgiven his brothers and has no plans to exact revenge on them. **God sent me before you:** Joseph sees the hand of God working all things for the good (50:20; Rom 8:28). Even his rejection by his brothers was part of heaven's larger plan to raise him up in Egypt and to make him a redeemer of the family of Israel, lest the covenant people dwindle and die in the grip of a famine. The theological lesson is that God can bring good out of evil and even fulfill his plan in spite of the faults and failures of those he intends to bless the most (CCC 312). • Stephen's defense speech in Acts makes an implicit comparison between Joseph and Jesus: both were spurned by their kinsmen only to become saviors of Israel. See note on Acts 7:9–16.

**45:10 Goshen:** A fertile plain in the eastern Nile Delta. The land was ideally suited for grazing and shepherding

land of Egypt. [9]Make haste and go up to my father
and say to him, 'Thus says your son Joseph, God
has made me lord of all Egypt; come down to me, do
not tarry; [10]you shall dwell in the land of Go'shen,
and you shall be near me, you and your children and
your children's children, and your flocks, your herds,
and all that you have; [11]and there I will provide for
you, for there are yet five years of famine to come;
lest you and your household, and all that you have,
come to poverty.' [12]And now your eyes see, and the
eyes of my brother Benjamin see, that it is my mouth
that speaks to you. [13]You must tell my father of all
my splendor in Egypt, and of all that you have seen.
Make haste and bring my father down here." [14]Then
he fell upon his brother Benjamin's neck and wept;
and Benjamin wept upon his neck. [15]And he kissed
all his brothers and wept upon them; and after that
his brothers talked with him.

16 When the report was heard in Pharaoh's
house, "Joseph's brothers have come," it pleased
Pharaoh and his servants well. [17]And Pharaoh said
to Joseph, "Say to your brothers, 'Do this: load your
beasts and go back to the land of Canaan; [18]and take
your father and your households, and come to me,
and I will give you the best of the land of Egypt, and
you shall eat the fat of the land.' [19]Command them[r]
also, 'Do this: take wagons from the land of Egypt
for your little ones and for your wives, and bring
your father, and come. [20]Give no thought to your
goods, for the best of all the land of Egypt is yours.'"

21 The sons of Israel did so; and Joseph gave them
wagons, according to the command of Pharaoh, and
gave them provisions for the journey. [22]To each and
all of them he gave festal garments; but to Benjamin
he gave three hundred shekels of silver and five festal garments. [23]To his father he sent as follows: ten
donkeys loaded with the good things of Egypt, and
ten she-donkeys loaded with grain, bread, and provision for his father on the journey. [24]Then he sent
his brothers away, and as they departed, he said to
them, "Do not quarrel on the way." [25]So they went
up out of Egypt, and came to the land of Canaan to
their father Jacob. [26]And they told him, "Joseph is
still alive, and he is ruler over all the land of Egypt."
And his heart fainted, for he did not believe them.
[27]But when they told him all the words of Joseph,
which he had said to them, and when he saw the
wagons which Joseph had sent to carry him, the
spirit of their father Jacob revived; [28]and Israel said,
"It is enough; Joseph my son is still alive; I will go
and see him before I die."

### Jacob Brings His Whole Family to Egypt

46 So Israel took his journey with all that he
had, and came to Be'er-she'ba, and offered
sacrifices to the God of his father Isaac. [2]And God
spoke to Israel in visions of the night, and said,
"Jacob, Jacob." And he said, "Here am I." [3]Then he
said, "I am God, the God of your father; do not be
afraid to go down to Egypt; for I will there make
of you a great nation. [4]I will go down with you
to Egypt, and I will also bring you up again; and
Joseph's hand shall close your eyes." [5]Then Jacob set
out from Be'er-she'ba; and the sons of Israel carried
Jacob their father, their little ones, and their wives,
in the wagons which Pharaoh had sent to carry him.
[6]They also took their cattle and their goods, which
they had gained in the land of Canaan, and came
into Egypt, Jacob and all his offspring with him, [7]his
sons, and his sons' sons with him, his daughters,
and his sons' daughters; all his offspring he brought
with him into Egypt.

8 Now these are the names of the descendants
of Israel, who came into Egypt, Jacob and his sons.
Reuben, Jacob's first-born, [9]and the sons of Reuben:
Ha'noch, Pallu, Hezron, and Carmi. [10]The sons of
Simeon: Jemu'el, Ja'min, O'had, Ja'chin, Zo'har, and
Sha'ul, the son of a Canaanitish woman. [11]The sons
of Levi: Gershon, Ko'hath, and Merar'i. [12]The sons
of Judah: Er, O'nan, She'lah, Per'ez, and Ze'rah (but
Er and Onan died in the land of Canaan); and the
sons of Perez were Hezron and Ha'mul. [13]The sons of
Is'sachar: To'la, Pu'vah, I'ob, and Shimron. [14]The sons

---

**46:6:** Acts 7:14, 15. **46.8–27:** Ex 1:1–4; Num 26:4–50.

---

(46:32). The Israelites were still settled in this area on the eve of the Exodus (Ex 9:26).

**45:19 take wagons:** Pharaoh approves and assists in the plan to move Jacob and his family from Canaan to Goshen (45:21).

**45:22 five festal garments:** Similar favoritism is shown in 43:34, where Joseph piles five times more food on Benjamin's plate than on that of any of his other brothers.

**45:24 Do not quarrel:** I.e., about things like (**1**) who bears most of the blame for selling Joseph into slavery or (**2**) about how to come clean with Jacob since lying to him about Joseph's death.

**46:1–4** The final appearance of Yahweh to the Patriarchs noted in Scripture. Not until Moses crouches before the burning bush, over 400 years later, will another Israelite encounter the voice and presence of God in this remarkable way (Ex 3:1–22). The promise made to Jacob on this occasion—that the Lord will be **with** him and **bring** him back to Canaan—recalls the similar promise made on the eve of his first departure from Canaan in 28:15.

**46:1 Beer-sheba:** A settlement in southern Canaan already consecrated for worship by Abraham (21:33) and Isaac (26:23–25). **offered sacrifices:** An important dimension of patriarchal religion (4:3–4; 8:20; 22:13; Job 1:5).

**46:3 a great nation:** Fulfills the promise made to Abraham at his call in 12:2. See topical essay: *The Abrahamic Covenant* at Gen 12.

**46:8–27** The family of Jacob settled in Egypt. The Hebrew text counts 70 descendants of the patriarch (46:27), a number reminiscent of the earlier table of 70 nations descended from Noah and his sons (10:6–32; Deut 32:8). The Greek LXX gives a more expanded list of 75 descendants that includes three sons and two grandsons of Ephraim and Manasseh (46:20). Stephen follows this latter tradition in Acts 7:14.

**46:8 came into Egypt:** A literal reading of biblical chronology puts the beginning of Israel's sojourn in Egypt around 1876 B.C., a full 430 years before the Exodus (Ex 12:40–41).

---

[r] Compare Gk Vg: Heb *you are commanded.*

of Zeb'ulun: Se'red, E'lon, and Jah'leel 15(these are
the sons of Leah, whom she bore to Jacob in Pad'dan-
ar'am, together with his daughter Dinah; altogether
his sons and his daughters numbered thirty-three).
16The sons of Gad: Ziph'ion, Haggi, Shu'ni, Ezbon,
E'ri, Aro'di, and Are'li. 17The sons of Asher: Imnah,
Ishvah, Ishvi, Beri'ah, with Se'rah their sister. And
the sons of Beriah: He'ber and Mal'chi-el 18(these are
the sons of Zilpah, whom La'ban gave to Leah his
daughter; and these she bore to Jacob—sixteen persons). 19The sons of Rachel, Jacob's wife: Joseph and
Benjamin. 20And to Joseph in the land of Egypt were
born Manas'seh and E'phraim, whom As'enath, the
daughter of Poti'phera the priest of On, bore to him.
21And the sons of Benjamin: Be'la, Be'cher, Ashbel,
Ge'ra, Na'aman, E'hi, Rosh, Muppim, Huppim, and
Ard 22(these are the sons of Rachel, who were born to
Jacob—fourteen persons in all). 23The sons of Dan:
Hu'shim. 24The sons of Naph'tali: Jah'zeel, Gu'ni,
Je'zer, and Shillem 25(these are the sons of Bilhah,
whom La'ban gave to Rachel his daughter, and these
she bore to Jacob—seven persons in all). 26All the
persons belonging to Jacob who came into Egypt,
who were his own offspring, not including Jacob's
sons' wives, were sixty-six persons in all; 27and the
sons of Joseph, who were born to him in Egypt, were
two; all the persons of the house of Jacob, that came
into Egypt, were seventy.

### Jacob Dwells in the Land of Goshen

28 He sent Judah before him to Joseph, to appear[s]
before him in Go'shen; and they came into the land
of Goshen. 29Then Joseph made ready his chariot
and went up to meet Israel his father in Go'shen; and
he presented himself to him, and fell on his neck,
and wept on his neck a good while. 30Israel said to
Joseph, "Now let me die, since I have seen your face
and know that you are still alive." 31Joseph said to
his brothers and to his father's household, "I will go
up and tell Pharaoh, and will say to him, 'My brothers and my father's household, who were in the land
of Canaan, have come to me; 32and the men are shepherds, for they have been keepers of cattle; and they
have brought their flocks, and their herds, and all
that they have.' 33When Pharaoh calls you, and says,
'What is your occupation?' 34you shall say, 'Your
servants have been keepers of cattle from our youth
even until now, both we and our fathers,' in order
that you may dwell in the land of Go'shen; for every
shepherd is an abomination to the Egyptians."

47 So Joseph went in and told Pharaoh, "My
father and my brothers, with their flocks and
herds and all that they possess, have come from the
land of Canaan; they are now in the land of Go'shen."
2And from among his brothers he took five men
and presented them to Pharaoh. 3Pharaoh said to
his brothers, "What is your occupation?" And they
said to Pharaoh, "Your servants are shepherds, as
our fathers were." 4They said to Pharaoh, "We have
come to sojourn in the land; for there is no pasture
for your servants' flocks, for the famine is severe in
the land of Canaan; and now, we pray you, let your
servants dwell in the land of Go'shen." 5Then Pharaoh said to Joseph, "Your father and your brothers
have come to you. 6The land of Egypt is before you;
settle your father and your brothers in the best of
the land; let them dwell in the land of Go'shen; and
if you know any able men among them, put them in
charge of my cattle."

7 Then Joseph brought in Jacob his father, and
set him before Pharaoh, and Jacob blessed Pharaoh.
8And Pharaoh said to Jacob, "How many are the
days of the years of your life?" 9And Jacob said to
Pharaoh, "The days of the years of my sojourning
are a hundred and thirty years; few and evil have
been the days of the years of my life, and they have
not attained to the days of the years of the life of
my fathers in the days of their sojourning." 10And
Jacob blessed Pharaoh, and went out from the presence of Pharaoh. 11Then Joseph settled his father
and his brothers, and gave them a possession in the
land of Egypt, in the best of the land, in the land
of Ram'eses, as Pharaoh had commanded. 12And
Joseph provided his father, his brothers, and all his
father's household with food, according to the num-

---

**46:27:** Acts 7:14.

---

**46:29 fell on his neck:** This emotional embrace, sodden with tears, is characteristic of family reunions in Genesis (33:4; 45:14).

**46:34 every shepherd is an abomination:** The reason for this is not specified, but it seems the Egyptians despised shepherds as offenders against their religion. This is because several herding and grazing animals were revered as symbols of Egyptian deities. Shepherding, which entailed eating these beasts for food and using their hides for various domestic purposes, was probably thought to profane and desecrate these sacred representations of the gods. For the explosive tension created by the sacrifice of flock and herd animals in Egypt, see note on Ex 8:26 and topical essay: *Sacrifice in the Old Testament* at Lev 9.

**47:7 Jacob blessed Pharaoh:** The elderly shepherd from Canaan pronounces a blessing over the mighty king of Egypt. Jacob is the more exalted of the two figures in the eyes of God (cf. Heb 7:7).

**47:9 my sojourning:** Not the 20 years that Jacob spent abroad in Mesopotamia (31:38), but the entire span of his life up to this point. The idea is that man is merely a pilgrim and wayfarer passing through this world, a concept that appears elsewhere in Ps 39:12 and Heb 11:13–16.

**47:11 land of Rameses:** Another name for Goshen in the eastern Nile Delta. Since the region's namesake, Pharaoh Rameses II, reigned in Egypt from ca. 1304 to 1236 B.C., long after the time of Joseph, it is clear that the name "Rameses" made its way into the story sometime after the 13th century B.C., presumably through an editor or copyist intent upon updating the book of Genesis for a later generation of readers.

**47:13–26** Egypt plummets into starvation and economic collapse as the famine grinds on. Soon the currency in circulation is depleted, and the Egyptian masses are forced to

---

[s] Sam Syr Compare Gk Vg: Heb *to show the way.*

ber of their dependents.

### The Famine in Egypt and Canaan

13 Now there was no food in all the land; for the
famine was very severe, so that the land of Egypt
and the land of Canaan languished by reason of the
famine. 14And Joseph gathered up all the money
that was found in the land of Egypt and in the land
of Canaan, for the grain which they bought; and
Joseph brought the money into Pharaoh's house.
15And when the money was all spent in the land of
Egypt and in the land of Canaan, all the Egyptians
came to Joseph, and said, "Give us food; why should
we die before your eyes? For our money is gone."
16And Joseph answered, "Give your cattle, and I will
give you food in exchange for your cattle, if your
money is gone." 17So they brought their cattle to
Joseph; and Joseph gave them food in exchange for
the horses, the flocks, the herds, and the donkeys:
and he supplied them with food in exchange for all
their cattle that year. 18And when that year was
ended, they came to him the following year, and
said to him, "We will not hide from my lord that
our money is all spent; and the herds of cattle are
my lord's; there is nothing left in the sight of my
lord but our bodies and our lands. 19Why should we
die before your eyes, both we and our land? Buy us
and our land for food, and we with our land will
be slaves to Pharaoh; and give us seed, that we
may live, and not die, and that the land may not be
desolate."

20 So Joseph bought all the land of Egypt for Pharaoh; for all the Egyptians sold their fields, because
the famine was severe upon them. The land became
Pharaoh's; 21and as for the people, he made slaves
of them[t] from one end of Egypt to the other. 22Only
the land of the priests he did not buy; for the priests
had a fixed allowance from Pharaoh, and lived on
the allowance which Pharaoh gave them; therefore
they did not sell their land. 23Then Joseph said to the
people, "Behold, I have this day bought you and your
land for Pharaoh. Now here is seed for you, and you
shall sow the land. 24And at the harvests you shall
give a fifth to Pharaoh, and four fifths shall be your
own, as seed for the field and as food for yourselves
and your households, and as food for your little
ones." 25And they said, "You have saved our lives;
may it please my lord, we will be slaves to Pharaoh."
26So Joseph made it a statute concerning the land of
Egypt, and it stands to this day, that Pharaoh should
have the fifth; the land of the priests alone did not
become Pharaoh's.

### The Last Days of Jacob

27 Thus Israel dwelt in the land of Egypt, in the
land of Go'shen; and they gained possessions in it,
and were fruitful and multiplied exceedingly. 28And
Jacob lived in the land of Egypt seventeen years; so
the days of Jacob, the years of his life, were a hundred and forty-seven years.

29 And when the time drew near that Israel
must die, he called his son Joseph and said to him,
"If now I have found favor in your sight, put your
hand under my thigh, and promise to deal loyally
and truly with me. Do not bury me in Egypt, 30but
let me lie with my fathers; carry me out of Egypt
and bury me in their burying place." He answered,
"I will do as you have said." 31And he said, "Swear to
me"; and he swore to him. Then Israel bowed himself
upon the head of his bed.

### Jacob Blesses Joseph and His Sons

48 After this Joseph was told, "Behold, your
father is ill"; so he took with him his two sons,
Manas'seh and E'phraim. 2And it was told to Jacob,
"Your son Joseph has come to you"; then Israel summoned his strength, and sat up in bed. 3And Jacob
said to Joseph, "God Almighty[u] appeared to me at
Luz in the land of Canaan and blessed me, 4and said
to me, 'Behold, I will make you fruitful, and multiply
you, and I will make of you a company of peoples,
and will give this land to your descendants after
you for an everlasting possession.' 5And now your
two sons, who were born to you in the land of Egypt
before I came to you in Egypt, are mine; E'phraim
and Manas'seh shall be mine, as Reuben and Simeon
are. 6And the offspring born to you after them shall

---

sell their livestock, their lands, and even their lives over to Pharaoh. Only Joseph is able to steer them through this crisis and is eventually hailed as a savior (47:25). The impression in 47:27 is that Israel continues to flourish in Goshen even while its host country struggles to survive.

**47:17 flocks ... herds ... donkeys:** That the Egyptians refuse to eat their livestock, even in times of hunger and desperation, shows how firmly they believed them to be sacred representations of the gods of Egypt. See note on 46:34.

**47:27 Israel:** The first time in Scripture where the new name given to Jacob becomes the national name borne by the covenant family descended from him. For its meaning, see word study: *Israel* at 32:28. **fruitful and multiplied:** In fulfillment of the promises God made to Abraham (17:2, 6), Isaac (26:4), and Jacob (28:14; 48:4). Israel continues to thrive and grow in Egypt up to the time of Moses (Ex 1:7).

**47:29 hand under my thigh:** A symbolic oath gesture. See note on 24:2.

**47:31 bed:** The Hebrew term can also be vocalized to mean "staff", which is the reading of the Greek LXX and Heb 11:21.

**48:1–22** The blind and bedridden Jacob adopts his grandsons, Manasseh and Ephraim. The boys are thus raised to an equal standing with the sons of Jacob and made founding fathers of two of the Israelite tribes. Despite being the youngest of all, Ephraim receives the first-born blessing (48:14) that was withheld from Reuben (49:3–4) and given to Joseph and his sons (1 Chron 5:1; Jer 31:9). See topical essay: *Blessings and Birthrights* at Gen 48.

**48:3 Luz:** Also known as "Bethel" (28:19).

**48:5 Reuben and Simeon:** The first two sons born to Jacob (29:32–33). Both are disqualified from receiving the blessing of the first-born, Reuben because he defiled his father's bed (35:22), and Simeon because of his violence (34:25; 49:5–7). Manasseh and Ephraim, the first two sons born to Joseph, take their uncles' places of honor in Jacob's family.

---

[t] Sam Gk Compare Vg: Heb *he removed them to the cities.*

[u] Heb *El Shaddai.*

be yours; they shall be called by the name of their
brothers in their inheritance. 7 For when I came
from Paddan, Rachel to my sorrow died in the land
of Canaan on the way, when there was still some
distance to go to Eph′rath; and I buried her there on
the way to Ephrath (that is, Bethlehem)."

8 When Israel saw Joseph's sons, he said, "Who
are these?" 9 Joseph said to his father, "They are my
sons, whom God has given me here." And he said,
"Bring them to me, I pray you, that I may bless
them." 10 Now the eyes of Israel were dim with age, so
that he could not see. So Joseph brought them near
him; and he kissed them and embraced them. 11 And
Israel said to Joseph, "I had not thought to see your
face; and behold, God has let me see your children
also." 12 Then Joseph removed them from his knees,
and he bowed himself with his face to the earth.
13 And Joseph took them both, E′phraim in his right
hand toward Israel's left hand, and Manas′seh in his
left hand toward Israel's right hand, and brought
them near him. 14 And Israel stretched out his right
hand and laid it upon the head of E′phraim, who
was the younger, and his left hand upon the head of
Manas′seh, crossing his hands, for Manasseh was
the first-born. 15 And he blessed Joseph, and said,

"The God before whom my fathers Abraham
and Isaac walked,
the God who has led me all my life long to this day,
16 the angel who has redeemed me from all evil, bless
the lads;
and in them let my name be perpetuated, and the
name of my fathers Abraham and Isaac;
and let them grow into a multitude in the midst
of the earth."

17 When Joseph saw that his father laid his right
hand upon the head of E′phraim, it displeased him;
and he took his father's hand, to remove it from
Ephraim's head to Manas′seh's head. 18 And Joseph
said to his father, "Not so, my father; for this one is
the first-born; put your right hand upon his head."
19 But his father refused, and said, "I know, my son,
I know; he also shall become a people, and he also

---

**48:9 God has given me:** Recognition that God is the Giver of children is a recurrent theme in Genesis (4:1; 21:1–2; 29:31; 30:22–24; 33:5).

**48:10 eyes ... dim:** Recalling 27:1, the narrator creates the impression that Jacob is about to make the same mistake as his blind father, Isaac, who gave the first-born blessing to his younger son, Jacob, instead of his older son, Esau. Jacob does precisely this, only his actions are deliberate (48:14), not misguided by an elaborate deception (27:1–35).

**48:12 his knees:** Sitting the boys on his lap signifies a legal claim of adoption. See note on 30:3.

**48:14 right hand:** The channel of the first-born blessing.

### Blessings and Birthrights

Genesis gives considerable attention to families and family life. Time and again the storyline twists and turns around the action of fathers and mothers, husbands and wives, uncles and nephews, brothers and sisters. This is not extraordinary in itself, but a distinct pattern emerges in Genesis that, for the most part, runs counter to the social and domestic customs of the biblical world. Several times we read in Genesis that God bypasses a first-born son and blesses one of his younger siblings instead. This was highly irregular in ancient tribal societies, where first-born sons were entitled by their position in the birth order to numerous family privileges not shared by their other siblings. The first-born, for example, was destined to receive a special blessing from his father and to inherit the largest share of his father's estate. He was seen as a father figure to his brothers because he stood in line to be the next leader, protector, and teacher of the family. First-born sons in the patriarchal age also succeeded their fathers in assuming priestly responsibilities in family life. In all essential respects, the eldest son who became the patriarch was the social and spiritual mainstay of the kinship group gathered around him.

Only three first-born sons in Genesis show themselves worthy of such blessings: Noah (Gen 5:28–30; 6:9), Shem (Gen 6:10; 9:26), and Abraham (11:27; 12:1–3). Every other identifiable first-born is passed over and loses his preeminent position to a younger brother. Often the eldest sons in Genesis are prideful and unworthy of the honors that await them; in effect, they disqualify themselves from their natural birthright. Other times the question of guilt or culpability goes unmentioned, and God simply elects the younger son over the older to carry his plans forward. Whatever the case, God's preference for the younger and weaker brother over the older and stronger is pronounced and forms a significant subplot in the book. Six times this pattern repeats itself in Genesis.

1. Abel is favored over Cain, the first-born of Adam (Gen 4:1–7).
2. Isaac is favored over Ishmael, the first-born of Abraham (Gen 17:18–21, 21:8–14).
3. Jacob is favored over Esau, the first-born of Isaac (Gen 25:19–34; 27:1–45).
4. Perez is favored over Zerah, the first-born of Judah by Tamar (Gen 38:24–30).
5. Joseph is favored over Reuben, the first-born of Jacob (Gen 35:22; 1 Chron 5:1).
6. Ephraim is favored over Manasseh, the first-born of Joseph (Gen 48:1–20). «

shall be great; nevertheless his younger brother shall be greater than he, and his descendants shall become a multitude of nations." [20]So he blessed them that day, saying,

"By you Israel will pronounce blessings, saying,
'God make you as E'phraim and as Manas'seh'";
and thus he put Ephraim before Manasseh. [21]Then Israel said to Joseph, "Behold, I am about to die, but God will be with you, and will bring you again to the land of your fathers. [22]Moreover I have given to you rather than to your brothers one mountain slope[v] which I took from the hand of the Am'orites with my sword and with my bow."

### Jacob's Last Words to His Sons

49 Then Jacob called his sons, and said, "Gather yourselves together, that I may tell you what shall befall you in days to come.

[2]Assemble and hear, O sons of Jacob,
and hearken to Israel your father.

[3]Reuben, you are my first-born,
my might, and the first fruits of my strength,
pre-eminent in pride and pre-eminent in power.
[4]Unstable as water, you shall not have pre-eminence
because you went up to your father's bed;
then you defiled it—you[w] went up to my couch!

[5]Simeon and Levi are brothers;
weapons of violence are their swords.
[6]O my soul, come not into their council;
O my spirit,[x] be not joined to their company;
for in their anger they slay men,
and in their wantonness they hamstring oxen.

[7]Cursed be their anger, for it is fierce;
and their wrath, for it is cruel!
I will divide them in Jacob
and scatter them in Israel.

[8]Judah, your brothers shall praise you;
your hand shall be on the neck of your enemies;
your father's sons shall bow down before you.
[9]Judah is a lion's whelp;
from the prey, my son, you have gone up.
He stooped down, he lurked as a lion,
and as a lioness; who dares rouse him up?
[10]The scepter shall not depart from Judah,
nor the ruler's staff from between his feet,
until he comes to whom it belongs;[y]
and to him shall be the obedience of the peoples.
[11]Binding his foal to the vine
and his donkey's colt to the choice vine,
he washes his garments in wine
and his vesture in the blood of grapes;
[12]his eyes shall be red with wine,
and his teeth white with milk.

**49:9, 10:** Num 24:9; Rev 5:5.

**48:22 mountain slope:** The Hebrew is *shekem*, which is identical in form to the city name, "Shechem" (33:18). There is probably an intended wordplay, since Shechem stands at the foot of Mt. Gerizim, near the border that will separate the tribal lands of Ephraim and Manasseh (Josh 17:7–8). This is also the place where Joseph will be buried (Josh 24:32).

**49:1–27** The twelve sons of Jacob gather around his deathbed to receive his blessing. The benedictions, uttered in poetic verse, are prophetic oracles about the future of the tribes of Israel. Allusions are made to the occupation of Canaan under Joshua and the Judges, the rise of the Israelite monarchy under David and his successors, and the dawning of the messianic age. The names of the sons are grouped according to their respective mothers: Jacob blesses first the sons of Leah (Reuben, Simeon, Levi, Judah, Zebulun, Issachar; 49:3–15), then the sons of his concubines (Dan, Gad, Asher, Naphtali; 49:16–21), and then the sons of Rachel (Joseph, Benjamin; 49:22–27). Judah and Joseph, who share the spotlight in the final portion of Genesis (chaps. 37–48), are given blessings conspicuously more exalted than the others (49:8–12, 22–26). For similar blessings by the elderly Moses, see Deut 33:1–29.

**49:1 days to come:** Renders a Hebrew expression that appears in other prophetic poems about Israel's future (Num 24:14; Deut 31:29; Is 2:2; Hos 3:5).

**49:3–4** Jacob's oldest son, **Reuben**, is rebuked for his pride and sexual aggression, having disgraced his father by sleeping with his concubine, Bilhah (35:22). This made him unfit to receive the honored blessing of the first-born (1 Chron 5:1).

**49:5–7** Jacob curses the fury of **Simeon** and **Levi**, who conspired to slaughter the defenseless city of Shechem, much to their father's irritation (34:25–30). The oracle foresees how the Simeonites will eventually divide and dissolve into various cities in the territory of Judah (Josh 19:1–9) and the Levites will disperse throughout Canaan to dwell in 48 separate cities (Josh 21:1–42).

**49:8–12** The tribe of **Judah** is destined to be the royal tribe in Israel. He is depicted both as a lion, sated with prey, and as a king, ruling over other nations with scepter in hand. Allusions to this blessing appear elsewhere in the OT in Num 24:9 ("lion"), Num 24:17 ("scepter"), and Ezek 21:27 ("until he comes").

**49:8 bow down:** Recalls how Joseph dreamed of his brothers bowing before him in homage (37:7, 9; 42:6). Here it indicates that all the tribes of Israel will acknowledge the kingship of Judah (cf. 2 Sam 5:1–3).

**49:10 to whom it belongs:** An international ruler is to come from the line of Judah. The oracle is preliminarily fulfilled in David and Solomon, both from the tribe of Judah, when they rule as kings over Israel and neighboring nations (2 Sam 8:1–14; 1 Kings 4:20–21). • Its ultimate fulfillment comes with the heavenly enthronement of Jesus Christ, who is both the Lord of all nations and the Lion of the tribe of Judah (Rev 5:5).

**49:11 blood of grapes:** A poetic description of wine or grape juice (Deut 32:14). The idea is that wine will be so abundant in the messianic age that people will use it for such menial tasks as washing clothes (Joel 3:18; Amos 9:13). • *Allegorically*, the wine stains point to the bloodstains of the Messiah, whose death cleansed the garment of the world from sin (St. Justin Martyr, *First Apology* 32).

**49:13** The tribe of **Zebulun** will prosper as a maritime people in northwest Canaan.

[v] Heb *shekem*, shoulder.
[w] Gk Syr Tg: Heb *he*.
[x] Or *glory*.
[y] Syr Compare Tg: Heb *until Shiloh comes* or *until he comes to Shiloh*.

13 Zeb'ulun shall dwell at the shore of the sea;
he shall become a haven for ships,
and his border shall be at Si'don.

14 Is'sachar is a strong donkey,
crouching between the sheepfolds;
15 he saw that a resting place was good,
and that the land was pleasant;
so he bowed his shoulder to bear,
and became a slave at forced labor.

16 Dan shall judge his people
as one of the tribes of Israel.
17 Dan shall be a serpent in the way,
a viper by the path,
that bites the horse's heels
so that his rider falls backward.
18 I wait for your salvation, O LORD.
19 Raiders[z] shall raid Gad,
but he shall raid at their heels.

20 Asher's food shall be rich,
and he shall yield royal dainties.

21 Naph'tali is a deer let loose,
that bears comely fawns.[a]

22 Joseph is a fruitful bough,
a fruitful bough by a spring;
his branches run over the wall.
23 The archers fiercely attacked him,
shot at him, and harassed him sorely;
24 yet his bow remained unmoved,
his arms[b] were made agile
by the hands of the Mighty One of Jacob
(by the name of the Shepherd, the Rock of Israel),
25 by the God of your father who will help you,
by God Almighty[u] who will bless you
with blessings of heaven above,
blessings of the deep that lies beneath,
blessings of the breasts and of the womb.
26 The blessings of your father
are mighty beyond the blessings of the eternal mountains,[c]
the bounties of the everlasting hills;
may they be on the head of Joseph,
and on the brow of him who was separate from his brothers.

27 Benjamin is a ravenous wolf,
in the morning devouring the prey,
and at evening dividing the spoil."

### Jacob's Death and Burial

28 All these are the twelve tribes of Israel;
and this is what their father said to them as he
blessed them, blessing each with the blessing suitable to him. 29 Then he charged them, and said
to them, "I am to be gathered to my people; bury
me with my fathers in the cave that is in the field
of E'phron the Hittite, 30 in the cave that is in the
field at Mach-pe'lah, to the east of Mamre, in
the land of Canaan, which Abraham bought with
the field from E'phron the Hittite to possess as a
burying place. 31 There they buried Abraham and
Sarah his wife; there they buried Isaac and Rebekah
his wife; and there I buried Leah— 32 the field and
the cave that is in it were purchased from the Hittites." 33 When Jacob finished charging his sons, he
drew up his feet into the bed, and breathed his last,
and was gathered to his people.

50 Then Joseph fell on his father's face, and
wept over him, and kissed him. 2 And Joseph
commanded his servants the physicians to embalm
his father. So the physicians embalmed Israel; 3 forty
days were required for it, for so many are required
for embalming. And the Egyptians wept for him
seventy days.

4 And when the days of weeping for him were
past, Joseph spoke to the household of Pharaoh, saying, "If now I have found favor in your eyes, speak,

---

**49:14–15** The tribe of **Issachar** will bow to the yoke of Canaanite slavery just to enjoy the fertile plain assigned to it in central Palestine.

**49:16–18** The tribe of **Dan**, though small, will take down larger enemies like a viper topples an unsuspecting horseman.

**49:19** The tribe of **Gad** will be forced to retaliate against desert marauders who invade and plunder his settlements east of the Jordan.

**49:20** The tribe of **Asher** will enjoy an abundance of choice foods.

**49:21** The tribe of **Naphtali** will be as fruitful and graceful as a mother deer.

**49:22–26** The tribe of **Joseph** will be exceedingly blessed, as suggested by the sixfold repetition of the Hebrew root for "bless" in the final stanzas. The similar stress on Joseph's fruitfulness in the opening stanza is an allusion to his son, Ephraim, whose name resembles the statement "God has made me fruitful" (cf. 41:52).

**49:24 the Shepherd ... the Rock:** Two titles for Yahweh, the first celebrating his guidance of Israel (Ps 23:1; Ezek 34:15) and the second his protection of Israel (Deut 32:4; Ps 18:31).

**49:27** The tribe of **Benjamin** will devour his enemies like a wolf that feasts upon its prey.

**49:28 twelve tribes of Israel:** Descendants of the sons of Jacob, renamed Israel. Note that the blessing bestowed upon Joseph in 49:22–26 was divided between Ephraim and Manasseh, who were adopted by Jacob in 48:1–22. This explains why Israel is hereafter a family of 13 tribes.

**49:29 in the cave:** Purchased by Abraham as a tomb for Sarah in 23:1–20. It became the burial place of all the Patriarchs and their first wives (49:31; 50:13).

**49:33 gathered to his people:** Means that Jacob entered the realm of the dead to rest with his deceased ancestors (25:8; 35:29).

**50:2 embalm:** The Egyptian art of mummification, a long and expensive process that involved dehydrating the body, smearing it with spices and preservative ointments, and wrapping it tightly with strips of linen cloth. Joseph will receive this same honor after his death (50:26).

---

[z] Heb *gedud*, a raiding troop.
[a] Or *who gives beautiful words*.
[b] Heb *the arms of his hands*.
[u] Heb *El Shaddai*.
[c] Compare Gk: Heb *of my progenitors to*.

I beg you, in the ears of Pharaoh, saying, 5My father
made me swear, saying, 'I am about to die: in my tomb
which I hewed out for myself in the land of Canaan,
there shall you bury me.' Now therefore let me go up,
I beg you, and bury my father; then I will return."
6And Pharaoh answered, "Go up, and bury your
father, as he made you swear." 7So Joseph went up
to bury his father; and with him went up all the servants of Pharaoh, the elders of his household, and all
the elders of the land of Egypt, 8as well as all
the household of Joseph, his brothers, and his father's
household; only their children, their flocks, and their
herds were left in the land of Go'shen. 9And there
went up with him both chariots and horsemen; it
was a very great company. 10When they came to the
threshing floor of Atad, which is beyond the Jordan,
they lamented there with a very great and sorrowful
lamentation; and he made a mourning for his father
seven days. 11When the inhabitants of the land, the
Canaanites, saw the mourning on the threshing floor
of Atad, they said, "This is a grievous mourning
to the Egyptians." Therefore the place was named
A'bel-miz'raim;[d] it is beyond the Jordan. 12Thus his
sons did for him as he had commanded them; 13for
his sons carried him to the land of Canaan, and buried him in the cave of the field at Mach-pe'lah, to
the east of Mamre, which Abraham bought with the
field from E'phron the Hittite, to possess as a burying place. 14After he had buried his father, Joseph
returned to Egypt with his brothers and all who had
gone up with him to bury his father.

### Joseph Forgives His Brothers

15 When Joseph's brothers saw that their father
was dead, they said, "It may be that Joseph will
hate us and pay us back for all the evil which we
did to him." 16So they sent a message to Joseph, saying, "Your father gave this command before he died,
17'Say to Joseph, Forgive, I beg you, the transgression of your brothers and their sin, because they did
evil to you.' And now, we pray you, forgive the transgression of the servants of the God of your father."
Joseph wept when they spoke to him. 18His brothers also came and fell down before him, and said,
"Behold, we are your servants." 19But Joseph said to
them, "Fear not, for am I in the place of God? 20As
for you, you meant evil against me; but God meant
it for good, to bring it about that many people should
be kept alive, as they are today. 21So do not fear; I
will provide for you and your little ones." Thus he
reassured them and comforted them.

### Joseph's Last Days and Death

22 So Joseph dwelt in Egypt, he and his father's
house; and Joseph lived a hundred and ten years.
23And Joseph saw E'phraim's children of the third
generation; the children also of Ma'chir the son of
Manas'seh were born upon Joseph's knees. 24And
Joseph said to his brothers, "I am about to die; but
God will visit you, and bring you up out of this land
to the land which he swore to Abraham, to Isaac,
and to Jacob." 25Then Joseph took an oath of the

**50:13:** Acts 7:16.

**50:7–9** Pharaoh grants Joseph and his grieving family a military escort to transport the body of Jacob back to Canaan. All this was to fulfill the charge that Jacob laid upon his sons to bury him in the tomb of the Patriarchs (49:29–32).

**50:10 threshing floor:** A stone or earthen platform, usually on a windy elevation, where grain was sifted in preparation for storage. **beyond the Jordan:** I.e., east of the Jordan.

**50:11 Abel-mizraim:** Involves a wordplay on the first element (*'abel*), which resembles the Hebrew word for "mourning" (*'ebel*).

**50:13 Mach-pelah:** The field near Hebron where the Patriarchs (Abraham, Isaac, and now Jacob) are buried with their wives (Sarah, Rebekah, and Leah). For the purchase of the site, see 23:1–20.

[d] That is *meadow* (or *mourning*) *of Egypt*.

**50:18 fell down before him:** A final realization of Joseph's dreams (37:7, 9). For earlier fulfillments, see 42:6 and 43:26.

**50:19 the place of God?:** A rhetorical question also uttered by Jacob in 30:2.

**50:20 God meant it for good:** A theological interpretation of the entire Joseph story. See note on 45:5.

**50:23 upon Joseph's knees:** Suggests that Joseph adopts his great grandchildren, just as Jacob adopted his grandchildren in 48:1–12. See note on 30:3.

**50:24 God will visit you:** Looks ahead to the Exodus event, when Yahweh will hear the groaning of Israel in Egypt and come to visit the nation with salvation (Ex 4:31).

**50:25 carry up my bones:** Fulfilled when Moses carts the bones of Joseph out of Egypt (Ex 13:19) and the next generation of Israelites bury them at Shechem in central Canaan (Josh 24:32).

**50:26 a hundred and ten:** Egyptian records list 110 years as the ideal life-span.

sons of Israel, saying, "God will visit you, and you
shall carry up my bones from here." 26 So Joseph
died, being a hundred and ten years old; and they
embalmed him, and he was put in a coffin in Egypt.

# STUDY QUESTIONS

## Genesis

### Chapter 1

*For understanding*

1. **1:1—2:4.** The note lists eight teachings of the first creation account. What are they? According to the note, what is the importance of the number seven?
2. **1:2.** Why is the RSV translation of "the Spirit of God" preferable to the translation "a wind from God" or "a mighty wind" in this verse?
3. **1:26.** If the plural "Let *us*" in God's speech does not imply a belief in multiple gods, how should it be read?
4. **Word Study: Image and likeness (1:26).** What do the Hebrew words for "image" and "likeness" often denote? To what concepts does Genesis associate this word pair? How does Genesis apply the prerogative of sonship in a manner different from that of the political ideologies of the ancient Near East?

*For application*

1. **1: 6–19.** Have modern discoveries of the size and nature of the universe challenged your view of God? How have you dealt with this challenge?
2. **1:26.** What does it mean to you that you are a created being? How does being created in the image and likeness of God affect your image of yourself?
3. **1:27.** How do you regard your own sexuality in view of that "image and likeness"?
4. **1:28.** How have your experiences of family shaped your attitudes toward procreation? How do those attitudes compare with the scriptural view of procreation as a blessing?

### Chapter 2

*For understanding*

1. **2:2.** For man, what does it mean to bear the image of God? Of what is the Sabbath the sign in the Old Testament? The New Testament?
2. **2:7.** What Hebrew wordplay is used to describe the creation of man? What does dust symbolize? What makes man unique?
3. **2:9.** If the "knowledge of good and evil" is not a moral awareness of right and wrong, what is it? What would Adam later presume to do, then?
4. **2:21–24.** What four characteristics is the marriage covenant designed by God to have? As a permanent union of the spouses, what does the marriage covenant symbolize?

*For application*

1. **2:15.** While there are many benefits for doing work, what personal benefits can work provide? How can physical work make people better as human beings?
2. **2:16–17.** How does setting limits help you discipline children? In your experience either as a child or as a parent, what function has the threat of awful consequences served in discipline? How should a parent train children to recognize the consequences of disobedience?
3. **2:24.** How does the view of marriage as a covenant differ from the view of marriage as a contract? Once a covenant that forms a family begins, when does it end?
4. **2:25.** What is the link between nakedness and shame? Aside from physical nakedness, what other kinds of nakedness might there be? What kinds of shame might be linked to them?

### Chapter 3

*For understanding*

1. **3:1.** Although the Hebrew term *naḥash* often refers to a snake, to what else can it refer? How is the serpent "subtle" or cunning? What does the serpent's question insinuate about God?
2. **3:6.** What makes Adam's capitulation to sin different from Eve's? If Adam's desire was not to "*discern* good from evil", what was it? What weapons did Christ use to conquer the devil?
3. **3:15.** To whom do the phrases "your seed" and "her seed" refer? What does the word "bruise" mean with respect to the deceiver? To the woman's offspring? How does Christian tradition interpret this text?
4. **3:17.** How does the curse of futility and decay affect the earth? How does it affect human toil? How does Jesus reverse this curse, according to St. Cyril of Jerusalem?

*For application*

1. **3:1–3.** What do you think is the most effective way to tell a lie? Why is the serpent's lie so effective with Eve? What mistakes does Eve make when the serpent first addresses her? (Compare with Jas 4:4–8.)
2. **3:7.** Reflect on those times when you did something of which you would rather God not have known. What were the consequences to your relationship with him? Have they been resolved?
3. **3:11–13.** How has playing the "blame game" affected your relationships with others? Why do you think it is so difficult to take responsibility for the harm you have done? What might be the antidote?
4. **3:16b–17a.** Have you experienced areas of tension and mistrust between the sexes? If so, in what were they? How have they affected your attitudes toward the other sex? How can you grow in healthy respect for the other sex?

### Chapter 4

*For understanding*

1. **4:4.** What does an offering of "firstfruits" represent? What appears to be the main difference between Abel's sacrifice to God and Cain's?
2. **4:7.** What does God warn Cain about sin? In addition to negligent worship, to what sins does Cain yield? What does the reality of sin in primeval times presuppose about the natural law?
3. **4:15.** What does the "mark of Cain" signify? What does it seem that Cain fears?
4. **4:17–24.** What good and shameful characteristics are the descendants of Cain described as having? What is the point of presenting Cain's genealogy in this way?

*For application*

1. **4:3–4.** What is the difference between an intimate and a casual relationship with an important person? How appropriate do you think it is for our worship of God to be casual? How might a casual attitude toward worship diminish a proper respect for God?
2. **4:6–7.** How might the danger of falling into sin seem like a wild animal ready to pounce? Look up Mt 5:21–22. Given the example of Cain's sin, what do you think Jesus means about anger and the danger of judgment or even the fire of hell?
3. **4:17–24.** Even though our age is one of great technological and scientific advancement, what dangers do you see in it for our civilization? What needs to happen for us to avoid them?
4. **4:23–24.** When have you felt the desire to get revenge? How did you deal with that desire? Given the Christian vocation, how should one deal with vengeful desires?

### Chapters 5—6:10

*For understanding*

1. **5:1–32.** What are some of the contrasts between Cain's line of descendants and Seth's? Whose line will the flood destroy, and whose will it preserve?
2. **5:5.** What are some of the approaches that have been taken to explain the immensely long life-spans of people before the flood? What are the difficulties with these approaches? What seems to be the best working hypothesis?
3. **6:1–4.** What are two interpretations from Jewish and Christian tradition that explain the meaning of the "sons of God" intermarrying with "the daughters of men"?
4. **6:6.** Why should the expression that "the Lord was sorry" not be taken literally? How does the Bible often describe the thoughts and actions of God, and why? What do these and similar word pictures communicate about God?
5. **6:9—9:19.** To what does the biblical flood story have close literary affinities? What is the theological significance of the story? What are the parallels with the creation story in the first chapter of Genesis? What allegorical significance do the Church Fathers find in the story?

*For application*

1. **5:4–31.** Why do you think young people want to live to be old and old people often want to die? What are your own attitudes about living to an old age? How do these attitudes reflect or contradict the Christian hope of heaven?
2. **5:28–29.** What hopes for their children do parents of newborns often have? How might these hopes be reflected in the names they select? What fears might parents have about their children?
3. **6:1–3.** Read the notes for vv. 1–4 and for v. 2. Why do you think it is morally and spiritually dangerous for committed Christians to marry persons who do not share their faith?
4. **6:5.** According to this verse, from where do evil thoughts come? How does this verse compare with what Jesus says in Mt 15:17–19? What is the antidote?

### Chapters 6:11—8

*For understanding*

1. **6:18.** What does the Hebrew expression concerning God's covenant with Noah imply about it? What does it presuppose?
2. **7:2.** Why are only single pairs of unclean animals brought onto the ark, whereas seven pairs of clean animals are taken aboard? What might the number seven symbolize?
3. **8:6–12.** Why does the raven, when released, return to the ark but not the dove?
4. **8:20—9:17.** As expressed in the sign of the rainbow, what covenant obligation does God take upon himself? Of what is the Noahic covenant a renewal?

*For application*

1. **6:18.** Have you ever sensed that God was preparing you for impending trouble? How did you respond? For example, what preparations did you make or fail to make?
2. **7:11–12.** Have you ever been caught in a flood or other type of natural disaster, or have you known anyone who has had such an experience? How does one cope with the sense of helplessness in such situations? How can faith in God help?
3. **7:21–23.** What is "survivor's guilt"? Why would someone feel guilty for having survived a catastrophe that claimed others? How can such guilt be assuaged?
4. **8:20.** Why do you think Noah took the clean animals and birds for sacrificial offerings instead of releasing them? In what way was such a sacrifice in keeping with Noah's character?

### Chapter 9

*For understanding*

1. **9:6.** Against what is murder a crime? Although the Lord can delegate his judicial authority to individuals or states to avenge wrongful deaths, what policy limits vengeance?

2. **9:22.** For what is the Hebrew idiom "seeing the nakedness of his father" a euphemism? Of what is Ham guilty? Of what does Ham's perversity most likely provide the backstory?
3. **9:24.** What might the detail of Ham being the youngest son suggest about his motive? What are other Old Testament examples of attempts by family members to usurp another's authority?
4. **9:26.** How is the blessing of Shem unique? When does the curse upon Canaan go into effect?

*For application*

1. **9:2–3.** Even though God gives animals and plants to man for food, "[m]an's dominion over inanimate and other living beings granted by the Creator is not absolute" (CCC 2415). What purpose is man's dominion over these creatures intended to serve?
2. **9:9–11.** To whom does God's covenant renewal apply? What does that suggest about what mankind's attitude toward creation should be?
3. **9:23.** What responsibility do we have to the victims of crime? What virtues might goven how we exercise that responsibility?
4. **9:25.** Given the explanation of Ham's crime in the note for v. 22, why does Noah curse Ham's son instead of Ham himself? What often seems to be the fate of the children of criminals, abusers, and alcoholics? Despite that fate, what is God's attitude toward them?

## Chapters 10–11

*For understanding*

1. **10:1–32.** What does the table of nations in this chapter tell us about the national, geographical, and linguistic diversity of the ancient Near East? Geographically, what does the table outline? Why is Palestine situated in the very center of this world map?
2. **10:21.** From whom are the Israelites descended? From where does the name *Hebrew* come?
3. **11:1–9.** What does the Tower of Babel incident explain? What are the mudbrick towers thought to represent?
4. **11:4.** What does the family of man band together to do? Who actually acquires the "name" that the sinners of Babel coveted? What fear motivates the building? What are its ultimate consequences?

*For application*

1. **11:4.** The citizens of Babel wanted to "make a name" for themselves. What has been your driving ambition in life (e.g., fame, wealth, athletic ability)? How well have you succeeded at realizing it? What has been its effect on your spiritual life?
2. **11:6.** What are some technological advances of the last hundred or so years that were considered impossible in prior centuries? What are some of the good and evil uses to which they have been put? How similar do you think the modern scientific mind-set is to that of the citizens of Babel?
3. **11:7–8.** Has a failure to communicate ever caused separation in your family? If so, what have been some of the difficulties in restoring communication?

## Chapter 12

*For understanding*

1. **12:1—50:26.** How are the patriarchal narratives often classified? What considerations favor the historicity of the narratives?
2. **Topical Essay: The Abrahamic Covenant.** What three promises did God make to Abraham? When does each promise become a covenant? How are the promises and covenants realized?
3. **12:7.** How does Abram sanctify the land of Canaan? What are some of the features of patriarchal religion? What religious role did the patriarchs perform in their families?
4. **12:10—13:1.** How does Abram's stay in Egypt foreshadow the story of Exodus?

*For application*

1. **12:1.** Have you ever felt that God was speaking to you personally? Why do you think he would or would not speak to you? How could you discern whether or not he did?
2. **12:4–5.** At what points in your life have you parted from your place of birth, your relatives, and your immediate family? What brought about the separations? What, if any, religious or spiritual consequences resulted from them?
3. **12:13.** Do you think Abram is simply keeping part of the truth hidden, or is he lying outright? What is a lie? Is it ever appropriate to divulge only a part of the truth in order to protect oneself or someone else? (Compare your answers with CCC 2483–84, 2489.)

## Chapters 13–14

*For understanding*

1. **13:2–18.** What is the point of the story of how Lot and Abram go their separate ways?
2. **14:18.** What does the title "Melchizedek" mean? Who do various scholars believe that Melchizedek was? Why did Melchizedek bring out bread and wine on Abram's arrival at Salem? Allegorically, what do the actions of Melchizedek prefigure?
3. **14:20.** What does Abram's tithe to Melchizedek anticipate?

*For application*

1. **13:8–9.** Abram settles a dispute by allowing Lot to choose between alternative solutions. How does Abram's approach demonstrate wisdom? How are disputes like this handled in your family?

2. **13:10–11.** Lot chooses what appears to be the better alternative, though the choice later proves disastrous for him and his family. How do you go about deciding on a course of action that could shape the direction of your life? On what do you base your decisions? How does your relationship with God figure into your decision making?
3. **14:18.** According to the note on this verse, Melchizedek may bring out bread and wine as a thank offering following Abram's victory. Does gratitude figure into your sense of personal accomplishment? How do you concretely express gratitude to God for what you have or have accomplished?
4. **14:20.** Abram gives Melchizedek "a tenth of everything". What do you give to the Lord? What limits do you place on your giving?

## Chapter 15

*For understanding*

1. **15:1–6.** How do these verses mark a critical juncture in Abram's spiritual journey? What opportunity is God giving Abram?
2. **15:6.** In the Genesis narrative, what acts indicate that Abram puts his trust in the Lord? What does the New Testament say that we learn from Abram about faith? What is "righteousness"?
3. **15:10.** What is the significance of cutting the animals in two? Who puts himself under threat of a curse in this ceremony?
4. **15:12–14.** What is implied about Abram's relation to the Promised Land when God tells him that Israel will experience 400 years of oppression before gaining possession of it?

*For application*

1. **15:1–6.** Scripture contains many promises that reveal God's loving care for us, such as salvation, everlasting life, and so on. How might promises like these test your faith? What stands in the way of trusting that God will fulfill them?
2. **15:8.** Abram asks how he can know that he will receive what God has promised. When you pray to obtain something for yourself or a loved one, for what kinds of assurance do you hope? How appropriate do you think it is to ask God for such assurance?
3. **15:12.** Abram experiences the approach of God as dread and great darkness. Have you ever felt the approach or presence of God? What was the experience like?
4. **15:13–16.** Sometimes, God's promises take time and the right circumstances to be realized. How easily do you give up waiting when someone promises you something good but does not say when the promise will be fulfilled?

## Chapter 16

*For understanding*

1. **16:1–6.** What are the consequences of Sarai's fateful decision to give Hagar to the embrace of her husband? What do archaeological finds show about the ancient practice of surrogate motherhood?
2. **16:2.** What were the rights of a man's lawful wife over the child born of a surrogate mother? Why is Abram's "listening" to his wife an ominous note in the narrative?
3. **Word Study: Angel of the Lord (16:7).** How does this figure sometimes appear? With what characteristic is the angel of the Lord endowed, and what are some of his many tasks?
4. **16:12.** Why is Ishmael called "a wild donkey" of a man?

*For application*

1. **16:2.** What are some of the methods available today to help childless couples have children? Of those you can name, which are morally allowable and which are not? (Compare your answers with CCC 2373–79.)
2. **16:4.** Have you ever regarded with contempt someone in your family, your circle of friends, or your work environment? What brought about that attitude? How do you think the Lord regards such contempt?
3. **16:5–6.** In your immediate family, about what do you most frequently argue? What role do you tend to play: the Wronged Victim, the Artful Dodger, the Cool Logician, or something else? How do you feel about yourself during an argument?
4. **16:12.** Do you know anyone with personal characteristics like Ishmael's? How do you relate to this person? How do you think the Lord would have you relate?

## Chapter 17

*For understanding*

1. **17:1–21.** What pattern does the circumcision covenant follow? What features does such a covenant have?
2. **17:4.** Which ancient peoples are descended from Abraham? What does the New Testament reveal about Abraham's destiny?
3. **17:5.** What are the original and the expanded meanings of Abram/Abraham's names? What does a change of name signify?
4. **17:11.** What roles does circumcision play in the Abrahamic covenant? Theologically, toward what does it point? Historically, who has practiced circumcision? In the New Covenant, how does Baptism act as the counterpart of circumcision?
5. **17:15–21.** What is the more precise definition of God's promise to Abraham in 15:18–21?

*For application*

1. **17:5.** What do you think of your given name? If you had the opportunity to change it, what name would you choose? What would be its meaning to you? For example, what might it suggest about your character or how you see your destiny?
2. **17:7.** As a member of the New Covenant, how do you experience your covenant relationship to God? How does your family experience it?

3. **17:10–11.** What is the "mark" of a Christian? What practical difference in your everyday life does it make to you that you are baptized?
4. **17:18–21.** Even though the older Ishmael is circumcised (v. 23), God's covenant blessings come through the younger Isaac's line (v. 21). Where does that leave Ishmael? Considering the whole Abrahamic narrative up to now, what factors might explain God's preference for the unborn Isaac?

## Chapter 18

*For understanding*

1. **18:2–3.** Who were the three men who came to visit Abraham? Why did Abraham worship only one of them?
2. **18:6.** Why did Abraham tell Sarah to prepare three measures of flour? In a moral sense, for what virtues do the three measures stand? What do they contain?
3. **18:14.** For what does this verse prepare? What is its New Testament echo?
4. **18:22–33.** What does this dialogue say about the character of God? How do these themes play out in the next episode?

*For application*

1. **18:1–8.** Have you ever received extravagant hospitality such as Abraham shows to the three men? What was your reaction when it was offered? When an opportunity comes for you to show hospitality to your guests, what do you offer them?
2. **18:11–12.** Have you ever questioned or doubted the Lord's ability to provide for you? What did the eventual outcome do to enhance or damage your trust in God's provision?
3. **18:14.** Many atheists question God's power because of the evil in the world, arguing that an all-powerful God should be able to prevent evil from happening. How would you answer them?
4. **18:20–32.** Have you ever found yourself, in fact or in effect, haggling with God regarding the outcome of a prayer intention? For what were you praying? How was the prayer answered?

## Chapter 19

*For understanding*

1. **19:1.** What might Lot's "sitting at the gate" indicate about him? How does he behave toward the two visitors?
2. **19:5.** What motive does the mob have for surrounding Lot's house? What form of sexual depravity was rampant among the Canaanites? How was it punished in ancient Israel?
3. **19:24–29.** What happens to the cities of the valley? What function does the memory of this catastrophe serve?
4. **19:30–38.** What do these verses recount? What other episode of drunkenness does it recall?

*For application*

1. **19:2.** What are some of the dangers of spending the night on the street, as homeless people often must do? What services for the homeless exist in your area? What service, if any, do you render at these facilities?
2. **19:12–14.** Why do you think people ignore warnings of impending disaster? If God were today to warn of approaching destruction unless people repented, what do you think the response might be? Can you think of any times in history when God provided such warnings?
3. **19:24–25.** When a natural disaster such as a flood, a volcanic eruption, or an earthquake occurs that causes numerous deaths, should the cause be attributed to God? What other causes for human casualties might there be?
4. **19:31–38.** What makes the act of deriding the ancestors of one's enemies so insulting? What function does slander or mockery serve for those who deliver the insult? What might be the Christian response to those who insult one's family?

## Chapter 20

*For understanding*

1. **20:1–18.** What does this episode show about God's promise to Abraham? What happens to Sarah?
2. **20:2.** What does the name Abimelech mean? What function does it serve? Who else encounters someone of this name years later?
3. **20:7.** What does the word "prophet" mean in connection with Abraham?
4. **20:12.** Is Abraham telling the truth about Sarah being his sister? When did prohibitions against marriages to close relatives arise?

*For application*

1. **20:3–7.** Have you ever had a dream that was so vivid or memorable that you felt the need to take it seriously? What sort of difference (e.g., moral or religious) did it make? In what way might it have been a grace from God?
2. **20:11.** Abraham admits to misrepresenting himself out of fear of an unfamiliar and possibly hostile community. When you enter a similar sort of community, how do you tend to protect yourself? Has this self-protection been justified or not?
3. **20:14–16.** Abimelech makes extravagant gestures to prove his good intentions and right the situation. When you are shown to be in the wrong, how do you know when a simple apology is sufficient and when to go beyond that to rectify things?

## Chapter 21

*For understanding*

1. **21:3.** What does the name Isaac mean? What does it recall?
2. **21:9.** What negative sense does the Hebrew word for "playing" have in this verse? What is the teenager Ishmael doing? How will Paul later interpret this incident?

3. **21:22–34.** What pattern does Abraham's covenant with Abimelech follow? What do both parties do during the ratification ceremony?
4. **21:31.** How are the two translations of the name Beer-sheba related? In this episode, how does Abraham enact his oath?

*For application*

1. **21:6–7.** Sarah responds to the birth of Isaac with a certain glee, saying that God has provided laughter for her. What part does laughter or mirth play in your relationship with God? How enjoyable is it to you? What do you think of God's "sense of humor" in happy coincidences?
2. **21:9–10.** What do you think of Sarah's sense of humor in this passage? If you are a parent or a childcare worker, how do you respond when you judge the conduct of your children's friends to be inappropriate?
3. **21:17.** An angel asks the outcast Hagar what troubles her and encourages her not to be afraid. What is it that most troubles you or makes you afraid? On a spiritual level, how do you deal with fear?

### Chapter 22

*For understanding*

1. **22:2.** What does the Hebrew version of this text convey about Isaac? How does the Greek Old Testament translate "only son"? How is Isaac a type of Christ? What is later located on Mt. Moriah?
2. **22:16–18.** According to Paul's discussion in Gal 3, what does the divine oath of this chapter indicate that God will do? What does Paul say the binding of Isaac prefigures?
3. **Word Study: Descendants (22:18).** To what can the Hebrew word for "seed" refer? What are its individual and collective meanings? How does Paul view Isaac (individual meaning) and Israel (collective meaning)?
4. **Topical Essay: The Sacrifice of Isaac.** How do some commentators interpret the significance of this episode? In terms of its spiritual significance, what part might it play in Abraham's developing relationship with the Lord? What is the importance of the lesson Abraham learns? In terms of the episode's theological significance, how does Judaism understand the significance of the binding of Isaac? How does Christian theology view the episode from prophetic and typological perspectives?

*For application*

1. **22:1.** What is a "test" from God? Do you think he has ever tested you? What was the outcome?
2. **22:2.** Many people avoid or delay surrendering everything to the Lord, fearing that he will take away from them something or someone they treasure. What do you fear the Lord will take away from you?
3. **22:16–18.** How might you be withholding from the Lord something of yourself? What would be the benefit of giving it over to him?
4. **22:18.** What does "obedience" mean to you? Does obedience to God's voice result in liberation or enslavement?

### Chapters 23–24

*For understanding*

1. **23:1–20.** What does this chapter stress about Abraham's negotiation for a burial plot for Sarah? What does the purchase of the site anticipate?
2. **23:9.** Who will be buried in the cave at Mach-pelah? Although the text says the site is in Hebron, where does Samaritan tradition locate it?
3. **24:2.** What do loins or thighs represent in Genesis? What kind of gesture is putting the hand under the thigh? In the context of this verse, what does the oath require of the servant?
4. **24:10.** Why does the servant take ten camels on his journey? What do we know about the domestication of camels?
5. **24:65.** What is the importance of the servant's reply, "It is my master", to Rebekah's question? Why does Rebekah cover herself upon hearing the answer?

*For application*

1. **24:3–4.** Because of God's call to him, Abraham does not want a Canaanite woman as a wife for his son. What relationships, personal or cultural, come along with the marriage partner one selects? What spiritual hindrances might some of those relationships bring into the marriage?
2. **24:6–8.** How does the locale in which you live affect your relationship with the Lord?
3. **24:12–14.** The servant prays for a sign to confirm his selection of a wife for Isaac. What standards do people of your acquaintance use in their selection of a marriage partner? How might one judge whether the selection is likely to be spiritually beneficial or not?
4. **24:67.** Isaac learns to love Rebekah *after* he marries her. Is this the order promoted by our modern culture? How might learning to love one's spouse after the wedding be good for the marriage?

### Chapter 25

*For understanding*

1. **25:19—36:43.** Although less attention is paid to Isaac than to Jacob in these chapters, why is Isaac an important link in the genealogical chain of Genesis?
2. **25:21.** In what way is Isaac like his father Abraham? Why?
3. **25:22.** For what are the unborn twins in Rebekah's womb already struggling? What does the struggle anticipate, both in this chapter and beyond the horizon of Genesis? What does Paul see in these events?
4. **25:26.** How does Jacob's name foreshadow his future?

*For application*

1. **25:21.** Isaac prays for his wife Rebekah. How often do you pray for members of your family? In general, for what do you pray? How have these prayers been answered?

2. **25:27–28.** Consciously or not, parents may prefer the personal or temperamental traits of one child over those of another. What dangers do such preferences pose for relationships within the family? What can parents do to minimize "favorite child" preferences?
3. **25:29–34.** In this episode, the rivalry between siblings in a seemingly trivial matter reveals traits that will mature later on. What is your experience of youthful contests among siblings? Have these contests revealed character traits that became settled as the children matured?

### Chapters 26–27

*For understanding*

1. **26:5.** What were the covenant benefits promised to Abraham, and why were they given? What does God mean by "my charge, my commandments, my statutes"?
2. **27:1–46.** In this chapter, what does Jacob do, and what is Rebekah's role? What is the attitude of the Genesis account toward Esau? What is the story intended to illustrate?
3. **27:13.** What price does Rebekah pay for her role in this story?
4. **27:29.** What does Isaac's blessing envision? When is the prophecy fulfilled?

*For application*

1. **26:14.** What is envy? Why is it described in the Catechism as one of the "capital sins" (CCC 2538–40)? How has envy affected your own life?
2. **26:17–22.** What do you think of Isaac's way of handling this situation? How would you deal with persons who took credit for—or even took over—your efforts? Which approach, yours or Isaac's, seems better able to achieve the Lord's designs for your life?
3. **27:5–19.** Who do you think bears the greater guilt for the deception of Isaac: Rebekah, who instigates the deception, or Isaac, who cooperates in it? What moral effect does deceiving others have on the deceiver?
4. **27:33–41.** Disputes over an inheritance often leave permanent scars on family relationships. How has your family handled distribution of the estate of a family member who has died? What might be a Christian way of handling disputes over such things?

### Chapter 28

*For understanding*

1. **28:12.** What kind of ladder does the Hebrew of this verse envision? Of what does the dream convince Jacob? How is Jacob's ladder a prophetic image of Christ?
2. **28:18.** Why does Jacob make a pillar of his stone headrest? What did Moses later instruct Israel to do with certain pillars?
3. **28:21.** Why is Jacob's vow to God conditional? What is Jacob thus doing with the Lord?

*For application*

1. **28:1–2.** Parents today seldom determine whom their children will marry—or even whether they will. Since a child's choice of a partner affects the entire family, do you think parents should have some say in the matter? What should the parents do if they disapprove of the child's choice, especially if they disapprove on religious or moral grounds?
2. **28:3–4.** In some families, the parents occasionally bless their children, e.g., before sending them out of the house. Are you familiar with this practice? What benefits do you see in it for both the parents and the children?
3. **28:16–17.** Not uncommonly, people have an almost physical sense of the presence of God in certain locations, such as in a particular church or in a forest. How and where have you experienced God's presence? What has been the religious or moral effect on you?
4. **28:20–22.** What is a *vow*? (Compare your answer with CCC 2102.) When might it be inappropriate for a vow to be conditional, as Jacob's was? How important is it to keep a vow made privately?

### Chapter 29

*For understanding*

1. **29:1–30.** What does divine Providence arrange for Jacob in the first of these two episodes? What happens to him in the second?
2. **29:16.** What do the names Leah and Rachel mean in Hebrew? What does their destiny of being married to the same man force the sisters to do?
3. **29:25.** How could Jacob have been deceived as to the identity of his bride? How is his blindness a just penalty for Jacob? What does Laban's trickery regarding the first-born sister recall about Jacob's own trickery?
4. **29:31.** What does it mean that Leah was "hated"? What might Leah's pregnancy indicate about Jacob's preferential love for Rachel?

*For application*

1. **29:10–12.** Family stories of how spouses met can sometimes hold lessons about God's provision for the family. What stories circulate in your family, and what can you learn from them about God providence?
2. **29:16–17.** Although physical good looks may initially attract, what characteristics should ultimately determine one's choice of a marriage partner? What qualities would you look for, and why?
3. **29:23–30.** Despite Laban's deception, Jacob fulfills his end of the service agreement. What obligation would you feel to complete an agreement if the other party had taken advantage of you on a technicality?
4. **29:31.** What pressures might the inability to conceive have on a marriage? What are some Christian ways of reducing these pressures or resolving these difficulties?

### Chapter 30

*For understanding*

1. **29:32—30:24.** What kind of wordplay do the names of Jacob's sons involve? What do their various names mean? When and where was Benjamin born?
2. **30:3.** To what ancient rite does the expression "bear [a child] upon my knees" refer?
3. **30:14.** What is the significance of mandrakes? What is the irony in this passage?
4. **30:27.** What is divination? What is Scripture's judgment about it?
5. **30:37–43.** What was the belief of ancient herdsmen about visual stimuli in the breeding of animals? How does Jacob act on this belief?

*For application*

1. **30:1–24.** In the context of their marriage to Jacob, why are Leah and Rachel locked in such a bitter contest to have children? Might such a rivalry between sisters occur even today? From which of the seven capital sins might such a rivalry stem?
2. **30:1–24.** What do you think of Jacob's role in this contest? How might his acquiescence contribute to the sisters' rivalry? How might a modern husband support his wife when she is distraught over infertility?
3. **30:31–36.** How does Laban try to ensure that he gets the better of Jacob in this agreement? If you were an employer, how would you determine an employee's wage so that you could still make a profit without cheating the employee?
4. **30:37–43.** Jacob retaliates by using his knowledge of animal husbandry to get himself the wage he was promised while minimizing the increase of Laban's wealth. How justified is Jacob in using this stratagem? Why is it inappropriate to cheat someone who has cheated you?

### Chapter 31

*For understanding*

1. **31:1–16.** What does the preceding narrative in chap. 30 highlight? Why is the story retold in the current chapter?
2. **31:39.** In the ancient Near East, what obligations did a shepherd have to his employer if an animal was stolen or mauled by wild beasts? How did Jacob go beyond the call of duty?
3. **31:43–55.** What do Jacob and Laban do to seal their covenant? What do they pledge? Why were covenants of this type made?
4. **31:47.** Why do Laban and Jacob call the same location by different names? What does the bilingual tradition mirror?

*For application*

1. **31:14–16**. Childhood grievances against parents often carry over into adulthood. Have you held grievances against your parents? What Christian virtues can help minimize or eliminate such grievances?
2. **31:19.** Not every child who leaves home steals from his parents, but everyone does take something of value when he leaves. Assuming you have left your parental home, what have you taken with you? Of what value is it to you? to your parents?
3. **31:20.** Review Jacob's motives in vv. 1–20 for fleeing Laban's service. What are they? As you reflect on your departure from your parental home, what were your motives? How mixed were they? Which were real, and which may have been rationalizations?
4. **31:36.** Have you ever been unjustly accused? How did you respond to the accusation? Given the example of Jesus at his various trials, how should you have responded?

### Chapter 32

*For understanding*

1. **32:4.** What do the titles that Jacob is using imply with regard to Esau? In effect, what is Jacob doing? What does this strategy accomplish?
2. **32:22–32.** What is the outcome of this mysterious wrestling match? Allegorically, what does the defeat of the angel represent? How does this interpretation apply to the people of Israel? On a moral level, what does it mean to wrestle with an angel?
3. **Word Study: Israel (32:28).** What is the wordplay involved in the name Israel? What is unusual about the compound character of this name? What is the name taken to mean in Scripture? In later biblical history, for what group does the name stand?
4. **32:30.** How does Jacob see God "face to face"? What does the name Peniel mean, and where was it located?

*For application*

1. **32:7–12.** How does Jacob manage his fear and distress at the approach of Esau? How do you typically handle fear? How does or could prayer enter into the way you handle fear?
2. **32:12–13.** Reflect on Jesus' exhortation in Mt 25–34 and the parallel passage in Lk 12:22–31. How much confidence do you place in God's promises in Scripture when you feel that your welfare is threatened? How readily, for example, do such promises even come to mind in times of anxiety?
3. **32:24–26.** The Catechism calls conversion a struggle (CCC 1426) and prayer a battle (CCC 2573ff.). In what ways are they a struggle and a battle for you? How like Jacob are you in continuing the struggle?
4. **32:28.** Through his struggle with God, Jacob "prevails." In prayer of petition, what changes: God's mind or man's? What does it mean to "prevail" in prayer?

### Chapters 33–34

*For understanding*

1. **33:18.** Where is Shechem? After whom is it named? What route is Jacob following?
2. **34:1–31.** With what does this chapter deal? What is Jacob's role in this episode?

3. **34:9.** What is Hamor negotiating between Israel and Shechem? What is in it for the citizens of Shechem? How do Jacob's sons react?
4. **34:15.** What is the condition for marital unions between Israel and Shechem? What do Jacob's sons intend by proposing it?

*For application*

1. **33:12–15.** Jacob's demurrals and his subsequent actions suggest that he does not fully trust his brother, even though the two are apparently reconciled. When trust is broken, how can it be rebuilt? How would you know when trust had been firmly reestablished?
2. **34:1–2.** The word "rape" comes from a Latin word meaning "to steal" by force. When a rape occurs, what is stolen? Compare your answer with that of the Catechism (CCC 2256).
3. **34:25–27.** Dinah's brothers take revenge by killing all the males in the city of Shechem and reclaiming their sister. In your area, what is the legal punishment for the crime of rape? In comparison with the revenge taken by Jacob's sons, do you think the modern legal punishment is adequate? What purpose should punishment for such a crime serve?
4. **34:30–31.** Jacob's sons dismiss their father's claim that their actions have brought disgrace and danger upon him. What impact does the crime of rape have on the family of the victim? on that of the perpetrator?

## Chapter 35

*For understanding*

1. **35:9–12.** What happens with Jacob at Bethel? How do the words spoken to Jacob parallel the divine discourse with Abraham in chap. 17?
2. **35:18.** How does Rachel die? What is the meaning of the name she gives her infant? What is the meaning of the name Jacob gives him? How does this name bring out what is unique in the child? What do later biblical narratives indicate about the tribe of Benjamin?
3. **35:22.** What is Reuben attempting by lying with Bilhah? What irony results from it? What will Jacob do with Reuben's birthright?
4. **35:29.** What impression is created by placing the story of Isaac's death here? Where else might it have been placed? What other story of a burial by feuding brothers does this one recall?

*For application*

1. **35:4.** Many people — perhaps you yourself — possess images or wear jewelry that are actually emblems of other religions, such as a bracelet charm or a garden statue of Buddha. What might be a danger, even in modern America, of possessing or wearing such images? What does the Catechism say about images of God? Compare your answer with that of the Catechism (CCC 476, 1159–62).
2. **35:11–12.** Why do you think God repeats the covenant promises to succeeding generations of patriarchs? Why do you think we need to hear promises repeated?
3. **35:17–20.** Why do families create burial markers, even if they have no intention of returning to the burial site? What do such markers indicate about those who are still alive?
4. **35:22–25.** Review the note for v. 22. With Jacob's favorite wife, Rachel, dead, why is Bilhah so important to Reuben? If you wanted access to a famous person, but that person was inaccessible, to whom would you go?

## Chapters 36–37

*For understanding*

1. **36:7.** What forces Jacob and Esau to separate their tribes? Why is the parallel with Abraham and Lot significant?
2. **37:1—50:26.** To what is this storyline devoted? What is the link between this material and that of the book of Exodus? What in this material has been verified as historically authentic?
3. **37:3.** What does Jacob's preferential love for Joseph do to his family? What is the significance of the robe Jacob gives Joseph? What is its allegorical significance?
4. **Word Study: Dream (37:5).** What did people in the ancient Near East believe about dreams? In the biblical tradition, why are dreams important? What does the Lord reveal through them? What role do they play in the life of Joseph?
5. **37:28.** Who are the Midianite traders? Does the sum of 20 shekels of silver, paid for Joseph as a slave accord with historical evidence for the price of slaves during that period? When did the price climb to 30 silver pieces?

*For application*

1. **37:3–4.** In a family with several children, how can the parents avoid showing favoritism? Why is such avoidance necessary?
2. **37:5–11.** In a family with several children, how do children tend to assert their own importance? In this passage, how does Jacob respond to his son? How should a modern parent respond?
3. **37:19–27.** In a family with several children, fraternal envy of a promising sibling may play out in a variety of ways behind the backs of the parents. Have you ever had experience of this sort of retaliation against a favored sibling? How has age or experience changed or confirmed the attitudes of other siblings (including yourself, if applicable)?
4. **37:34–35.** In comparison with Jacob's expression of grief over the loss of a child, what attitude should a Christian parent display?

## Chapter 38

*For understanding*

1. **38:1–30.** On whom is the spotlight in this chapter? What does the story hint, and what does it explain?
2. **38:8.** To what "duty" is Judah referring here? When was this duty made into law?

3. **38:9.** In addition to interrupting sexual intercourse, what else made Onan's sin so gravely displeasing to the Lord? What is the twofold reason for the seriousness of what he did? In its codified form, what is the usual punishment for violation of the levirate law in Scripture? In Catholic moral theology, what does the sin of "Onanism" cover?
4. **38:21.** What is the meaning of the Hebrew word used in this verse? What does the shift in terminology suggest?
5. **38:26.** What is Judah's point in saying that Tamar is "more righteous" than he?

*For application*

1. **38:2.** Read the note for this verse. What standards have your parents had regarding their children's selection of a marriage partner? What role has religion played in those standards? What role should it play?
2. **38:9.** According to Catholic Church teaching, "each and every marriage act must remain open to the transmission of life" (*Humanae Vitae* II). What are some reasons modern couples give for wishing to avoid or delay having children? Which means of regulating births are morally acceptable, and which are not? What makes contraception inherently contradictory to the marriage covenant? (Refer to CCC 2368–71.)
3. **38:13–19.** What is Tamar trying to accomplish by her actions with Judah? Given the levirate custom of the time, how justified is she in taking matters into her own hands?

## Chapters 39–40

*For understanding*

1. **39:4.** What does authority over Potiphar's palace and possessions anticipate?
2. **39:6–18.** How does Joseph resist the advances of Potiphar's wife? Aware of his own weakness, what does he refuse and what does he avoid?
3. **39:20.** Why is prison a mild punishment for Joseph?
4. **40:13.** What is the meaning of this wordplay for the butler? for the baker?

*For application*

1. **39:7–12.** Have you ever dealt with sexual temptation? What have such temptations taught you about yourself? Why might it be better to flee from such a temptation than to fight it?
2. **39:21–23.** What talents or skills do you have that have brought you success over the long run, despite setbacks? Might the Lord be responsive to them? To whom do you generally give credit for them?
3. **40:8.** Despite the Church's condemnation, many Christians still practice some form of divination, such as consulting horoscopes. What is the difference between using divination to interpret dreams and the way Joseph interprets them? Why does the Church condemn practices such as divination? (Refer to CCC 2116.) What harm can they do to the person who uses them?

## Chapter 41

*For understanding*

1. **41:1–57.** How does God arrange for Joseph's elevation to royal power in Egypt? What are some of the parallels between this chapter and chap. 2 of the Book of Daniel?
2. **41:39–44.** As vizier of Egypt, what authority does Joseph have? What do the symbols of his office signify? In addition to Egypt, what other Near Eastern countries recognized the position of vizier?
3. **41:45.** What are the meanings of some of the Egyptian names in this verse? What was the Greek name for the city of On, and for what was it famous? What does Joseph's marriage into the priestly caste mean?

*For application*

1. **41:8.** Whenever you have a significant personal or spiritual problem, how do you seek resolution? To whom do you turn for help? How willing are you to take the advice that is offered?
2. **41:14.** Of what importance is it to appear clean and well dressed in the presence of important officials? What do you think explains the current trend to appear in casual or worn attire in the presence of God in the liturgy? How would you rate your own dress when you attend the liturgy?
3. **41:16.** The Catechism discusses charismatic gifts as ways by which the Holy Spirit "makes the faithful 'fit and ready to undertake various tasks and offices for the renewal and building up of the Church' [*Lumen Gentium* 12 §2]" (CCC 798). What charisms has the Holy Spirit given you for that purpose? How do you recognize them?
4. **41:47–57.** Because the spiritual life alternates between spiritual "uptimes" and "downtimes", how should you prepare yourself spiritually for the periods of dryness and desolation that tend to follow periods of growth and consolation? For example, which spiritual practices should you strengthen, and which should you begin that you have not yet undertaken?

## Chapters 42–44

*For understanding*

1. **42:34.** What threat and what promise do Joseph's brothers hide from Jacob?
2. **43:32.** Why was there separate seating arrangements at this meal? Why did Egyptians refuse table-fellowship with Hebrews? What other references in the Pentateuch support this interpretation?
3. **44:5.** How was a drinking cup used for divination? What indication do we have that Joseph practiced these superstitious arts?
4. **44:16.** About what guilt is Judah speaking in his reply to Joseph? What is the irony here?

*For application*

1. **42:28.** When a disaster strikes, particularly one that claims many lives, where do people tend to lay the blame? What challenges to faith can such disasters pose? What answers should faith give to these challenges?

2. **43:1–14.** How true is the saying, "Not to decide is to decide"? Have you ever put off making a vital decision out of fear of the consequences? What were your reasons? What finally brought about a decision?
3. **44:1–13.** After having treated Benjamin with such elaborate kindness at the feast in chap. 43, Joseph stages a trick that puts the blame on Benjamin for theft, the penalty for which is slavery in Egypt. What do you think is Joseph's motive? What "message" may he sending to Benjamin's brothers? How might this message be related to what happened to Joseph himself?

### Chapter 45

*For understanding*

1. **45:5.** What do Joseph's words to his brothers imply about his attitude and intention? How does Joseph interpret his rejection by his brothers? What theological lesson is contained here? What comparison between Jesus and Joseph does Stephen imply in his defense speech in Acts?
2. **45:10.** Where is Goshen? For what was the land ideally suited?
3. **45:24.** About what does Joseph admonish his brothers not to quarrel as they journey home?

*For application*

1. **45:4.** Pope John XXIII, whose given name was Giuseppe (Joseph), greeted a delegation of Jews at the Vatican by quoting this verse. What do you think he meant to tell them? How are Christians, in the words of Pius XI, "spiritually Semites"?
2. **45:7–8.** Can you think of other incidents in history where God brought good out of evil? How might a setback or disaster in your own life have been a blessing in disguise?
3. **45:24.** Read the note for this verse. Why would Joseph suspect that his brothers might quarrel after such good fortune? What might be the motives for such quarreling?

### Chapter 46

*For understanding*

1. **46:1–4.** Why is this appearance of Yahweh to Jacob important? How long will it be before another Israelite encounters the presence of God in this way? What does the promise made to Jacob on this occasion recall?
2. **46:8–27.** In this inventory of the family of Jacob in Egypt, how many descendants does the Hebrew text count? Of what is that number reminiscent? How does the Greek OT expand that list, and which tradition does Stephen follow in the NT?
3. **46:8.** Around what year does a literal reading of biblical chronology place the beginning of the sojourn in Egypt?
4. **46:34.** Why is "every shepherd an abomination" to Egyptians? Of what were some herding and grazing animals a symbol, and what aspects of shepherding made that profession represent a profanation of their religion?

*For application*

1. **46:5–7.** How often has your family made a major move from one location to another? What was the occasion of each move, and how difficult was it? What have been the long-term effects of the moves on your family?
2. **46:8–27.** Genealogies occur frequently in Scripture. How well do you know the genealogy of your own family? Of what importance to you is it to know who your ancestors were, where they came from, and what kind of people they were?
3. **46:32–34.** Do you regard your occupation as a vocation, as a career, or as a job? What is the difference? How did you select your occupation, and how do you feel about it? How can you use it to honor the Lord?

### Chapter 47

*For understanding*

1. **47:9.** What does Jacob mean by "my sojourning"? What is his point?
2. **47:11.** For what is Rameses another name in this verse? Who updated that name? When did the region's namesake actually reign?
3. **47:13–26.** How do the Egyptians fare as the famine grinds on? Who steers them through the crisis? What impression is given in 47:27 about Israel?
4. **47:27.** How is the name Israel used here for the first time in Scripture? How are the promises of God to Abraham and Isaac fulfilled here?

*For application*

1. **47:12–13.** Care for an aged parent or disabled relative is not a single-event situation; rather, it is ongoing, often for years. What is involved in such care? What effects does ongoing care have on the caregiver and the caregiver's family? How does such care reflect obedience to the fourth commandment?
2. **47:13–26.** Joseph's rationing policy involves selling grain to the Egyptians or bartering for their service rather than giving grain to them. Considering its effects on the populace, what do you think of the policy? How might a modern government handle a similar food emergency?
3. **47:29–30.** What do you think are Jacob's reasons for wanting to be buried, not in Egypt, but with his fathers? Why is the place of burial significant? What religious importance might the place of burial have?

### Chapter 48

*For understanding*

1. **Topical Essay: Blessings and Birthrights.** What distinct pattern emerges in Genesis that tends to run counter to the domestic customs of the biblical world? What were some privileges that first-born sons typically had? Who were the only

first-born sons in Genesis to receive the customary blessings? Why did most first-borns lose their positions? How often does the pattern of God's preference for younger sons repeat itself, and who benefits?

2. **48:1–22.** What is the blind and bedridden Jacob doing in this chapter? What is its significance for Joseph's sons? What blessing is given to Ephraim, the youngest?
3. **48:5.** How did Reuben and Simeon disqualify themselves from receiving the blessing of the first-born? Who takes their places?
4. **48:22.** What is the Hebrew wordplay on the term translated "mountain slope"? Where is the city of Shechem located? What is its connection with Joseph?

*For application*

1. **48:1–2.** When notified that a parent is dying, children will often rush to be present before death occurs, even if the parent is not conscious. What are some of the reasons why they might feel compelled to come? What religious motives might prompt them, even if they are not religious themselves?
2. **48:3–4.** Jacob reminds Joseph of God's covenant promises to him. What makes the last words of a dying person important to those left behind? What are the reported or actual last words of people you have known or read about that have impressed you the most? What makes them memorable?
3. **48:15–16.** Jacob's blessing seems to pass on to Ephraim and Manasseh the blessings he has received from God. If you had a blessing to pass on to loved ones, what would it be?

## Chapter 49

*For understanding*

1. **49:1–27.** What sort of benedictions are the blessings that Jacob gives his sons? How are they grouped? How are the blessings given to Judah and Joseph different from the others?
2. **49:5–7.** What does Jacob have to say about Simeon and Levi? What does the oracle foresee about their tribes?
3. **49:8–12.** What is the destiny of the tribe of Judah? How is Judah portrayed? Where else in the OT do allusions to this blessing appear?
4. **49:10.** Who fulfills the oracle of an international ruler from the line of Judah? When does its ultimate fulfillment come?
5. **49:11.** What is the "blood of grapes"? What idea does it convey? Allegorically, to what do the wine stains point?
6. **49:24.** What do the two titles for Yahweh celebrate?

*For application*

1. **49:3–27.** The attitude of parents toward their children can indicate for good or ill the kinds of persons their children will become. In what ways have the attitudes of your parents determined the course of your life so far? Have you consciously or unconsciously resisted your parents' expectations for your life? If you are a parent, have you passed on such attitudes to your children?
2. **49:9.** Jesus is described in Rev 5:5 as the Lion of the tribe of Judah. What leonine traits does Jesus have? How is this an apt description of him?
3. **49:11.** Read the note for this verse. What connection do you see between the expression "blood of the grape" and the cup of the Eucharist?

## Chapter 50

*For understanding*

1. **50:2.** What was Egyptian embalming? What did the process involve?
2. **50:10.** What was a threshing floor? To what direction does "beyond the Jordan" refer?
3. **50:25.** When was Joseph's request to carry his bones out of Egypt fulfilled? Where did the Israelites bury them?

*For application*

1. **50:7–13.** Aside from burying a deceased person, what is the purpose of a funeral? Why does the funeral liturgy of the Church include such elements as draping the casket with a pall, incensing it, and sprinkling holy water on it?
2. **50:20–21.** Read carefully Joseph's reply to his brothers' plea for forgiveness. What does he say about his brothers' transgression? In what way might his reply serve as a model of true forgiveness?
3. **50:24–25.** In the OT, the prediction of a "visitation" by God may be either a promise or a threat, depending on the circumstances. Which is Joseph predicting? Have you personally experienced such a "visit" by God? How would you characterize the experience?

# BOOKS OF THE BIBLE

## THE OLD TESTAMENT (OT)

| | |
|---|---|
| Gen | Genesis |
| Ex | Exodus |
| Lev | Leviticus |
| Num | Numbers |
| Deut | Deuteronomy |
| Josh | Joshua |
| Judg | Judges |
| Ruth | Ruth |
| 1 Sam | 1 Samuel |
| 2 Sam | 2 Samuel |
| 1 Kings | 1 Kings |
| 2 Kings | 2 Kings |
| 1 Chron | 1 Chronicles |
| 2 Chron | 2 Chronicles |
| Ezra | Ezra |
| Neh | Nehemiah |
| Tob | Tobit |
| Jud | Judith |
| Esther | Esther |
| Job | Job |
| Ps | Psalms |
| Prov | Proverbs |
| Eccles | Ecclesiastes |
| Song | Song of Solomon |
| Wis | Wisdom |
| Sir | Sirach (Ecclesiasticus) |
| Is | Isaiah |
| Jer | Jeremiah |
| Lam | Lamentations |
| Bar | Baruch |
| Ezek | Ezekiel |
| Dan | Daniel |
| Hos | Hosea |
| Joel | Joel |
| Amos | Amos |
| Obad | Obadiah |
| Jon | Jonah |
| Mie | Micah |
| Nahum | Nahum |
| Hab | Habakkuk |
| Zeph | Zephaniah |
| Hag | Haggai |
| Zech | Zechariah |
| Mai | Malachi |
| 1 Mac | 1 Maccabees |
| 2 Mac | 2 Maccabees |

## THE NEW TESTAMENT (NT)

| | |
|---|---|
| Mt | Matthew |
| Mk | Mark |
| Lk | Luke |
| Jn | John |
| Acts | Acts of the Apostles |
| Rom | Romans |
| 1 Cor | 1 Corinthians |
| 2 Cor | 2 Corinthians |
| Gal | Galatians |
| Eph | Ephesians |
| Phil | Philippians |
| Col | Colossians |
| 1 Thess | 1 Thessalonians |
| 2 Thess | 2 Thessalonians |
| 1 Tim | 1 Timothy |
| 2 Tim | 2 Timothy |
| Tit | Titus |
| Philem | Philemon |
| Heb | Hebrews |
| Jas | James |
| 1 Pet | 1 Peter |
| 2 Pet | 2 Peter |
| 1 Jn | 1 John |
| 2 Jn | 2 John |
| 3 Jn | 3 John |
| Jude | Jude |
| Rev | Revelation (Apocalypse) |